HOW DID
IT BEGIN?

The Origins of Our
Curious Customs
and Superstitions

DR. R. & L. BRASCH

MJF BOOKS
NEW YORK

THIS REVISED EDITION IS DEDICATED TO THE
MEMORY OF ITS AUTHOR BY HIS EVER-LOVING WIFE.
IT WAS HIS FIRST BOOK ON "ORIGINS," TO BE
FOLLOWED BY MANY, MANY OTHERS.

Published by MJF Books
Fine Communications
322 Eighth Avenue
New York, NY 10001

How Did It Begin?
LC Control Number: 2014940135
ISBN 978-1-60671-271-9 (hardcover)
ISBN 978-1-60671-072-2 (paperback)

MJF Books hardcover reprint edition published in 2014.
First published as an MJF paperback reprint in 2011.

This revised edition published in Sydney, Australia, by ABC Books
for the AUSTRALIAN BROADCASTING CORPORATION in 2006.
This North American edition is published by arrangement with HarperCollins
Publishers Australia Pty Limited.

Printed in the United States of America.

MJF Books and the MJF colophon are trademarks of Fine Creative Media, Inc.

QF   10 9 8 7 6 5

CONTENTS

Introduction   vii

1 The Origin of Superstitions   1

Spilling Salt • Unlucky Number 13 • Knocking on Wood • Lucky Four-
leafed Clovers • Lucky Horseshoes • Third Time Lucky • Breaking a
Mirror • Walking under Ladders • Getting out of Bed on the Wrong Side
• Lighting Three Cigarettes with One Match • Opening an Umbrella
Indoors • Stumbling • Meeting a Black Cat • A Rabbit's Foot for Luck
• Lockets of Hair • Whistling at Sea • Dogs Howling • Aversion to Red
Hair • Spitting • Pointing • Pointing the Finger

2 Birth and its Customs   24

The Stork and Babies • Blue for Boys and Pink for Girls • The Pram
• Birthday Cake and Candles • The Queen's Birthday

3 The Ritual of Courting and Marriage   28

The Kiss • *X* for a Kiss • Spooning • The Valentine Card • Leap-year
Proposals • The Best Man • Bride on the Groom's Left Side • The Bride's
Veil • Orange Blossoms • The Wedding Ring • The Ring Finger
• Throwing Confetti • Throwing an Old Shoe • The Wedding Cake
• Carrying the Bride over the Threshold • The Honeymoon • The
Honeymoon Destination • The Helpmate • The Marriage Certificate
• Bill of Divorce

4 Death and Mourning   52

To Kick the Bucket • To Go West • Stopping the Clocks at a Death
• Black for Mourning • The Mourning Arm Band • Half-mast • Candles
and Death • The Coffin • The Wreath • The Hearse • The Funeral
Procession • The Tombstone • Crocodile Tears • The Grass Widow

5 Everyday Courtesies   68

Etiquette • Shaking Hands • Raising One's Hat • The Curtsy • "God
Bless You" when Sneezing • Hand in Front of the Mouth when Yawning

6 Table Manners and Eating Habits   73

Three Daily Meals • Knife and Fork • Crossing the Knife and Fork
• Chopsticks • The Serviette • The Difference between Tea and Coffee
Pots • The Sundae • Welsh Rabbit • Peach Melba • Melba Toast • The
Adam's Apple • To Eat One's Hat • Pork as Forbidden Food

7 Drinking Customs   85

Host Pouring Wine into His Own Glass First • The Toast • Clinking
Glasses • The Cocktail • Beer • Wine • Champagne • The Champagne
Glass • The Teetotaller • Glass

8 The History of Dress   98

Trousers • Turn-ups • The Waistcoat • The Bottom Button on a
Waistcoat • Buttons on Sleeves • To "Laugh up One's Sleeve" • The
Different Way of Buttoning for Men and Women • The Slit in the Lapel
• The Handkerchief • The Wig • The Fan • The Umbrella • The Hatband
• The Mad Hatter • To Run the Gauntlet • Spectacles

9 Beauty Culture   118

Perfume • Lipstick • Shaping Eyebrows • Painting Nails • Soap • The
Barber's Pole • The Beard • Parting the Hair • Hair Standing on End

10 Animals in Language   131

The White Elephant • A Red Rag to a Bull • To Put a Flea in One's Ear
• To Go the Whole Hog • The Mad March Hare • To Let the Cat out of
the Bag • To Have Kittens • Raining Cats and Dogs • A Cat's Nine Lives
• No Room to Swing a Cat • The Cheshire Cat

11 The Story of People's Dwellings   143

The Palace • The Drawing-room • The Attic • The Lumberroom • The
"W.C." • Windows • Gothic Style • Jerry-built

12 Magic   152

The "First Footer" • The Door Knocker • Elephant Ornaments • "Break a
Leg" • The Magic Carpet • The Witch's Broom • The Three Wise Monkeys

22 The Beginnings of Writing   251

The Alphabet • "To Mind One's P's and Q's" • The Question Mark •
Paper • Foolscap • Ink • Blotting Paper

23 Counting and Accounting   261

"Once in a Blue Moon" • The Fortnight • A Baker's Dozen • "By Rule of
Thumb" • The Piggy Bank • The Rim on Coins • The Traveler's Check •
The Pawnbroker's Three Brass Balls • Blackmail

24 The Measurement of Time   269

The Calendar • The Numbering of Years • Ordinary Time • The Months
• The Days of the Week • Red-letter Days • April Fools' Day • May Day
• Boxing Day • The Clock • The Naming of the Clock • The Watch

25 Religion and its Symbols   286

The "Dog Collar" • Joining Hands in Prayer • Kneeling • The Rosary
• Fish on Friday • The Communion Service • Covering the Head in a
Synagogue • Church Bells • The Halo • The Cross • The Fish • The
Crescent Moon • The Christmas Tree • Tinsel • Holly • Christmas
Pudding • The Mince Pie • The X in Xmas • The Christmas Card
• The Christmas Stocking • Good Friday • Hot Cross Buns • The Easter
Egg • The Easter Bunny • In the Lap of the Gods • "Amen"

Index   318

13 Medicine 157

The Emblem of the Staff and Serpent • Surgeons Addressed as "Mr." • The Caesarean • "Not to be Sneezed at" • The Quarantine

14 Sources of Justice 162

"Justice is Blind" • The Ordeal • The Jury • Twelve Jurymen • The Derrick • Lynching • Boycott • The Guillotine • The Scapegoat

15 Parliamentary Procedure and Royal Regalia 174

The Chamber • The Speaker • The Mace • The Whips • "Hear! Hear!" • The Coronation Stone • The Anointment • The Crown • The Scepter

16 Symbols of Nationhood 185

The Flag • The Union Jack • The Australian Flag • The Stars and Stripes • The Israeli Flag • The Red Flag • National Anthems • "God Save the Queen" • "Waltzing Matilda" • "The Star-spangled Banner" • The Israeli Hymn • The Passport

17 Naval Customs 204

The Christening of Ships • Tattooing • The Sailor's Bib • The Blue Peter • Fathom • The Ship's Bell • The Dog Watch • Crossing the Line • The Albatross • "Tell it to the Marines" • The "Senior Service"

18 In the Army 218

Khaki • The Baton • The Drum-major's Staff • The Busby • Medals on the Left Side • The White Feather • The Emblem of the Rising Sun • The Digger • The Slouch Hat • ANZAC • Anzac Day • Three Volleys over the Grave

19 The Origin of Sporting Terms and Pastimes 229

Chess • Dice • Playing Cards • The Ace • Love in Tennis • The Crossword Puzzle • The Quiz • Blue for First Prize • The Clue • The Jigsaw Puzzle • Backgammon • Smoking Cigarettes

20 On the Stage 242

The Theater • The Tragedy • The Pit and the Stalls

21 In the Way of Speaking 246

The Real McCoy • Fair Dinkum • "O.K."

INTRODUCTION

To explore the origin of customs and superstitions is a great adventure and its reward a goldmine of fascinating information. Everyone wants to know how it all began. We are anxious to discover the reason why we do certain things and why we express our attitudes, feelings and convictions in definite prescribed ways.

Blue for boys and pink for girls, black cats that augur good luck or portend misfortune, the little slit in the lapel, the throwing of confetti at weddings and fish on Friday—they all have found their place in our patterns of life, manner and dressing and religious tradition not just accidentally. Though we may now take them for granted, there is nothing in life that has not its initial significant meaning and purpose.

The story of our customs is not always easy to trace. Frequently they go back into the obscurity of the most distant past. Many of them owe their existence not merely to one single desire, need or fear, but are the result of a combination of factors and thus present a mosaic which, in many cases, consists of pagan beliefs, primitive superstition and modern reinterpretations.

Layers of legend are woven around historic facts and early, but now obsolete, practical explanations. Again, most misleadingly, many present-day explanations are manifestly false and mere rationalizations. Often several possible roots offer themselves.

The study of the origin of our customs is thus significant for many reasons. By exploring and explaining, the history of people and the curious working of the human mind are revealed. Moreover, to know the purpose of our habits and actions inevitably enriches our appreciation of their value. In the case of superstitions, however, the very act of digging up their roots helps to kill them and thus to rid ourselves of fears that otherwise would go on haunting us even in our so-called enlightened age.

This book is the result of many years of research all over the world. Its object is twofold: to serve as a handy source of information as well as to help the readers in their search for a meaning in the things we do and say (often so thoughtlessly) from birth to death, at play and work, within and without the realm of religion.

R.B.

CHAPTER 1

The Origin of Superstitions

Superstitions have been with people from the earliest days and even in the scientific age of today the most enlightened are often tempted to keep them, as there might be "something in them." For superstitions are not always as irrational and illogical as may be imagined. They have a reason, a background, and a practical explanation.

From the beginning of time people assumed the existence of powers which could influence their lives for better or worse. To placate the anger of these forces or to buy their goodwill became (to some people) almost an obsessional neurosis, which has been responsible for many habits and customs that are meticulously observed even nowadays.

The fact is that, at some time or other, everybody, no matter what their education or place in life, is a slave to superstition. Mostly, however, we do not realize it. We cleverly rationalize the meaning of superstition and refer to them as beautiful customs. No doubt they belong to the social life of both the civilized and the savage. To trace their origins is a rewarding adventure, prompting one whether to be or not to be—superstitious.

Spilling Salt

From the beginning of civilization, salt was important in daily diet and was considered a holy substance. No sacrifice, whether according to biblical rite or pagan tradition, could be offered without the addition of salt. Its presence at every table was regarded as a necessity and a meal without it thought to be profane. Salt is still used today in the baptismal ritual of the Catholic Church.

Even everyday speech testifies to the importance of salt. It is said of some people that they are "not worth their salt." The word salary is derived from the Latin for "salt"—*sal*—and recalls the

1

practice of paying soldiers in the Roman Empire with lumps of salt or an allowance to buy salt.

Salt purifies. Hence it became a symbol of incorruptibility. That is why the Greek philosopher Pythagoras saw in it an emblem of justice which had to belong on every table. It was to remind all those participating in the meal of this essential virtue. To upset the salt was already seen then as a forewarning of an injustice.

Salt is a preservative. This made it a sign of lasting friendship, as well as of immortality. Therefore Arabs to this day put salt in front of strangers to assure them of their goodwill, and in many countries salt was put into the coffin as a reminder of the soul's survival. When the Bible wished to stress God's everlasting bond with humans, it spoke likewise of "the covenant of salt." In Scotland, brewers used to throw a handful of salt on top of the mash, believing that its purifying character would ward off witches.

It was a combination of these various traditions and factors that from Roman days to the present time made the spilling of salt an omen of ill luck which could be averted only if the offender threw a pinch of it with the right hand over his left shoulder. The superstitious persons who have accidentally spilled salt will take immediate remedial action to cancel out any unfortunate after-effect by throwing a pinch of it over their left shoulder. They do so for a variety of significant reasons. As the result of the "upsetting" incident, they thought that the devil was about to pounce on them. Being a most cunning creature, he would do so not only from the rear where he could not be seen, but also from the left—the weaker (and sinister) side.

An explanation frequently given, though confusing cause and effect, relates to the famous painting of *The Last Supper* by Leonardo da Vinci. On his canvas the salt, facing Judas, is depicted as being upset. The scene captured the moment when, according to the Gospels, Jesus startled his Apostles with the announcement that one of them would betray him. Their faces vividly show consternation and grief. But Judas, to appear as innocent as the rest, whilst clasping in his right hand the bag with the thirty pieces of silver, raises his left hand as if in a gesture of horror. By that very movement he upset the salt.

The fact that this Passover meal immediately preceded the betrayal of Jesus made people assume that there was a causal connection between the spilling of salt and Jesus's crucifixion. However, there is no confirmation of any such occurrence. It is obvious that da Vinci merely made use of the much older superstition to further dramatize his painting.

The commonly held superstition that the spilling of salt would bring bad luck, in addition to its various other explanations, has a sexual interpretation as well. According to some psychoanalysts, the salt symbolized man's semen. Spilling it presaged premature ejaculation (*ejaculatio praecox*). The very superstition, in fact, revealed people's unconscious apprehension of such incomplete intercourse.

Unlucky Number 13

The numeral "13" shares the fate of the black cat in people's ambivalent attitudes. It all depends on who and where you are, and whether the cat and the "13" mean good luck or misfortune. Thirteen has not always been considered the unlucky number it is generally assumed to be now. The Aztecs saw in it a divine figure, and used thirteen steps leading up to the sacred platform on which they kept their holy fire burning for exactly four times thirteen years at a time. The Mayas, prior to the Aztecs, had worshipped "the 13 gods of the upper world" and regarded them as so holy that they saw the "13" as one collective deity.

Thirteen indeed was an important magical, if not cosmic numeral. Various myths all over the world told of a group of twelve who, by the addition of one, grew to the consequential number of thirteen. Thus, the sun, added to the twelve signs of the Zodiac, made thirteen. Indians in their temples paid homage to thirteen Buddhas.

In the Jewish faith, thirteen has always had a happy and sacred connotation. Interpreting a passage in the book of Exodus (34:6–7), God was believed to reveal himself by thirteen of his attributes, all of which expressed his bountiful mercy. The divine name itself, as it appeared in the tetragrammaton—the four-lettered Yahveh (YHVH)—added up to a value of twice "13," so numerologists pointed out. (Y was the numeral for 10, H for 5 and V for 6.) Still part of every orthodox Jewish prayerbook are the "Thirteen Principles of Faith." They were drawn up by Moses

Maimonides, the renowned twelfth-century philosopher, whose constant aim was to be "a Guide to the Perplexed," the very words with which he entitled his main work. Up to this day, Jewish boys celebrate their confirmation, known as *Bar Mitzvah*, at the age of thirteen, when they become full and responsible members of the community.

Circumstance gave the figure "13" an especially significant role in the history of the United States. Because of the nation's original thirteen states, the American flag continues to display thirteen stripes and the American eagle to count thirteen feathers on each wing. Thirteen was the favorite number of the German composer Richard Wagner. Not only did he take note that his name counted thirteen letters, but he was born in 1813, composed thirteen operas and completed *Tannhauser* on March 13, 1845.

The notion of the unlucky "13" is deeply rooted in people's minds, going back to earliest times.

The ability of primitive people to count was limited. They could do so only up to "12," but no further. That is why numbers beyond "12" have no individual and independent names, but are composed of a combination of previous numbers. If "12" was the end of the line, as it were, "13," which followed it, had no exact value and definite meaning at first. An uncertain number, so to speak, it was fraught with mystery. This enigmatic quality of the "13" made people fear the numeral, regarding it as fateful and foreboding, an attitude that never died out but, even if only unconsciously, continues to haunt and obsess people.

No doubt, a subsequent observation deepened the ominous quality attached to the "13." While "12" was a most "fortunate" number in the way it could be divided and could be seen as a multiple of 3 times 4 and twice 6, "13" stood on its own. Completely indivisible, it seemed not to mix with any other number, and because of its isolation, it came to be shunned. Other factors and traditions further contributed to the ominous quality of the "13." There was the Norse myth of the twelve gods who gathered for a banquet in Valhalla. Loki's gate-crashing of the party increased the number of gods to thirteen, which supposedly led to the death of Baldur, the most beloved of the gods.

In Christianity "13" came to play yet another role. At the Last Supper, Christ and his twelve disciples made up a company of thirteen. No doubt, they had dined together many times previously, but it was this one occasion that made Christians give the "13" its fateful meaning. Because they had been thirteen Jesus was crucified. The Last Supper and subsequent execution of Christ therefore were seen not as a chronological sequence alone, but a chain of cause and effect. The crucifixion had actually been the consequence of the presence of thirteen at Christ's last celebration of the Jewish Passover eve. It was all a matter not of *post hoc* but *propter hoc*. At least, this idea became fixed in many Christian minds centuries after the event. It seemed only to confirm the widespread pagan tradition of the disastrous effect of "13."

Later, when satanic cults tried to ridicule Christian tradition, they introduced the Black Mass as a mockery of the Last Supper and the Holy Communion service which evolved from it. When the followers of black magic met in their secret covens, it was said that on each occasion they made sure to number thirteen: twelve ordinary witches plus their leader, or "warlock." The Christian Church was convinced that satanic cults had deliberately chosen this quorum and, like so many features of its Black Mass, was deriding the Church's sacred tradition. One theory holds that it was the association of the number "13" with witchcraft and devilry that caused Christians to decry the numeral as evil. As an omen of misfortune and an integral part of satanism, no good could come of it.

By proclaiming "13" the most unlucky of numbers, Christians felt they could keep people away from the satanic gatherings, a practice so abominable in their eyes. It was like a chain reaction which by diverse means seemed determined to establish 13 as the unlucky number. The malevolence of the numeral was further reinforced by the thirteenth card in the fortune-telling deck, which represented Death and was depicted as a skeleton carrying a scythe.

Belief in the unlucky "13" is the real reason why the thirteen loaves bakers once supplied in bulk were never called by their real number, but described as "a baker's dozen."

Perhaps to make the irrational fear of "13" respectable, the sophisticated like to refer to it as "triskaidekaphobia." Derived from the Greek, it joined *triskaideka* (13) and *phobia* (fear).

Knocking on Wood

Fear often haunts people, not least in moments of happiness. They are afraid that some jealous agency, real or imagined, may try to deprive them of their good fortune. To talk of personal good luck became almost a challenge of fate, which in turn gave rise to many precautionary measures, some belonging to the psychopathology of everyday life. One of these is the custom of touching wood.

The usual explanation associates it with the cross of Christ. Churches in various parts of the world treasure pieces of wood which, they believe, were once part of the real cross and to touch them would ensure sustained happiness. Touching any kind of wood, in memory of the cross, was an obvious further development of the custom.

Another interpretation, still in the realm of religion, recalls the ancient days when a church offered sanctuary to pursued persons. Once these reached the holy precinct and touched the church's wooden door, nothing could happen to them. They were under the protection of the cross. No one would have dared to apprehend them there, as that would have been tantamount to sacrilege.

Yet a further explanation dates back to the more distant past, when people lived in wooden huts. Those who were prosperous were afraid of talking about it, lest evil spirits would envy their luck and try to interfere with it. Thus, when discussing their good fortune, people knocked loudly on their wooden walls. The noise was meant to drown their conversation and prevent any ill-meaning eavesdroppers hearing what they were saying about their luck.

However, the custom most probably stems from pagan times, when trees were deified. The fact that these were often struck by lightning led to the belief that divine power had entered them, and they were soon identified with particular deities. It was thought, for example, that the oak was the dwelling place of the god of lightning and thunder. Hence to touch its timber would get magic results.

Lucky Four-leafed Clovers

The origin of the belief that a four-leafed clover is lucky is lost in antiquity. Only a biblical legend that offers an explanation survives. This relates that when Adam and Eve were expelled from paradise, Eve took a four-leafed clover with her, which flourished in the garden of Eden. She wished to retain at least something that would remind her always of her happy existence in the now-lost paradise. That is how its presence in one's own garden came to be looked upon as an omen of good luck.

Lucky Horseshoes

There are several explanations as to why horseshoes are thought to be lucky. Best known is the legend about St. Dunstan. He was noted for his skill in shoeing horses. One day, the devil himself, in disguise, called on him "for repairs," presenting his single hoof. But St. Dunstan recognized the "evil one." He fastened him tightly to the wall and then set to work so roughly that the devil roared for mercy. St. Dunstan, however, did not let him go until he had promised never to enter a home on which a horseshoe was fixed.

Another tradition associates the horseshoe superstition with an early and widely held belief in witches. All over the world and until late in the Middle Ages, people feared them and their nefarious work. Though it was commonly supposed that one was immune from their evil spells while outdoors, it was equally assumed that they could do harm in the home. People thought that witches were afraid of horses, for which reason they rode on a broomstick. It followed that a horseshoe at the door of the house would be a protection, as the mere sight of it would frighten away the witches.

The horseshoe has always been considered lucky. Its shape was that of the crescent moon, in which primitive people saw a sign of good fortune. It indicated fertility and the increase of all that was good. The ancient Romans held that evil could be nailed, and the hammering of nails on the doors of their houses was a means of curing or diverting ill luck and disease. The horseshoe cannot be hung just any way. It must be fixed with its points upward, lest the luck run out.

Third Time Lucky

The proverbial saying "third time lucky" is not just an encouragement never to give up trying—"If at first you don't succeed, try,

try, try again." It has its ancient and sacred associations and is based on the belief, spread throughout the West and the East, in the significance of the figure three.

The sixth-century-B.C. Greek philosopher Pythagoras called 3 "the perfect number." It was the sign of completion and fertility. That is why in some languages the figure "3" and the word "tree" have the same root, meaning the power of reproduction. In Aryan tongues, "3" is the first expression of plurality and the multiplication of things.

This concept of "the perfect 3" is inherent in people's thinking and imagination. It can be found as much in ancient mythology as in modern psychology. That is why, all through history, the idea of the essential triangularity of matter and of the trinity of the spirit has prevailed. Shakespeare wrote that there is luck in odd numbers, especially three.

Most prescriptions of folk medicine contain three ingredients, their number being necessary to ensure a cure. Indian philosophy speaks of the three worlds, heaven, sky and earth, just as it is thought that there are three parts of a person, body, mind and soul. In pagan lore Neptune appears with the trident and Jupiter with three-forked lightning. According to biblical tradition, humans are the descendants of three families—of Ham, Shem and Japhet. In modern times Professor Freud distinguished the three aspects of superego, ego and id.

Breaking a Mirror

The superstition that the breaking of a mirror means bad luck is so old that it leads back to times when mirrors could not be broken because they were made of metal. They were preceded by the still water of lakes and pools. People looked into them not out of vanity, but to view their fate. The way their image appeared on its surface was interpreted as an indication of what the future held for them. If the face seemed distorted, broken into many pieces, as it were, it was taken as a definite portent of evil, of the forthcoming disintegration of the viewer's life. Foes could easily disturb a calm and pleasant reflection by maliciously throwing pebbles into the pond.

Other beliefs were soon added, making the breaking of a

mirror even more ominous. Mirrors were used for divination, just as nowadays people gaze into crystal balls. Primitive people imagined that the picture they saw was not the reflection of their personal image but of their soul which, they were convinced, had an independent existence. It could detach itself from the body and actually be in the mirror. If this was broken the soul, too, was shattered, and thus the very substance of their existence destroyed. By losing their soul through the shattered glass, the man or woman was bound to die.

Belief in magic further increased the unfortunate associations with the breaking of mirrors. It was assumed that any injury done to the reflection would affect the person whose likeness it bore, just as people believed that by piercing the eyes of a foe in a picture of him, they would cause him to go blind.

There was yet another fear that the breaking of the mirror would anger the spirit dwelling in it so much (because it had been hurt) that it would seek vengeance on the offender, or a member of his family. Equally, as mirrors were used to foretell a person's future, their being broken was interpreted as intentional, and not just an accident. It was an act deliberately committed by the gods who wished to prevent people from seeing in it an intimation of coming disaster.

Chinese people used to fix mirrors over idols they kept in their homes. The mirrors, so they believed, were a potent power against evil spirits which, seeing themselves in the mirror, were scared away. Thus, if a mirror was broken, the only defense against malevolent powers was lost, and the home was wide open for them to take possession.

Though nowadays people decorate their dwellings with numerous kinds of mirrors, both to beautify them and to look into them, when broken they still reflect the ancient superstitious past, and out of the shattered pieces the spirits of old rise again. George Bernard Shaw rightly observed that one of the laws still ruling in modern times is the conservation of credulity. It may be that beyond this multitude of irrational fears and phobias a very mundane consideration has made people afraid of breaking a mirror. It is costly to replace and the resulting glass splinters might cause serious injury.

Walking under Ladders

It is commonly held that to walk under ladders is unlucky. At first sight it seems a logical deduction. Accidents do happen and a painter working on top of the ladder might splash down some paint or perhaps drop the pot itself. Or, worse still, a tool or a tile might drop onto the person below. Such explanations, however logical they might appear, are not the real ones but what psychologists term rationalizations. The true origin of the superstition leads back to the ancient, pre-Christian belief in the sanctity of the trinity. A ladder, leaning against a wall, forms a triangle. This has always been the most common symbol of the Holy Trinity. To pass through its area would be tantamount to defiance of sacred power and an intrusion into sanctified space. It would be a dangerous play with supernatural forces. Worse still, such action might disturb, if not annul, the trinity's potency as a guard against satanic forces which, thus released, would immediately start their evil work.

Another explanation relates to an ancient taboo observed by some primitive races. This concerned the head, which was considered not as the seat of wisdom but of guardian spirits. By walking under a ladder, this spirit would take offense and, simultaneously, become ineffective, thereby delivering the trespasser to malevolent agencies.

Early Christian tradition took due cognisance of the superstition about ladders. However, trying to interpret it in its own way, it pointed to the fact that because a ladder was used in connection with the crucifixion of Jesus, it has been associated ever since with evil and death.

Getting out of Bed on the Wrong Side

It is said of people who show ill temper that they must have got out of bed "on the wrong side." But in doing so, it is not realized that the phrase has any deeper meaning or ominous sense. It is used merely in the way of picturesque speaking. In reality and originally, it was meant quite literally. People firmly believed that the way they rose in the morning affected their mood and dealings throughout the ensuing day. The simple act of getting up was therefore of almost magic significance.

Matters were aggravated further by the fact that the most important question was left unanswered. If there was a wrong side from which to get out of bed, which was it? From long ago two different interpretations were given.

First, people assumed that it was inviting disaster to get up the same way as they had retired. They must complete the "magic circle" and rise from the opposite side of the bed. A more deeply rooted belief was that, no matter which way one had gone to bed, in the case of rising the left side was always the wrong side. Getting out of bed, one must put down one's right foot first.

In all ages the left has been linked with evil and, therefore, with superstitious fear. This might have been brought about by people's experience that the average person's left hand was less powerful than the right, and even clumsy. For centuries left-handedness has been associated with debility of mind. Even a criminologist of the standing of the Italian Cesare Lombroso claimed that left-handedness was a common occurrence among the insane and criminal.

The ancient Romans already had identified the left side with the "evil one." Therefore they considered it unlucky to enter a house with their left foot first. To avoid any such possibility, noble families employed a servant whose sole duty it was to ensure that guests entered his master's home right foot first. Appropriately, this slave's office became known as that of a *footman*. The title is still retained, but the original meaning has been forgotten. The English word *sinister*, likewise, dates from the Roman civilization and the identical superstition. It was the Latin word for the *left* side. Its very association with evil made it a term denoting what is underhand, base and bad.

Lighting Three Cigarettes with One Match

The holy trinity, commercial interests and self-protection in time of war are cited as the direct cause of the aversion to lighting three cigarettes with one match.

Three is the symbol of the trinity. To make a mundane use of it was to defile its sanctity and to transgress the holy law. People would invite disaster and put themselves into the power of the "evil one." Thus a match, trebly used, would light the fires of hell for one's own soul.

Another less fearful tradition claims that the superstition first arose among British troops during the Crimean War. They learned from Russian captives of the danger of using any light for a three-fold purpose. They were told that it was the sacred rule of the Orthodox Church that the three candles on the altar were not to be lit from a single taper, except when the high priest used it.

However, a more likely explanation of the origin of the custom is that British soldiers, entrenched against Dutch foes in the Boer War, learned by bitter experience of the danger of lighting three cigarettes from one match. When the men thriftily used one match to serve three of them, they gave the Boer sniper time to spot the light, take aim and fire, killing "the third man."

Ivar Kreuger, the Swedish match king, did not create the super-stition, as has been alleged, but he made the widest possible use of it to promote sales. People, innately superstitious, did not mind wasting a match. After all, there might just be something in it! Certainly there was much profit for Mr. Kreuger who thus, by fostering for his own purpose a realiztic wartime precaution, was able to increase his sales manifold.

Opening an Umbrella Indoors

It is a common superstition that opening an umbrella indoors brings bad luck. A belief in magic and in the right order of things may have given rise to it.

An umbrella is meant to be a shield in the open air, no matter whether it is used against the rain or the sun. Therefore to open it where it does not belong, as it were, is a defiance of the natural order and an insult to the spirit of the umbrella which, personi-fied, would surely punish the offender.

There was also an ancient fear of having an unjustified cover over one's head. People believed that evil forces enveloped them all the time, watching out for every possible opportunity of doing harm. But beneficial mystical powers protected them by their invisible radiation. Opening an umbrella indoors, however, would put up an impenetrable screen against the rays of good fortune.

In modern times practical consideration reinforced the ancient superstition. An open umbrella in a room obstructs vision and can easily become the cause of breakage, damage and injury. Even the most enlightened person, therefore, was well advised to deem it "dangerous" to open an umbrella indoors.

Stumbling

People about to embark on a new adventure instinctively and superstitiously look out for signs which will either encourage or deter them. A bride on her wedding day will welcome sunshine and a blue sky as happy auguries. To stumble, on the other hand, has been associated with bad luck and "explained" as a warning of misfortune to come. As early a writer as the Roman Cicero mentioned the fear as one of the many omens at which weak minds are terrified. Seventeen hundred years later, Shakespeare could still record the identical obsession:

> For many men that stumble at the threshold
> Are well foretold that danger lurks therein.

Historic and biographical examples, ancient and modern, seem to support this superstition. Tiberius Gracchus stumbled on the threshold of his home and died the same day.

When leaving his tent, pitched on a battlefield, Antigonus slipped. His men immediately interpreted the accident as a prediction of the gods' ill will. To all appearances they were confirmed in their opinion, because Antigonus was killed that very afternoon. One day during his invasion of the East, Napoleon's horse stumbled. The General, so it is said, defied the sign. Ridiculing it and considering himself above "fate," he continued his campaign—with disastrous results.

About to embark on his second—and fatal—expedition to Africa, Mungo Park took leave of Sir Walter Scott. Immediately afterwards, on crossing from the moor to the road, his horse stumbled. Sir Walter, watching the incident, expressed his apprehension and tried to stop his friend from proceeding. But Park rejected the warning, saying that "omens follow them who look to them." He was never seen again.

Such examples, however numerous they are, prove nothing. They are mere rash rationalizations. After all, how many people have stumbled and nothing has happened to them! On the other hand, how many people who had never slipped did not return from their ventures or died tragically.

Originally, stumbling was taken as a revelation of the agency of unseen evil forces, determined to frustrate persons in the task on which they were about to embark. They made them stumble, as it were, to give them a last warning. If they still did not heed the sign and refused to turn back, they would see to it that their will was done.

Common sense offers a more obvious explanation. Stumbling is perilous at all times. Persons who trip up or, worse still, whose horse misses a foothold, might easily break their neck.

Modern psychology, however, points to a much more rational answer. A close relationship exists between body and mind. Feelings can condition actions. The way a task is approached— with confidence or with fear—will greatly determine its final execution, its success or its failure. Hence people who are not sure of themselves and hesitant in what they are doing would come to grief, even without stumbling. Subconsciously they miss their footing. Their stumble is not a superstitious omen, but a symptom of their own mood. No wonder therefore that eventually, already preconditioned to defeat, they miss their objective.

Meeting a Black Cat

To meet a black cat is considered both lucky and unlucky; it all depends in which country it happens.

The belief that black cats are lucky goes back to Egypt, where they were mostly of a sandy color. An all-black cat was a rarity. Mice and rats destroyed the grain in silos and when Egyptians found that by keeping cats the vermin were greatly reduced, they protected and eventually deified the cat, as it ensured their food supply.

The cat became sacred to the goddess Isis, and her daughter, the goddess Bast or Pasht, was represented with the face of a cat. Indeed, a cat was thought to be so holy that anyone who killed it, even by mere accident, was put to death. Frequently, mummified cats were buried with their worshippers. Cat cemeteries were unearthed by archaeologists in Egypt and a shipment of embalmed cats was taken to England. Thus, the belief that a black cat crossing one's path brought good luck is rooted in Egyptian mythology.

A tradition which arose in medieval Europe made the black cat not a god, or one of its associates, but a companion of witches and their familiars. People believed that a witch could assume the form of a black cat, black being the color of the powers of darkness. Therefore, all black cats were suspected of being transformed witches. Hence to have a black cat cross one's path came to be regarded as an omen of bad luck.

Once again, legends did their part to increase the occult stature of the black cat. The Greek goddess Hecate and the Scandinavian deity Hel, who were both linked with death, had black cats as their feline aides. No wonder that by this association in the eyes of people black cats themselves appeared as omens of misfortune and death.

In Lincolnshire, England, a popular story was told of a father and his son meeting a black cat which they suspected of being a witch. They pounded it with stones. When next day they encountered the witch in her real form, her face was bandaged. Not long afterwards she passed away.

The two contradictory beliefs about a black cat thus are the result of two strands of tradition: that of the Egyptian idolized cat, and of the European witchy one. It is just a matter of geographical circumstance whether the black cat one meets augurs good luck or warns of impending misfortune.

A Rabbit's Foot for Luck

Widespread is the belief that a rabbit's foot brings luck. Children were brushed with it at birth, and well-wishers used to present one to young actors when first they appeared on stage, to be used ever after when applying make-up. The rabbit's foot was deemed a guarantee of good fortune, and its loss a threat of disaster.

As with many other customs and superstitions, there was a variety of reasons that caused the rabbit's foot to become a lucky charm. It may be a survival of ancient Totemism, which claimed that humans were descended from the beast. These early evolutionists thought that each tribe had its own kind of animal ancestor, which they worshipped, refrained from killing, and frequently used—either as a whole or only in parts—as their lucky charm. They called it their totem.

This ancient concept can be traced in biblical literature as the root of many dietary laws which prohibited certain (totem) animals being eaten. In much the same way, the modern regimental mascot, whether a sheep or a goat, is believed to secure luck for the regiment.

It is probable that the rabbit, too, is a long-forgotten totem which became the guardian spirit of its descendants, thus, its foot is still considered a bringer of good luck.

But then again, rabbits were taken to be evil, a view possibly quite feasible to those accustomed to speak of the Australian pest. The story is told of a ship's crew of God-fearing men who, having landed on a far-off island, being hungry, chased and killed rabbits. When they sailed for home, their ship was lost on the high seas— "because of the rabbits"!

The rabbit's burrowing habits undoubtedly further contributed to the suspicion with which it was once regarded. What was the animal doing down under? People asked themselves that question and some surmised that the rabbit had a secret communication with the underworld's evil forces. So it was that rabbits were said to have the power of the evil eye, an assertion reinforced by the erroneous notion that young rabbits are born with their eyes wide open.

It was the rabbit's fecundity that helped give its foot an association with good luck and prosperity. The rabbit was so prolific that people considered it the outstanding example of all that was creative, and thus it became symbolic of an abundance of life. It did not take people long to assume that by carrying part of a rabbit, its proximity or touch would transfer to them the animal's good fortune. The choice of the foot was not accidental. Even before Freudian sexual interpretations were known, a foot was recognized as a phallic symbol and regarded as a sure means to foster fertility.

Lockets of Hair

To give a locket of hair to a cherished person is a beautiful custom. But its real meaning is much more profound.

Though now considered an ornament or, perhaps, a charm—a constant reminder of someone loved—originally, it was worn or carried to dominate the donor.

The gift of a lock was an act of surrender, based on the ancient superstition that the hair was the seat of one's vital spirit. Whoever had even a single strand of it was able to influence or bewitch the person to whom it belonged. Thus, whoever bestowed a lock of hair on a chosen person, entrusted their lives to them. Certainly, nothing could surpass such testimony of love and trust.

Whistling at Sea

In the old days of sail the sailor's calling was especially hazardous and it was small wonder that superstition permeated much of his life. In numerous ways seafaring people tried to ensure that the sea would be friendly. They left nothing undone that might help them to escape disaster by propitiating the many invisible, hostile forces on whose goodwill they depended so much and whose whims they could not guess. These agencies, sailors believed, hovered all over the sea and peopled ships. They could cause terror and destruction.

One way of dissuading them from any evil intentions was by sympathetic magic, of the potency of which primitive people were firmly convinced. Thus, some African tribes would never heat milk. If they did so, they imagined that the cow which had provided the milk would suffer, in sympathy, from the heat and perish.

Gales were one of the most frightening hazards at sea. To avoid them by every possible means was a matter of common sense. Sailors believed it was possible to call up a gale by the accidental use of sympathetic magic—if a noise like a storm were made, a storm would come.

The sound of whistling resembled that of a gale in the rigging and for that reason it was assumed that anyone who whistled, magically started a gale. Whistling on board ship was thus considered an invitation to bad luck. Of course, when the sea was becalmed circumstances changed and on such an occasion a whistle could become the right charm. However, sailors who then whistled for the wind did so with utmost caution lest they roused the wrong type, in both strength and direction. They whistled softly and only towards the point from which they wanted the wind to blow.

The view that it is "common" and wrong for a woman to whistle, whether on land or at sea, is rooted in the same belief in the magical power of a whistle. It was considered that a woman's place was in the home and that for her to meddle in male concerns was dangerous at the best of times. But if she did so with a whistle, it could prove fatal. She could rouse winds from the wrong direction and in destructive, gale force.

Apart from that, a woman who whistled usurped a male privilege. An old-established custom gave a man the right to "whistle up" a girl he fancied, which was not, as it is today, a rather vulgar way to attract her attention. As in the case of the wind, it was thought that a man's whistle magically brought the girl to him.

Dogs Howling

It is a long-held belief that the howling of dogs portends misfortune, if not death. People were convinced that everything had a reason and they could not imagine that a dog would howl just for the sake of howling.

It was assumed that the dog, a friend of humans, tried to give them a message. The dog's prolonged doleful cry, full of wails, suggested that the message was of a calamitous nature. This is the most obvious explanation of how people began to believe in the clairvoyance of dogs and to credit them with the faculty of seeing ghosts and spirits. There were other contributory factors.

A dog's perception, at least in part, extends beyond that of a human. Its senses of smell and hearing far excel those of its master. Thus, it took note of many things which to humans did not seem to exist.

Unable at first to find a natural cause of this phenomenon, people endowed dogs with supernatural gifts and mysterious instincts. These, it was thought, gave them the power not just to "sense" spirits and ghosts—especially the approaching figure of Death—but literally to see them, even though people could not perceive their presence. To warn them that Death was hovering over their home, the animal began to howl. It was the least it could do.

Many examples of such "supernatural" gifts of dogs can be found in literature from early times onward. Best known is the account given in the *Odyssey*, where it is told how the dogs of the swineherd Eumaeus, "with a low whine shrank cowering to the stalls' far side" in the presence of Athene, whom Telemachus was unable to see because "the gods in no wise appear visible to all."

Again there is the story of Hecate, associated in Greek lore with the realm of the uncanny and ghosts. Hovering at the crossroads, she foretold death. But only dogs were aware of her. They gave warning by their show of terror and barking.

It is hard to determine whether the numerous tales of that kind were the result or actually the origin of the superstitious notion. At any event, they certainly helped in spreading it. Gullible people, not always capable or willing to differentiate between fact and fiction, soon took the myth for reality.

There may be a much simpler and more rational basis to the belief in the ominous nature of the dog's howl. When rabies was rampant, the whining and howling, no doubt, were linked with the dog going mad. By its bite, it transferred the sickness and consequently caused death. Unaware of the medical facts, people considered the symptoms of the disease as a supernatural omen of death.

Aversion to Red Hair

In some parts of the world there is still a prejudice against red-haired people. It may be that one of its causes is the psychological law of the dislike by the like for the unlike. Certainly, red-haired people almost everywhere are in a minority. However, the unjustified, irrational attitude has other significant foundations as well.

It has historic roots. Anglo-Saxons dreaded their red-haired Danish foes. In the subconscious memories of many English people the otherwise long-forgotten association of hostile invaders with red hair lingered on.

Nature itself has played a part in rendering red an ominous color. Red-yellowish sand was found in the desert which spelled drought, thirst and disaster to many. That is how Egyptians first came to depict one of their evil gods in a red-yellowish sandy color. A medical fallacy has equally been quoted as the virus which poisoned people against red-haired neighbors. Doctors used to diagnose illness by the patient's color and, at some time, a red complexion was considered a symptom of a "gross humor" and ill blood. Possibly scared of infection and because illness was regarded as the result of sin, people shunned and despised those with red hair.

It has been suggested that neither fear of sickness nor horror of sin created the prejudice, but pure envy. Red hair, this much more pleasant fallacy claimed, was an indication of the purest blood, a most clarified spirit and, consequently, the finest of intellects. Red hair showed the best balanced constitution, poised exactly halfway between the blond (phlegmatic) and the black (melancholic), the fickle and the authoritarian. It was for this reason that other people, lacking such a gift, jealously derided and abused those who by the very color of their hair could not disguise their superiority. An Italian proverb asserted that "face without color, either a liar or a traitor."

There are biblical sources as well. Scarlet was the color of sin, and artists therefore painted evil men with yellowish-red hair. The best examples are those of murderous Cain and treacherous Judas Iscariot. And it may have been their portrayal most of all that was responsible for the antipathy towards red-haired people.

Spitting

The habit of spitting on things for luck has a sacred origin. It leads back to belief in magic and several Gospel stories. In antiquity people regarded spittle as representative of the soul. To expectorate, therefore, was like making an offering to the gods who, in return, would extend protection to the spitter.

On the other hand, primitive races believed that if they could get hold of their foe's spittle, they would be able to bewitch them. That is why on the Sandwich Islands, for instance, chiefs were accompanied by a servant who carried a portable spittoon. He carefully buried its contents every morning at a secret spot, lest sorcerers use it for their nefarious purposes.

Human saliva served as a charm against witchcraft and enchantment and was considered a potent antidote against every type of poison. The magical rite of spitting thus found its place in primitive medicine, especially in treating the eyes.

In ancient days, fighters in pugilistic bouts spat on their hands, expecting this would magically increase the strength of their blows.

Authorities, quoted by Pliny, asserted that the pernicious powers of toads, frogs and serpents were rendered innocuous by spitting into their mouths. Tacitus recorded how Vespasian healed a blind man in Alexandria by wetting his eyes with spittle.

Above all, it was the narrative of the Gospels that spread the belief in the miraculous power of spittle among Christian nations. It is told in several passages of the New Testament (Mark 7:32f, 8:22f and John 9:1–7) how Jesus, by its use, worked wonders in restoring sight and speech:

> And they brought unto him one that was deaf and stammered . . . and he took him aside from the crowd, and put his fingers into his ears, and touched his tongue with spittle. And looking up to heaven, he sighed and said to him, "Be opened!" . . . and straightway his tongue was loosed, and he spoke plainly (Mark 7:32f). And they brought a blind man unto him . . . and he took the blind man . . . and he spat into his eyes, and put his hands upon him, and asked if he saw anything, and he looked up, and said, "I perceive men . . ." (Mark 8:22f).

It was stories of that kind, both sacred and profane, which were remembered by the people. They hoped that what had worked once might prove successful again in their own case. Eventually, spitting was credited not only with possessing the power of curing disease, but with acting as a general prophylactic against evil of any kind. As it would ward off misfortune, so it would attract good luck.

People spat, if possible three times, at anyone thought to possess the evil eye. This was not done out of contempt. Spittle, regarded as a holy substance, as part of the soul power, a divine ingredient indeed, would be inimical to evil forces.

Pointing

It is considered bad manners to point at people. This is merely a rationalization of an ancient superstition and a primitive practice. In some parts of the world to point at a celestial body was taken as an affront to divine power, which would punish the offenders. Their action could not harm the sun, moon or stars but only themselves. By a natural development the danger of pointing was generalized.

Pagans, while worshipping idols, pointed at their image. It was thus a natural reaction for Christians to view with disfavor any type of pointing. However, black magic is the most likely source of the disapproval. Widespread and most feared among savage people was the practice of pointing. It was a supernatural way of killing. Possibly at first the savages pointed at an adversary whose death they desired. They did so with a bone taken from a dead man's body, believing that with it they could best express and attain their aim. Survival of this magic death ritual among primitive races rendered the act, if no longer fatal, reprehensible. To avoid any possible ill effect, yet—consciously or unconsciously—not wishing to admit knowledge of the original murderous background, any sort of pointing was decried as uncouth.

Pointing the Finger

Children are taught that it is rude to point a finger at anyone. Why should this be so? In fact, the warning has nothing to do with etiquette or good manners, but is a survival of people's magic past. They believed that psychic power was concentrated in their finger, like in a magic cone, and by aiming at a target, they could achieve miraculous things. It is not difficult to trace the origin of this notion to early times when humans, aware of the omnipotence of sex, worshipped the phallus. It was the source of life. They could not fail to recognize in their outstretched finger the image of the male organ, in a state of erection ready to eject its sperm. The finger thus could prove equally "productive" in the creation of both good and evil.

The use of the outstretched finger in the gesture of blessing was not a symbolic bestowal of the gift but was intended to generate good fortune for whomever it was pointed at. Conversely, the finger was used to inflict harm, as in primitive society the phrase "to point the finger" had become synonymous with killing a person.

Eventually, the pointing finger became detached from the hand

and stretched. Helped by the rod, it evolved into the magic wand, now totally independent of the hand but no less effective. The Bible tells how Moses produced the plagues that hit Pharaoh and his people by "pointing." By stretching his hand towards the sky, he made the sun vanish and darkness envelop the land. When at Moses's bidding Aaron pointed his rod towards the River Nile, he caused the frogs to come up and cover the land. Whether a rod or hand (this fivefold multiplication of the finger), they all reflect the identical magic of the phallus as represented by the digit. It was therefore not simply used as a powerful metaphor by the Egyptian magicians, who when referring to the plagues that had befallen their land, said, "This is the finger of God!" (Exodus 8:15). The ancestral memory has not forgotten the original ominous connotation of the pointing finger, and the gesture of pointing continues to be decried as rude. But at the back of people's minds remains the ancient fear.

CHAPTER 2

Birth and its Customs

Birthday celebration are rather a paradox. Who but children would be happy because a calendar date reminds them that another year of their lives has gone?

Originally, birthdays looked into the future and their celebration was regarded as ensuring continuation of life. It was held that life was renewed on that day, which was thought magically to repeat one's actual birth. If properly observed, the birthday ritual meant life, health and prosperity for the next twelve months. This is why the birthday wish is for "many happy returns of the day."

The Stork and Babies

Dutch, German and Scandinavian mothers particularly used to tell their children that babies were brought by the stork. They also claimed that the stork, when depositing the baby, bit the mother's leg, forcing her to stay in bed. In its very name the stork carries a tradition of love. The English word comes from the Greek *storge*, meaning "strong natural affection," and in Hebrew literally speaks of it as the "pious one."

Several factors combined in creating the belief in the stork as the bringer of babies. First, there was the bird's remarkable tenderness towards its young and old. Legend grew up which described how the young ones looked after the aged, blind and weak parents; how they carried them around on their own wings and fed them.

People watched the stork's care in making its home and noted how it loved to return to the same spot each year. This made them regard the stork's very presence as a sign of good fortune. Indeed, German peasants often encouraged it to build its nest on the roofs of their houses by putting a wagon wheel there for a foundation. The stork soon used it for that very purpose.

The bird's regular trips abroad added to the mystery. At the time, people knew nothing of the migratory habits of birds and legend assumed that during the winter storks went to Egypt, to change there into men. It was believed that the stork had once been a human being.

Finally, there was the fact that storks loved water and frequented swamps, marshes and ponds. Ancient tradition held that it was in those watery places that the souls of unborn children dwelled. It was easy to link all these beliefs and superstitions to make the stork, so conspicuous in appearance, all-important in the propagation of humans.

Blue for Boys and Pink for Girls

The practice to dress boys and girls in different colors is linked with their sex. All babies look alike, and what better means could there be to identify them readily than colors—blue for boys and pink for girls, a color scheme adopted all over the world. But who would ever suspect that the choice of blue was also linked with the haunting fear of anxious parents, deeply concerned for their baby's future?

Already in antiquity it was believed that evil spirits hovered menacingly over the nursery. They were thought to be allergic to certain colors, the most potent among them being blue. It was considered that its association with the heavenly sky rendered satanic forces powerless and drove them away. To this very day Arabs in the Middle East continue to paint the doors of their homes blue in the belief that it will frighten away demons. The display of blue on a young child thus was not merely an adornment, but a necessary protective precaution.

As girl babies were regarded as vastly inferior to male infants, it was assumed that evil spirits would not be interested in them. It explains why blue was reserved for boys, whilst any distinctive color for girls was deemed unnecessary. It was possibly because later generations were unaware of the original reason for "blue for boys" but very much conscious of the neglect of girls, that the new pink look was introduced for them.

European legendary tradition suggests another beautiful explanation of the color scheme for babies. This tells that baby boys are found under cabbages whose color—on the continent of Europe—is mostly blue. Baby girls, on the other hand, were born inside a pink rose.

The Pram

The modern pram was first constructed in 1848 in New York City by Charles Burton. His newfangled idea did not catch on, mainly because the pram collided with too many pedestrians. Burton, however, was determined to make a success of his invention. He went to Britain and opened a factory there. The change of site brought him a change of luck. His pram appealed to the common sense of mothers and became fashionable when Queen Victoria (and later Queen Isabella of Spain and the Pasha of Egypt) ordered the new type of baby carriage for their families. The choice of the word perambulator for the new baby vehicle is interesting. Its literal meaning, derived from the Latin, is "to walk through." The shortened version "pram" first appeared in the vocabulary in its new sense in 1857.

Birthday Cake and Candles

The purpose of birthday candles is to honor the birthday child and to bring it good fortune for the ensuing year.

The custom goes back to the ancient Greeks. According to the writings of Philochorus, worshippers of Artemis, goddess of the moon and hunting, used to put honey-cakes on the altars of her temples. They did so in honor of her birthday. The cakes were round like the full moon and lit with tapers.

No further record of this custom exists between the days of those Greek moon-worshippers and its reappearance among German peasants in the Middle Ages, who again used to light candles on birthday cakes, doing so at the moment the child wakened. The candles were then kept burning until the cake was eaten at the family meal. If necessary, they were replaced by new ones. The number of candles indicated the age of the child. Always added was an extra taper representing the light of life.

Like in the case of sacrificial fires, from the earliest days burning tapers were endowed with a mystical significance. It was believed that the birthday candles had the power to grant a wish and ensure a happy year for the child. However, the wish, which had to remain secret, would only come true if all the candles were blown out with one puff.

The old belief that the candles symbolized life is retained in many sayings. Thus we warn people of not "burning the candle at both ends" and Macbeth spoke of life as a "brief candle."

The Queen's Birthday

British sovereigns have two birthdays every year—on the real date of their birth and on an official, proclaimed day. This explains why, for instance, although Queen Elizabeth II was born on April 21, her birthday is celebrated on the second Saturday in June. The day was not chosen because any particular monarch was actually born then. Indeed the choice had nothing to do with the needs or convenience of the monarch.

Concern for the people's enjoyment was the major reason for fixing the date in June. Because the day fell during the summer season, it was most likely that the sky would be blue and the weather pleasant and therefore conducive to all types of outdoor events, games and sports. Other considerations of a practical kind also supported the new date.

Traditionally, the king or queen awards titles and decorations twice annually, with honors lists being published both on New Year's Day (on Australia Day in the Antipodes) and the monarch's birthday. To prevent the occasions from being too close together or, worse still, falling during the same month, the middle of the year was chosen as the most feasible time to fix the monarch's official birthday.

"Trooping the Color" forms the stirring climax of the celebrations. It attracts vast crowds. With the ever-increasing weekday traffic causing congestion in London streets, people experienced great difficulty in reaching the Horse Guards parade off Whitehall, where the ceremony is being held. To eliminate this problem it was decided to move the celebration to a weekend—a "Saturday early in June."

CHAPTER 3

The Ritual of Courting and Marriage

The history of courting is a mirror of human civilization and technological advance. Its duration and speed have varied enormously. Its time and pace have fluctuated between the fourteen years it took Jacob to woo Rachel and the lightning speed of modern times.

The range of intensity, likewise, has differed greatly. It extends from the reticence of young lovers making polite conversation in the presence of ever-watchful chaperones in Victorian parlors to the impetuous petting of today's teenagers in the complete privacy, propinquity and mobility of their car.

Even the choice of one's partner has undergone many significant changes. There were times when the bridal couple met for the first time on the day of their marriage, which had been arranged—independently of their own wishes and desires—by the tribe or the family. Then marriage brokers took over the task, on a strictly commercial basis, yet they were not unaware of human factors. Rome had its lottery for lovers.

For the sake of marriage God gave Eve to Adam. Ever since, people have married. They have made many mistakes and have often taken the bond for something that it is not.

We speak of wedlock and imagine that a marriage is something that locks people up and chains them together like prisoners. The original lock is no lock at all but the Anglo-Saxon for "gift," as "wed" means a promise. Wedlock thus pledged the finest of all gifts—the happiness of a man and a woman. To achieve that aim, numerous customs have been followed down the ages.

The story is told that ever since God created woman out of one of Adam's ribs, men have been rushing all over the world, seeking their missing rib. Some never get hold of it and they rationalize their failure by calling themselves confirmed bachelors. Others actually find "a rib." But it is not theirs and that is why it does not really fit, and both parties concerned experience much anguish and pain. However, there are the lucky ones. They retrieve the rib which belongs to them and thus become once more "complete," with all the happiness this implies.

Beautiful and romantic are the numerous customs which are now associated with courtship and marriage. Nearly all of them can be traced to primitive ritual and early practice designed to ensure—by magical rites and armed force—the fertility of the union.

The Kiss

The mystery of the kiss is its very paradox. To the Western mind so fundamentally erotic, expressive of affection and "natural," other races have never known it. Kissing—of one kind or another—has its prominent place even in nature. The origin of the kiss has been explored from almost every angle, and views still differ as to how it all started.

Fish kiss—mouth to mouth. Some races kiss—by rubbing noses. No matter what the technique, every kiss, though in varied proportions, involves several senses. First of all, there is the sense of touch. It is necessary to feel the object of one's affection. That is why a cat rubs itself against people to whom it has taken a fancy. Insects make contact with their antennae and birds with their bills or beaks: all just to tell how much they love each other. This tactile pleasure may well go back to the conjugation of the earliest unicellular organisms. These linked their mouths—temporarily—to exchange their hereditary nuclei. Then, enriched, they separated again. Possibly, kissing is a vestige of this initial sexual union and its sublimation.

From very early days onward, smell has also played a role in kissing, at times significantly so. It has been suggested that when blind Isaac asked Jacob to kiss him (before bestowing his divine blessing actually meant for his brother Esau), his secret intention was to smell him, to make quite sure of his identity. Only Jacob's deception by having donned Esau's clothes made Isaac proceed: "And he smelled the smell of his garments" (Genesis 27:27).

Eskimos and Maoris still "rub noses." A number of primitive races, completely unfamiliar with the mouth kiss, also "rub noses" instead. In their case this is an inaccurate description as in reality what they do is place the mouth and nose against the cheek of the other person and inhale! In some of their languages, tellingly the very word for kissing denotes "smelling," and Borneans do not "greet" but "smell" a visitor.

A beautiful fable tries to explain what it was that gave the sense of smell such importance in loving. A mother sheep had lost one of her baby lambs. Greatly distressed, she started searching for it. She went about sniffing everywhere until, at long last, she recognized her missing lamb by its special odor. From that moment onward, to smell each other gave extra satisfaction and a feeling of happiness. A dog still sniffs its master. No doubt scent has its sexual appeal and is erotically exciting. This, of course, accounts for the creation of the whole industry of perfume.

Of all parts of the body, the mouth alone can taste and feel at the same time. Its proximity to the nose and the labial contact serve equally well the senses of smell and sound. Above all, the combination of mucous membranes and a complex network of nerves have rendered the lips supremely sensitive. With such a focus of love, the mouth was bound to become one of the prominent erogenous zones that could easily activate the very fires of passion. That kissing is really an atavism is a widespread conviction. Subconsciously it recalls in the grown-up man and woman, so psychoanalysts claim, the earliest days of their babyhood when they were suckled at their mother's breast. Thus, in people's fervent passion survives memories of infantile drinking habits and their supreme bliss.

Another theory of the birth of kissing also links it with early nourishment, though detached from the nipples. Just as in nature, among birds for instance, the mother premasticates the food in her mouth then transfers it by means of a kiss into the mouth of her little one, so did humans in the remote past. And it is the ancestral memory of that early stage that made kissing so wonderful.

An early belief, if not accounting for the mouth kiss, well added to its importance. The dead do not breathe. No wonder, therefore, that breath was identified with the life force, a person's spirit or soul. It was so easy to escape through that largest of orifices—the mouth. This is why yawning was regarded as dangerous and children were taught to cover the gaping mouth with their hand. It was to keep in their soul and thereby stay alive. People used to kiss the mouth of the dying. They did so not out of affection but to catch the departing spirit and preserve it for the generations to come.

The magic of kissing thus has played its part in various spheres of life. Fairytales keep alive the ancient belief that the kiss could undo spells and remove taboos. It is the recurring motif of the prince who, with his liberating kiss, awakens the sleeping princess.

X for a Kiss

That X—a mere cross—came to represent a kiss has its own story to tell. Some have seen in the choice of that figure from mathematics a most appropriate symbol. It may signify nothing at all, a mere "zero," or stand for (an) infinity (of delight). On the other hand, it can "multiply" joy and love. However, the prosaic explanation for this affectionate sign may be twofold. Originally it represented the formalized, stylized picture of two mouths—><— touching each other—X. But then the cross came to express a kiss by odd circumstances, namely people's lack of education. Early illiterates signed documents with a cross. They did so for an obvious reason.

A cross was so simple to draw and yet, being also a sacred symbol, implied the promise of truth. To solemnly confirm the veracity of what they had endorsed, the writers kissed their signature, as they were accustomed to do with the Holy Book. And that is how, finally, by its very association, the cross came to be identified with a kiss.

Spooning

Three possible explanations offer themselves for the use of the word "spooning" to describe courting. Far from being slang, the term recollects a beautiful custom.

Young men in Wales used to carve a wooden spoon that they presented as a token of love to the girl of their choice. Often this took the place of an engagement ring. If she accepted the spoon, it was as good as a promise of marriage.

The spoon itself was elaborately carved. Frequently it was decorated with intricate floral patterns, both on the handle and the bowl. It was stained and embossed with the lovers' initials, suitably intertwined. Only the progress of civilization, with its mass production of spoons, discontinued this lovely mode of courting. Engagement rings, easily purchased, took the place of the spoon, now merely retained in the way of speaking.

A less romantic interpretation relates the spoon to childish behavior, and implies that the spooning couples are not serious about their love-play. There is also the suggestion that "spooning" refers to the lying closely together of two people, like spoons that fit into each other. Lastly, the father of the girl made the young man carve a spoon in order for him, whilst courting, to keep his hands occupied, to stop them from wandering!

The Valentine Card

On February 14 millions of Valentine cards are sent to people of the opposite sex. Once individually written and now mass-produced, they are light-hearted missiles of love. Either in prose or in rhyme they voice amorous feelings. Mostly they are humorous, sometimes vulgar and often accompanied by illustrations.

It is all a play of love, strongly spiced with sentimentality and fun. Who would ever think that this jolly and harmless custom of budding romance began long ago and has its origins in pagan tradition about the love-life of birds, an ancient lottery for sweethearts and, most of all, the martyr's death of a Christian bishop? The popularity of Valentine cards also testifies to the success of the early Church in its endeavor to Christianize heathen practices.

Many years prior to the advent of Christianity, the middle of February was considered propitious for love. It was the season of spring and the time when birds started mating.

Roman mythology associated the day with the goddess Juno, worshipped especially by women at all crises of life. She was the "venerable ox-eyed" wife of Jupiter and the queen of heaven. Identified with the Greek Hera, she became the guardian of women and marriage, though significantly also a goddess of war. Part of the pagan ritual honoring Juno was a unique kind of lottery. Young girls wrote their names on slips of paper which they placed into a drum from which the boys drew their luck. There were no blanks. The girl drawn by a young man became his sweetheart until the next annual draw.

All the world loves a lover, and Christianity was unable to uproot a day dedicated to the enjoyment of life and love. This made the early Church appropriate February 14 for its own calendar, linking it with the martyrdom of St. Valentine.

Originally, Valentine was a third-century pagan priest. Converted to Christianity, he became a bishop. The story is told that at the time, the Roman Emperor Claudius, feeling that husbands did not make good soldiers, had decided to abolish the institution of marriage. He tried to enforce the new law with the utmost rigor.

Valentine, however, considered such policy against the spirit of God and of human nature. Secretly he married young lovers. But not for long. He was arrested, imprisoned and brutally murdered—on February 14, 269.

Another (and more plausible) account relates that Valentine frequently aided persecuted Christians, and that this was the reason that he was thrown into prison. But even there he continued his saintly work, miraculously restoring vision to his jailer's blind daughter. However, he was doomed and on February 14 he was clubbed to death. The date coincided with the ancient pagan feast of Juno, and ever since has been celebrated as St. Valentine's Day.

The Church's desire to Christianize pagan practice did not end here. There was still the most popular part of the feast—its lottery for love. Those early theologians were men of the world and certainly did not live in an ivory tower. They knew only too well that one cannot suppress people's deepest urges, including their love of gambling—no matter for what.

Therefore they retained the ancient lottery but changed its prizes. They substituted the names of saints for those of girls! The lucky winners were now expected in the ensuing year to match their life to that of the saint whose name they had drawn. This bored the participants. The girls recaptured the lottery drums, putting into them once again their own names, with the ancient love-play starting all over again.

Then a final development took place. People were no longer satisfied with having their sweethearts chosen for them by chance. Their own choice, they felt, should take the place of luck. Thus on February 14 they began sending a gift, a card or a set of verses to whomsoever they considered nearest their heart.

Often the cards were sent anonymously and it was left to the recipient to guess their author. Their text either stated briefly but to the point that "the honey's sweet and so are you" or went into most elaborate and passionate musings. Those who could not write their own words selected them from specially published handbooks, such as *The Young Man's Valentine Writer*, which appeared in 1797. That is how, eventually, the printed Valentine card came into existence. Its popularity was greatly fostered by the introduction of cheap postal rates.

Leap-year Proposals

The right of women to "pop the question" every fourth year goes far back into the past. The choice of a leap year is rather significant. According to ancient tradition, many things happened then that were topsy-turvy; even beans were thought to grow the wrong way during that year.

That specially appointed day—February 29—really was not counted and had no status in English law, for which reason it was "leapt over," which explains the year's name.

Just as the extra day every fourth year brought at least a partial correction of the discrepancy which developed between the calendar and the seasons, so the privilege of leap-year proposals gave women an opportunity of correcting, temporarily, a state of affairs that was one-sided and completely unjust. Especially at a time when there was a surplus of females, they could try to ensure that they were not "left on the shelf."

The origin of the custom has been explained both as the result of a specific (but fictitious) Royal Act and rebellion by some nuns. It is alleged that in 1288 Queen Margaret of Scotland decreed through her Parliament that in a leap year any woman could propose to any man she liked who could refuse her only if he was already engaged. If, defying the law, he still insisted on preserving his single state and rejected the woman's advances, he was liable to a fine of $150, reducible only in cases of hardship.

From the Scots the rule was adopted in Genoa, Florence and France, though at no time—at least officially—by the English themselves.

Yet in spite of the fact that this so-called Act of the Scottish Parliament has been quoted numerous times, investigation has proved it to be a myth and nonexistent and thus for hundreds of years women based their "right" on a legal fiction.

Scottish people are renowned for their wisdom. No wonder therefore, that their men were not slow to guard themselves from being taken unawares by a female pursuer. They conceded that women had the privilege of proposal during a leap year, but stipulated that they indicate their intention by wearing a scarlet petticoat with a clearly visible hem. It gave bachelors due warning and a sporting chance to get out of the way.

Celibacy among priests and nuns was not always the rule and certainly not at the time of St. Patrick, which makes at least a little more feasible an otherwise completely outrageous myth. It tells how one day Patrick was approached by St. Bridget, who was in tears. The nuns under her supervision were in revolt, strongly resenting the unfair institution that gave only men the right to propose and barring women from taking the initiative in selecting a mate.

Patrick himself had vowed to stay single. Nevertheless, he sympathized with the rebellious women and saw their point. Total equality was out of the question. Hence he suggested that they should be permitted to propose during one full year every seven years.

Bridget was still dissatisfied and did not see her way clear to accept the offer. She knew men's weakness and threw her arms around Patrick, calling him "my jewel" and saying that she dare not go back to the nuns with such a proposition. "Make it a year in four!" she begged.

The future saint had rather enjoyed her embrace and promised that, for another of those "squeezes," he would accede to her request. Moreover, he undertook to make it not only every fourth year but the longest at that—the leap year.

The agreement took effect at once. Bridget was not slow to take advantage of it for herself and immediately proposed to Patrick.

Having taken a vow of celibacy, he could not help but refuse. However, to soften the blow, he gave her a kiss and a silken gown as a consolation gift.

From this legend came the custom, observed until recent years, of acknowledging the right of a rejected woman to claim as compensation a new dress of pure silk.

The Best Man

The best man has always been the bridegroom's best friend, but for different reasons. Originally, his duties were neither pleasant nor particularly safe.

At the beginning of history a bridegroom's best man had to excel in many qualities which are now completely unnecessary and even forgotten. Then he was chosen for being strong, brave and a good fighter. He accompanied his friend as an armed escort, to help him in capturing a bride! No wonder, therefore, that he was called the best man. For such a purpose only the best was good enough.

In some parts of the world warriors considered it undignified to woo a woman themselves. They let others do the job for them. When all was ready for the marriage, they set out with their companions—to wrest the bride from her original owner. That is why the actual wooer surrounded himself with an armed guard, his "best men." They were there to repel any counterattacks and defend the "goods."

Times changed. Men no longer captured their brides, either from their homes or their rightful "owners." And yet, on the day of the actual wedding, they needed extra protection and support. There still was the danger of a rival who, at the last moment, might carry off the bride. To avoid this the best man was in attendance, armed and on the alert. It was for this reason, too, that Scandinavians used to hold their weddings under the cover of night. Behind the High Altar of one of the Swedish churches, so it was said, were kept lances with sockets for torches. These served the best men in their hazardous task, as weapons and sources of illumination, to detect and repel possible abductors.

It was only logical that at first the best man accompanied not the groom but the bride, whom obviously he was there to guard and retain. Only when rough times increased vulgarity on the part of the men, and brides seemed even less safe under their protection, a separation of the sexes proved advisable. From then onward the best man was always near the groom, whilst bridesmaids closed their ranks around the bride.

Bride on the Groom's Left Side

Procedure at a wedding follows definite rules. Its processions and paraphernalia are therefore carefully studied and rehearsed by all parties concerned.

The bride and groom stand and walk together in a way that is traditional. At the ceremony, the bride takes her place on the left side of the groom. Once the bond is sealed, her husband places her hand within his left arm to follow the officiant to the desk to sign the register. Finally, on the way out, the bride passes down the aisle, once again on the left arm of the bridegroom.

That on each of these occasions the groom offers his left arm and hand to the bride is not just a matter of meaningless etiquette. It is the result of ancient and most anxious considerations. Once, he did so purposely and not merely because it was "the right thing" to do. He placed her on his left not to honor but to safeguard her. It enabled him to keep his right (and sword) hand free, to be ready to defend her (and himself) from attack and capture by jealous rivals, or in ancient days, her former owner from whom he had wrested her.

The Bride's Veil

A complexity of old traditions, fears and obsolete social conditions are interwoven in the bridal veil. It is also a relic of the early custom of capturing a wife. Naturally the newly acquired "goods" were safely wrapped up before being taken away. What now consists of a thin lace or net covering was once a large sheet big enough to envelop the body.

As times grew more polite, the veil assumed more subtle and psychological meanings. It indicated a woman's original complete submission to her husband. She should not even be seen. Hidden goods tend to appear more precious and attractive than those openly on display. It was yet another significant reason for the concealment of the bride's face and explains why in ancient times (and still today in some primitive groups) the bridegroom was not permitted to set eyes on his bride until the very moment when they were about to consummate their marriage.

The veil used to express humility on the part of the bride. It recalls the ancient biblical account of how Rebecca, when she first met Isaac, her future husband, shyly "took a veil and covered herself with it." People are most superstitious at moments when great happiness is about to be theirs. Fear of jealous demons who might carry off a lovely bride led to the custom of disguising her identity—and hiding her face behind a "curtain." This was also thought to be effective against the "evil eye," once considered to be a ubiquitous and potent malevolent force.

Yet another interpretation points to the use of a veil not only at weddings but on all occasions when a person assumed a new identity. Thus initiates into religious communities are veiled, and even the dead, as they, too, enter a totally new circle of associates. The bride, likewise, by the fact of man and woman becoming "one flesh," was considered to change completely her personality. The veil "shut out" magically her old former being. She was now to be a new person altogether—"for better or worse."

Finally, the veil might be the last relic of the "care-cloth," as it was called among Anglo-Saxons. This enveloped both bride and groom. Aware and afraid of higher powers, the couple thereby acknowledged their presence and, even more so, tried to protect themselves from them.

Orange Blossoms

Flowers have expressed, without words, many a significant message, not least on behalf of a bride on her wedding day. The orange blossoms that traditionally adorned her were originally not meant as an ornament. They were used to tell—in silent language—facts and hopes which it would be too difficult and embarrassing to voice in so many spoken words. The white blossoms were, first of all, a symbol of innocence and purity. They were worn publicly to make it known that the bride was a virgin. As few trees bear greater crops, the orange blossoms were also intended to convey the hope that she, too, may be blessed with an abundance of offspring. They tried magically to ensure the realization of this wish.

Only on rare occasions does life bestow on people all they desire. Mostly it is a question of one thing or the other. Various qualities are thus distributed among different individuals, and only in the most fortunate cases combined in one person.

In former days a man hoped to wed a wife who was not only beautiful in both looks and character but, at the same time, prolific, the future mother of many children.

The orange tree, an evergreen, was one of the few plants which produced both fruit and flowers simultaneously. Therefore its blossoms could most suitably voice the hope and wish that the bride, too, far from being merely "a worthless flower of beauty," would be blessed with the two virtues of the orange tree.

Orange trees are a common sight in countries of a warm climate, but in northern Europe they were known as something exotic. As they were rare and costly, only the rich could afford to import them. For this reason their blossoms were chosen to adorn brides from the wealthy and noble classes. Consequently they became a symbol of high rank.

To imitate the rich has always been the desire of those less fortunate, who were anxious to do so especially on their wedding day, when only the best was good enough. That is how all the brides, no matter at what cost, wanted to wear them.

In England the custom is of a comparatively recent date, having been introduced from France about 1820. The French had adopted it from the Spaniards who many centuries earlier, tradition claims, received their first orange trees from the Moors.

A beautiful legend tells the story of the origin of the custom, associating it with a poor Spanish girl. Soon after the trees had been introduced into Spain, the then reigning monarch planted them in his palace garden, treasuring especially one tree.

The French ambassador often expressed the wish to obtain an offshoot for himself but, possibly jealous of his possession, the king refused. His gardener's daughter knew all about this. She was in desperate need of a dowry to marry the man she loved. Her father was too poor to give her one. Secretly, she cut a slip from the prized tree and sold it to the ambassador at a high price.

On the day of her wedding she felt that, somehow, she had to acknowledge her debt to the tree to which, after all, she owed her happiness. For that purpose she took some of its blossoms and put them into her hair. Thus she inaugurated the fashion which became universal.

The Wedding Ring

The ring, now an essential part of the wedding ceremony, adopted by the Christian Church as late as the ninth century, had its beginning in the pagan world. Its origin leads back to ancient superstition, to magic and the kidnapping of one's wife. Its shape was both utilitarian—best adapted to secure a precious property—and symbolic, as in the Egyptian hieroglyphic script the circle represented eternity and marriage was seen as a permanent bond.

From the East, it was copied by the ancient Greeks, from whom, like so many other customs and traditions, it was taken over by the Romans, finally to be introduced worldwide. Now a small ring worn around a finger, it developed from large bands that circled the wrist, the ankles or even the waist.

Primitive man, believing in magic, bound a rope around the woman he chose for himself, being convinced that this "magic circle" would fetter her to him and cause his spirit to enter her body. She was thus tied to him by supernatural forces which could never be broken. Yet another primitive belief regarded the ring as an amulet that would ward off evil spirits hovering around the bride to threaten her marital bliss.

The early custom of capturing one's wife survives in many a legend with the ring leading back to that primitive beginning of matrimony, when the man bound fetters around the wrists and ankles of the woman he carried away to become his property and servant.

Actually, the wedding ring developed from the engagement ring. It was a pledge of future intentions and, therefore, it is also closely connected with the purchase of women, once prevalent and still remembered by the dowry. The ring, bestowed in this manner, was an old Roman custom confirming betrothal. It was a commercial promise that the contract would be carried out. In modern terminology the ring served as the first instalment of a lay-by plan. From the moment this had been paid, the ring, conspicuously displayed, told all other men that this woman was no longer "for sale."

Among the Jewish people the ring was first introduced in the eighth century A.D. It replaced the custom of handing the bride a small coin as a promissory "note" of the husband's ability to meet all future financial obligations towards his wife.

The purpose of the ring was not ornamental, but a practical means to enable the woman not to lose (or lose sight of) that precious token. From early antiquity onwards, as excavations and biblical records testify, rings had a signet. This provided a seal with which orders were signed. To hand such a ring to another person symbolized, and actually carried out, a transfer of authority. That is why Pharaoh took off his ring and handed it to Joseph, so that "you shall be over my house and according to your word shall all my people be ruled."

To hand one's wife the signet ring implied, likewise, that she had come to share all responsibilities and had been admitted as an equal partner in the management of the home. Its circular shape indicated the lasting character of the contract.

It was only Pope Nicholas who—in A.D. 800—first distinctly referred to the Christian use of the ring. Once adopted by the Church, it came to represent not merely a commercial transaction but a token and pledge of fidelity, a sacred covenant. Its shape now signified "the eternity, constancy and integrity of love." It was there to perpetually remind the wife and others of the sanctity of wedlock. As the circle symbolized harmony and perfection and its lines were endless, so the ring indicated the continuity of the sacred bond and reminded the couple that their mutual love and affection should flow from one to the other in a circle, continually and forever. Psycho-analysis, with its early sexual interpretations of almost every aspect of life, saw in the finger a representation of the male and in the ring the female which—at marriage—were joined together.

The Ring Finger

A variety of traditions account for the choice of hand and finger for the wearing of the wedding ring. The selection of the third finger of the left hand has been attributed to ancient faulty anatomy, according to which a vein led straight from there to the heart. However erroneous, it is still a beautiful explanation. Another reason is linked with early symbolism where the right hand represented dominance and the left submission. By placing the ring on the bride's left hand, the groom made her understand—without saying it in so many words—that from now on she was his property and that he was the master of their home.

In some countries, the ring is placed on the right hand. The choice is associated with this hand's traditional use in taking an oath. To confirm the truth of a statement, people either raised their right hand or placed it on the Bible. Likewise, as a token of the marriage vow, the ring belonged to this hand. It also expressed rather poetically how a wife was "like a man's right hand."

Solely utilitarian is yet another explanation. The third finger is the least active of the hand and a ring placed there will not inconvenience its wearer. There is also less likelihood of it being worn out or damaged.

An equally practical consideration was the retention and span of the ring finger. Whereas every other finger can be stretched independently, the third one cannot be extended to its full length on its own. This prevented a wedding ring from easily slipping off, thereby making that finger the most secure safeguard for so precious an object.

Nowadays, the ring is immediately put on the finger on which it is to stay at the marriage ceremony. However, this was not always the case. Thus, in an ancient Church ritual, still being practiced in the sixteenth century, the ring used to be systematically moved three times prior to finding its permanent place. Each change was introduced or accompanied by successive parts of the trinitarian formula. With the words "In the name of the Father," the priest placed the ring on the thumb. Whilst saying, "In the name of the Son," he moved it to the forefinger and then, with "and of the Holy Ghost," to the middle finger. With the closing word "Amen," he slipped the ring onto the third or ring finger, sealing the marriage bond.

Throwing Confetti

The word "confetti" comes from the Italian, being of the same root as the word "confectionery." It refers to "sweetmeats"—a recollection of the time when nuts and sugared almonds were thrown over the bride and groom.

The custom, in turn, derived from the ancient pagan rite of showering the happy couple with grain. Most of the wedding ritual was designed to expel evil. But in this case the intention was to ensure bliss. The missiles of grain or rice were a standard feature of pagan marriages. Their purpose was not just symbolically to express wishes for a fruitful union. It was believed the fertility of the seeds would be magically transferred to the pair on whom they fell.

Confetti is the inexpensive paper-substitute for the rice, wheat or nuts originally thrown on the newlyweds. It is strange to imagine that present-day society, which has become so proficient in birth control, still enthusiastically applies—in its paper version— the ancient magic of birth promotion!

Throwing an Old Shoe

In modern times, the throwing of a shoe, or the tying of it to a carriage, is restricted to wedding celebrations—when a bridal couple is about to go away on their honeymoon. It expresses people's wish for good luck to the newlyweds. Not so long ago, however, people threw shoes after anyone starting on a trip. Ben Jonson could thus say—

> Hurl after me an old shoe
> I'll be merry whatever I'll do.

Who would guess that such a simple custom as throwing a shoe contains a wealth of meaning, good and bad? It was observed as a magic means of ensuring plenty of children and lots of luck. The shoe is an ancient fertility symbol. Eskimo women, for instance, used to carry on them a piece of an old shoe to make themselves prolific. At some time shoes were part of a worker's wages and greatly esteemed as such for the same reason.

The choice of an old shoe for throwing was not a matter of economics. On the contrary, it was a most thoughtful selection. People believed that the soul lived in their shoes. These preserved the essence of the life of the person who wore them. Therefore to throw them, or just one of them, after a bridal couple or, better still, to tie them to their carriage, gave to those embarking on a new life all the additional good luck and experience of the shoes' former owner. Indeed, it was not only the cheapest, but the most precious of gifts.

For thousands of years slippers and shoes have also served as an emblem of power and possession. To cast one's sandal on a piece of land actually meant to take possession of it. Holy Scripture supplied an example, when God says, "Over Edom itself I cast My shoes." Still prevalent in various languages is a phrase that speaks of having a person "under one's slipper" or "under one's heel," meaning that one dominates them.

In the case of the sale or transfer of property, the former owner would take one of their sandals or shoes and give it to the new owner. The shoe was the ancient equivalent of the modern title deed to goods or property. The ceremony was therefore a legal procedure, not restricted to marital occasions alone.

In antiquity, a wife was considered a man's chattel. Her parents sold her to her future husband and the transaction was confirmed in the then customary way of a business deal, in which a sandal was given as a token of faith and of the transfer of property. By throwing shoes after the bride, parents indicated—in the presence of witnesses—that they had relinquished their authority over their daughter who now legally belonged to her new master.

Yet another explanation links the custom with the ancient institution of capturing one's bride. In this case the throwing of shoes is a last remnant of the old (but later merely mock) battle between the bride's family, anxious to retain the girl, and the bridegroom's party, set on abducting her.

There are two further interpretations. Throughout marriage, the wife formally had to present shoes to her husband. She thereby symbolically reaffirmed her inferior position and his lordship. To help build up a stock of shoes, friends tossed some to her on the day of the wedding. It has also been suggested that not men but unmarried women were the original shoe-throwers, out of happiness and in self-congratulation. The shoe was the symbol of woman's serfdom to man. But so far they had escaped from that fate and preserved their liberty. Happy for themselves, but sorry for the bride, they cast shoes after her, as she was being carried off as a slave!

The Wedding Cake

The wedding cake has its history and even the sugar-coating, like the veil, covers up quite an exciting past. The Romans were the first to use it but only at the nuptials of the Patricians, their upper class. It was part of a ceremony known as the *confarreatio*, meaning "eating together."

Initially, the bride and groom shared a small part of the cake, which was a sort of unleavened scone made of flour, salt and water. It was thought to secure for them a life of plenty, in both children and happiness.

Then the cake was broken over the bride's head and the guests scrambled for the fragments, believing that thus they, too, would share in the blessings these symbolized.

Only children born of a marriage solemnized in this fashion, with a cake and in front of ten witnesses, qualified for the high sacred offices in Roman life. The cake therefore not only provided the guests with some tasty morsels of food (and a little extra luck) and the couple—magically—with future fertility, but even their still-unborn children—legally—with opportunities for advancement!

The wedding cake rites, with the food symbolizing fertility, were followed all over the world, with local variations and developments. American Indians used the simple, scone-type cake, which the bride herself had to bake and present to her groom. The early Anglo-Saxons supplied at a wedding a huge basket of small dry biscuits, of which each guest took one, with those left over being distributed among the poor. In a further development the guests brought their own cakes. Often spiced buns, they piled them into a large heap. If the bride and groom were able to kiss each other across the mound, it was considered a good omen for their life-long happiness. Eventually, around the time of King Charles II, the many buns were combined into one big cake. Legend credits the idea to a French chef who was visiting Britain. Watching the cumbersome way of piling numerous little cakes insecurely on top of one another, he decided it would be much more practical to ice the mound of buns into one mass, the very origin of the elaborately decorated, many-tiered iced wedding cakes of today.

Carrying the Bride over the Threshold

Several reasons could account for the custom of carrying the bride across the threshold. Dating back to a superstitious past, they do not reflect favorably on the beginnings of matrimony and might well be a recollection of the days when wives were captured. They did not come willingly but had to be taken by force into the man's house.

Quite differently, psychologists may recognize in it a wise and not-so-romantic way to make the woman realize who runs the house and who determines where to go. On the other hand, it is a common experience that a sham opposition creates greater desire, and perhaps the bride loved to appear as if she entered the new home under duress.

A superstition dating back almost to prehistoric times makes people afraid of stumbling. It was thought to be a sign of ill luck, especially if falling over one's own doorstep. To avoid any possibility of such an ominous accident that might doom the marriage from its very beginning, the cautious bridegroom carried his bride across.

In ancient Rome the threshold was sacred to Vesta, the virgin goddess. Therefore it was considered not merely bad taste, but sacrilegious, for a bride, who was about to lose her virginity, to touch the threshold. There was no better way to avoid any such untoward event than to carry her across.

Indeed, an old belief in the sanctity and evil properties of the threshold most of all may account for the custom. People assumed that demons dwelt there and to avoid any contact with them, they jumped across. More so, to propitiate those evil forces, they buried stillborn babies under the door or smeared blood on its lintels. To save his wife from any possible contact with the demons lurking under the doorstep the bridegroom carried her across.

The Honeymoon

There are several opinions as to the origin of the word "honeymoon." The moon gave birth—on the loom of language—to the "month." In ancient days (and still today among Arabs and Jews) the duration of a month coincides with the period of one revolution of the moon. One had only to look at the moon to ascertain the approximate date. A new moon always signified the first day of the new month. Hence the "honeymoon" was the first month of marriage, when all was sweet.

Other lunar observations turned away from the sunny side of the moon—and life—and noted their ever-changing character. The moon never appeared the same and was subject to constant variation. A dismal way of thought indeed, the honeymoon likewise referred not so much to the period of one month, as to the fickleness of love, its intensity growing so much less after the first white heat of passion. Indeed, not a few misanthropes explained that the honey was bound to change—like the moon—but to water and gall . . .

> But of all the lunar things that change,
> The one that shows most fickle and strange,
> ʼ And takes the most eccentric range,
> Is the moon—so called—of honey.

Thomas Hood

The most likely origin of the honeymoon, however, is an old Scandinavian and generally northern European custom for the newlyweds to drink honeyed wine or other kinds of diluted and fermented honey during the first month of marriage, believing in their effectiveness as an aphrodisiac.

The Honeymoon Destination

Many a newlywed couple does not like to reveal, even to their closest friends, the place where they are going to spend their honeymoon. They really do not know why it is that they keep it a secret and mostly, superstitiously, believe it to be for good luck.

The practice has also been rationalized by the explanation that they want to be left alone and, by the added air of secrecy, make the occasion all the more romantic. Actually, the custom originated in the days when the man used to capture his bride-to-be. There was every reason, therefore, for the couple not to make known their whereabouts, lest the woman's family catch up with them, causing much unpleasantness or, at the very worst, reclaim the woman as their property. Once the honeymoon was over, the young couple hoped, tempers would have cooled down and the new situation be accepted as final.

The Helpmate

When referring to a helpmate, the term (going back to the second chapter of Genesis and to a later, rather confusing English translation of the original Hebrew text) should really be pronounced (and spelt) help-meet, because that is its original spelling and meaning— man's most suitable companion, meeting all his requirements, to assist him in life.

At first, man was all alone. It did not take long for God to realize that solitude was not good for him. Man was meant to be a social being. So God decided to revise his creation and give man a companion to share his life and help him in his work.

When King James I authorized a group of scholars to prepare a "modern" English translation of the books of the Bible, they encountered great difficulty in rendering correctly, and in the idiom of their own time, certain Hebrew terms. Among them was the passage which referred to God's creation of Eve as Adam's companion. The scholars rejected an earlier translation by Wycliffe which had God say, "Make We to hym help like hym." Neither did they favor Miles Coverdale's choice of words in his version of 1535, describing Eve as "an helpe, to beare him company." Adopting the then current word meet (for "suitable"), they rendered the passage as saying, "I (God) will make him (Adam) an helpe meet ('suitable') for him."

By the time this new "Authorized Version" of the Bible was published—in 1611—people had stopped using "meet" in the sense of suitable. But as it was now part of the new English Bible, which had been given official status throughout the English-speaking Protestant Churches, people were reluctant to replace it, even by a word that would make sense and be intelligible to the average person. Thus, for hundreds of years, the Bible went on printing a text that was incomprehensible and perplexing. Those who read the word and could not make it out eventually imagined that somehow it must be a special term for a wife.

In 1673 Dryden tried to improve matters by using a hyphen, rendering the obsolete term as help-meet. Later generations, still in search of a meaning yet more puzzled than ever, again dropped the hyphen and fused the two words into one—creating the helpmeet. The stage was set for just one more change: less than another fifty years later, helpmeet became helpmate, with a new meaning as well as spelling. It is a word born of misunderstanding and former generations' reluctance to update expressions.

The Marriage Certificate

Originally the usual form of contracting a marriage was the simplest. The mere act of cohabitation made a man and a woman husband and wife. With the refinement of taste, the growth of moral consciousness and the development of a sense of social responsibility, this type of union came to be considered legally insufficient and shameful.

Initially, a woman counted for nothing. She was captured or purchased as a mere chattel and became her husband's property. Her price widely differed, depending on supply and demand, on the girl's qualities (again assessed differently according to the tribe), her age and her family's status in the community.

Central Africa's Nandi tribes, for instance, considered six cows a fair price for a good wife, fourteen years old. Most expensive among African Bantus was a girl who was already an unmarried mother, as she had proved that she was able to bear children.

The fixing of the purchase price led to the issuing of a certificate, which itself is not mentioned in the Bible. However, its antiquity is shown by the discovery of a document of this type, possibly the earliest "marriage certificate" in existence. It was found among Aramaic papyri, relics of the Jewish garrison stationed at Elephantine in Egypt in the fifth century B.C.

The certificate had become a regular document among Jewish people well before Christian days. Its text was influenced by pagan marriage contracts of a similar nature, some of which, dating back to that early period, are still preserved. In them the husband agreed to give his wife all the food, clothes and amenities she needed, and the wife, on her part, pledged to conduct herself blamelessly.

The marriage certificate was officially introduced among the Hebrews in the first century of this era. Jewish religious law then stipulated that a marriage without the contract having been drawn up was not properly consummated. It was not a mere formality or the result of ecclesiastical bureaucracy, but due to important considerations which took into account that a woman was still without rights of her own and completely at the mercy of her husband, who could disown or dismiss her on the slightest pretext. It was to safeguard her for all eventualities and to give her a more secure status, that the new kind of marriage certificate was introduced. Its dual purpose was clear.

The terms laid down in the certificate made any husband think twice before sending away his spouse as, ridding himself of a companion he no longer desired, he also had to surrender a considerable part of his fortune! Likewise, the document guarded a widow against greedy heirs who might try to deprive her of sustenance. The original marriage certificate was thus most realiztic. Though presented to the couple when they were on the very pinnacle of happiness, it lacked all romance. At the moment of marriage, it was concerned with the possibility of an untimely end to the relationship by the death of the man or divorce. Its text was rigid, following prototypes of Roman law.

Early on the Christian Church adopted and adapted its text, adding an obligation on the wife to "love, cherish and honor" her husband who, on his part, had to do all that a free-born wife expected from a worthy husband. Yet from the sixth century onwards its use among Christians lapsed, except in the case of marriages between persons of high rank. As if to compensate for the legal and dry nature of the document, people began to ornament it. Apart from portraits of the bride and groom, they added all kinds of artistic creations, including nude figures representing Adam and Eve in paradise.

Bill of Divorce

Divorce among primitive and pagan people was free and easy, lacking any kind of documentation. It was devoid of all formalities and purely a private matter, with which tribal and "state" authorities were unconcerned.

Anglo-Saxons, on the other hand, demanded grounds for divorce. However, it was not too difficult for a husband to find an excuse.

He had the right to dismiss his wife if she was barren, passionate, luxurious, rude, habitually drunk, quarrelsome or abusive.

Early Romans considered a spouse's dislike of a partner reason enough to terminate their union. Later Roman law continued to view divorce, just like marriage, as a private affair between two parties. All that had to be done was for one spouse to inform the other, through a messenger or in the presence of seven witnesses. This private "writ" had both to express the intention to end the marriage and to state that in future the other may keep his or her own property. A judicial inquiry was necessary only when the parties disagreed regarding the future of their children or the division of their assets.

Not so with the Hebrews. They permitted divorce, but a merely private or oral declaration, however formal, was insufficient. A written official statement was essential, a Bill of Divorcement, according to biblical legislation. This is all the more surprising as Scripture does not do so regarding any need of a marriage certificate.

CHAPTER 4

Death and Mourning

Life is a continuous progression toward death. The latest drug may extend the life span by many years, but it cannot remove the inevitability of passing. Thus Victor Hugo could comfort the condemned criminal, standing in the shadow of the guillotine, by saying that "all humans are condemned to death—only the date of execution is uncertain."

The mystery of death puzzled and haunted the primitive savage as much as modern people. Was death merely a portal to a further existence, a gate through which everyone had to pass, or was it complete extinction?

Mourning is a universal reaction to death, but the way grief is expressed varies widely. Likewise, several factors account for one's sorrow which is not just, as it is believed, the result of piety and loving remembrance of the departed.

There are psychological reasons. These include an unconscious but healthy desire to externalize sorrow which otherwise might cause serious harm to the bereaved. People are sorry for themselves. They have lost a companion and are all the poorer for it. Ashamed to admit that it is for their own selves and their loneliness that they mourn, they rationalize their grief.

Many mourning customs at present, however, are a legacy of obsolete fears of the dead and of their power to haunt and harass the living.

To Kick the Bucket

To "kick the bucket" is a description of someone's passing from this world into the next. On the surface it might seem to be mere slang. It has, in fact, an interesting history.

The ancient Egyptians used the bucket not only in the construction of their pyramids, but equally in the symbolism of their faith.

It became their sign of death. Hieroglyphic script employed it as
the representation of a body without life. To kick, in this context,
had nothing whatsoever to do with "striking out with the foot." It
is an ancient Egyptian word that, as if it were mummified, has
survived in the modern way of speaking. It is the Egyptian *khekh*,
meaning to "return," to "send back." Therefore, to "kick the
bucket" really meant to send back and return the empty bucket—
a lifeless body.

Another interpretation of the phrase dates back to the late
sixteenth century and to British farm life. Farmers usually killed
their own cattle and pigs, using a heavy three-legged contraption
with a pulley in the center. The animal's legs were tied to a
wooden beam which was hoisted by a rope. As this reminded the
farmer of pulling a bucket from a well, it was not long before the
beam itself was called a bucket. Often, as the animal was being
lifted, its feet were thrown against the beam or bucket which gave
the impression that it was kicking it. As in reality by that stage the
beast had become a carcass, the phrase "to kick the bucket"
assumed a deadly significance.

A third derivation of the term comes from the act of suicide.
A common form of taking one's own life was by hanging, with
people standing on a bucket to adjust the noose around their
necks. When they were ready to die, they kicked the bucket
(away). Soon the description of this suicidal method was adopted
for any kind of dying, no matter who cut the thread of life.

To Go West

Although the saying "he has gone west" became especially
popular during World War I, its origin goes back to most ancient
days. Its obvious reference is to the setting sun, which "goes west"
to expire there.

There are various other claims as to its origin. The Egyptians of
old considered the west as the home of departed spirits. It made
mourners, standing on the banks of the Nile, as if to speed and guide
the dead in the right direction, call out to them, "To the west. . . ."

Another suggestion links the phrase with early American history.
The saying was first used by American Indians. They said that those
who had died had "gone west" to meet the setting sun. Following

on, in later years, bitter experience of the white pioneers gave the phrase a tragic meaning. Prospectors, advancing westward beyond the Mississippi, often failed to return because Indians, anxious to keep their territory for themselves, had murdered them, with the result that to the friends of anyone who was reported missing, the words "gone west" soon became synonymous with his having lost his life out there.

According to an English claim, the phrase was first introduced in London, and in totally different circumstances. It was used by criminals on their last trip—to the gallows. They did so quite correctly, as west was the actual direction of their final journey.

Newgate Prison, built in the thirteenth century, was situated near the New (western) Gate in the wall surrounding the City of London. Just outside that gate, at the site of the present Marble Arch, was the famous Tyburn Tree, London's place of execution for 600 years. Accordingly, those sentenced to death were led out due west of the prison to the gallows, and that is how to "go west" assumed its lethal meaning. Ultimately, the term became so general that by the year 1592 it was applied to all who had died, and had lost completely its ignominious significance.

Stopping the Clocks at a Death

Clocks and watches have been closely linked with human life and its vanishing hours. No wonder, therefore, that they have stirred people's imagination for centuries and given rise to many a fallacy and superstition.

Some people claimed that the "electricity" of their body made it impossible for them to carry or wear a watch. Others refused to turn back its hands because they wrongly thought that this would damage its works.

The superstition that some clocks stopped at the moment of their owner's death is deep-rooted. It sounds so sentimental and, as it were, assumes that even a clock can feel or, among the more primitive-minded, that it was regulated not just by an intricate mechanism but by sympathetic magic. Several other factors and considerations may well serve as a much more likely explanation.

First of all, though exceedingly rare, there is always the possibility of mere coincidence. It might just have happened that, accidentally, a clock stopped at the hour of death. And who could blame people, already emotionally upset, for regarding sole chance as a matter of cause and effect? They would tell the story to others, and tales of that kind are always easily spread and accepted as accurate by those susceptible to the mysterious.

A more feasible theory relates the superstition to facts. A clock used to be a rare and precious possession. Hence its owner, who was always the head of the house, treasured it and it was his jealously guarded privilege to perform, like a solemn regular rite, its winding up.

It was only natural that at his death his family was confused and harassed and forgot all about the clock and its needs. But even if they did remember the necessity of winding it up, they still refrained from doing so. They were reluctant to undertake—at least immediately—a task so long reserved for the head of the house. Otherwise it might appear that he was not being missed and that his passing had not really upset the smooth running of the home. With its works run down, the clock inevitably stopped.

Visitors could not help but notice that in the house of mourning time was standing still. They did not draw the obvious conclusion that this was due to natural causes. Gullible, ignorant and in awe of the dead, they saw in the stoppage a supernatural phenomenon. They further assumed, and later asserted, that the occurrence had actually coincided with the exact moment of death.

In many places it was believed that a clock must be stopped at the hour of death or bad luck would stay in the home. The gesture was prompted by deference to the dead and a wish to express symbolically that, in this home at least, life itself had come to a stop and the world was at an end.

It was a moving custom. Yet its original purpose was not concerned with the dead. The clock was stopped not to honor the deceased but to guard the living. The action told Death to get out of the house; that, having done his nefarious work, the time of his rule there was over, and a new era of life was about to begin. People's memory is short and indulges in rationalizations. That is why the true sequence of events is often forgotten. Possibly driven by some unconscious urge, they really came to believe after some time that not they themselves, but Death had stopped the clock!

Black for Mourning

To wear black for mourning in Western countries is a custom that dates back to pagan days. Its origin had nothing to do with piety or a wish to show grief. On the contrary, it expressed fear. It arose not out of respect for but dread of the dead.

People put on black as a disguise, so that the ghost of the deceased might not recognize and then start haunting them. The same purpose, it is thought, applied to the mark of Cain, branding him after his brother's death, lest he be identified by his victim's spirit.

The wearing of black, just as at times the veiling of one's face, was also believed to act as a protection against one's own death. It was hoped to confuse any demon still hovering around and bent on snatching more lives. Among some races the custom to paint one's face white or black was supposed to trick the dead into the belief that the mourners themselves were ghosts and not living creatures to be envied.

Indeed, there is no real difference in intention between the wearing of black and the even more primitive custom of gashing the flesh and tearing the clothes.

The modern explanation of the use of black for mourning is a superb example to spiritualize and rationalize ancient superstition. Black is symbolic of the night, and the absence of color seemed best suited to express a person's abandonment to grief. The color of mourning, too, was meant to serve as a constant reminder of the loss one had suffered. To the people one met, it indicated one's state of mind, making them in turn considerate, and reminding them to refrain from saying anything that might hurt or offend. The dark color itself not only expressed the sorrow of the bereaved but created inward tranquillity and serenity.

Black, however, has never been the universal color of mourning. Henry VIII wore white when "mourning" Anne Boleyn, just as many Chinese do. Burmese chose yellow and Turks violet. Ethiopians preferred a grayish-brown and the South Sea Islanders a combination of white and black stripes, perhaps to symbolize how joy and grief, light and darkness, are always intermingled in life. In some parts of China, however, the traditional mourning color was purple, which influenced American trade in a most unexpected way. When a U.S. manufacturer of chewing gum changed its wrapper from green to purple, its export sales to China dropped alarmingly. It was subsequently discovered that the Chinese believed that gum of this color was meant to be chewed at funerals only!

The Mourning Arm Band

The wearing of black arm bands for mourning originated in England where, to start with, according to eighteenth-century regulations, they were restricted to military personnel. A Gazette of May 20, 1775, specifically stated that "His Majesty does not require the Officers of the Army should wear any other mourning, on the present melancholy occasion than a black crepe round their left arm with their uniforms." From England it found its way to the Continent, where it became prevalent.

Traditionally, those who had suffered a bereavement showed their grief and honored the departed by dressing entirely in black. They continued to wear this color to the very end of the mourning period, which differed according to the degree of relationship. An exception related to Queen Victoria who chose to wear black permanently after the death of her consort Prince Albert. In English society it used to be the custom for the entire household, including the staff, to show their sense of loss by donning black. However, as to fit out servants in black clothes was too costly, a black arm band had to suffice for them. The latter therefore generally owes its existence to reasons of economy. It equally recalls an age in which class distinctions were pronounced.

Half-mast

The flying of a flag at half-mast is an international sign of mourning. Tradition demands that the flag should be hoisted to the top of the mast, stay there for a moment, and then be lowered.

The custom had its origin in early naval battles. Initially, it was possibly not just the defeated vessel's flag which had to be lowered, but its topsail. The beaten foe had to haul down his flag (halfway) so that the victor's colors could take its place and show his superiority.

It was with this background that in later years the lowering of the flag became a mark of respect, especially to one of superior station. The practice developed, also, of passing ships dipping the ensigns as a gesture of courtesy. The original practical purpose to make room for another flag above was completely forgotten. That is how, finally and far removed from its first martial context and naval warfare, the flying of a flag at half-mast became a token of respect to the dead, expressing the homage people wished to pay to a worthy departed.

Candles and Death

Ingeniously and in every possible way people have tried to defeat their last and greatest enemy—death. With that aim in mind, Egyptians first built their majestic pyramids, learned to mummify bodies, and composed the *Book of the Dead*, which has been called "Everyman's Guide to Immortality."

Jews, Christians and Muslims alike believe that burial in consecrated ground helps to ensure resurrection. The washing of the corpses was not entirely a reflection of cleanliness: hygiene even after death. It was based on the superstition that demons and witches had an aversion to water and therefore, by its application to the bodies of the deceased, they were kept at bay. The burning of candles or lights, linked with death and the dead from primitive times onward, is still maintained to shine upon a bier and to give special expression to grief.

When, in the sixteenth century, the tomb of Tullia, Cicero's daughter, was discovered in the Via Appia outside Rome, it was said that a light had been burning inside it for nearly 1,500 years. This was not necessarily an incredible, miraculous tale, but could have been accounted for by a supply of natural gas or oil.

A perpetual light burns in Christ's tomb in the Church of the Holy Sepulchre in Jerusalem.

Catholics light votive candles on All Souls' Day in memory of the faithful departed. Jews burn a light for twenty-four hours (from sunset to sunset) every year on the anniversary of their loved ones' death. Japanese celebrate the Feast of Lanterns.

The word "funeral" has been derived from the Latin *funus*, meaning "torch." It was based on the belief that torches at a funeral could guide the departed soul to its eternal abode. Lamps, it was thought, aided the dead to find their way through the darkness. Later times rationalized the flickering light of a candle as a simile of life and saw in its steady glow a symbol of the soul, itself a spark from the never-dying flame of the divine.

Originally, however, candles, torches and lights near a corpse or a grave served a completely different purpose. They were relics from the days when fires were lit around the dead to frighten away supernatural evil beings anxious to reanimate the corpse and take possession of it. Their domain was darkness and they were afraid of light.

The ghost of the departed was believed to be afraid of light, and thus, by the burning of candles, was prevented from returning to haunt the survivors.

Another early source of illumination at funerals was the wish of primitive people to provide the dead with the very comforts they had enjoyed in life, which included light. Fear of the dead also was responsible for the use of tapers. The burning flame was to show the deceased that they were well remembered by their family and therefore had no reason to attack any of its members for forgetting them. More so, the light kindled in their honor should remind them to guard their family in reward for the loyalty thus expressed.

It was thought as well that the dead loved to revisit their old haunts, especially on certain days, not least the anniversary of their passing. To guide them home and light their way, candles were lit.

The Coffin

The English word coffin stems from the Greek *kophinos*, meaning a "basket." It goes back to the custom of the ancient Sumerians and Egyptians who used to enclose their dead in a structure of plaited twigs which resembled a basket.

From earliest days, a kind of wooden coffin, in its most primitive form, was equally known. It was a tree (often an oak, which was considered sacred) split into two. One half served as the bed for the dead and was suitably hollowed. The other half was used as a lid.

Such early tree-trunk burial had its roots in ancient pagan belief, linked with the myth that humans had grown out of a tree. More significantly, there was a striking resemblance between this "tree of the dead" and the dugout, the primitive form of canoe. The original coffin was not just a "bed," but a boat, ready to transport the dead on their last journey across the waters.

The modern commercialization of death took due advantage of the coffin. To be properly "boxed" was made almost a status symbol, thereby adding further to the cost of dying. The bereaved were led to believe that it was the right thing to enclose their beloved dead in a substantial "casket" (which is the modern, American-born term, replacing the outlived "coffin"). This had to be of the finest wood, highly polished, with comfortable lining within and precious ornamentation without.

Nevertheless, this is not a recent development either. Hundreds of years ago, a "chested burial" was considered to be an attribute of the privileged classes alone and, therefore, reserved for people of wealth and social standing. The poor had to be satisfied with occupying a coffin only for a short time, as a temporary place of abode. It merely conveyed the body from the house of death to the graveside, where the corpse was removed and, wrapped only in a shroud, put into the grave. The coffin, aptly described as a death-hamper, was returned empty, to await further use in others' funerals.

Apart from the social significance of the casket, many other reasons account for its use. They lead back, through the centuries, to prehistoric times. No doubt, they reflect the various stages of civilization, religious belief and attitudes. They can be divided into two main objects—protection of the corpse and safeguarding the living.

There is, first of all—especially so in more recent times—the wish to pay due respect and deference to the dead. To preserve the body from decay as long as possible, it had to be enclosed in a chest. This protected the corpse against the weather and microbes in the soil, for a time at least. But there were other dangers that threatened the body as well. Wild animals might dig it up.

During the early days of anatomy, when religious authorities frowned on the dissection of human remains, corpses were at a premium. Body-snatchers abounded and coffins served as a most suitable means to hamper their activities.

The ancient belief in bodily resurrection, still observed by the orthodox sections of many faiths, was a contributory reason for using coffins. At the end of days, all the dead would rise again. Therefore everything possible should be done to keep their bodies in perfect condition. A right kind of chest was the first and most obvious need, and the more durable it was, the better.

If one digs deep enough in search of the original coffin, however, pious considerations for the dead suddenly change into crude self-interest on the part of the living. Indeed, this was the prime motive in its invention. Survivors were concerned to protect themselves from anything their dearly beloved could do to them, now that they had moved to realms beyond their power.

Thus, everything had to be done to prevent the dead person from returning and haunting the living. With this purpose in mind, frequently their feet were fettered and sometimes, for the identical reason, even their head was cut off and placed between the legs. On the way to the graveside, devious means were employed further to bamboozle the dead, lest they might find their way back to their family and former home. They were carried out of the house feet first and, in many communities, not through its door, but by way of a hole in the wall made for that one occasion alone and immediately closed up again. Once outside and on the way, the longest and most circuitous route to the burial ground was chosen. It was for this reason not least—to keep the dead away—that coffins were first introduced. Often they had heavy stone lids, to make doubly sure that the departed stayed inside. Nailing or screwing down the lid served the same purpose!

The Wreath

The story is told of a soldier who in a foreign land visited a former comrade's grave, to place flowers on it. On his way, he met a native who was carrying an offering of food to his ancestors' tomb. The soldier stopped him, to point out the absurdity of his action. "When do you think," he asked, "your relatives will come out of their graves to enjoy the meal?" "At the same time as your friend will come up to smell the flowers!" was the immediate retort.

To send a wreath to a funeral and to lay it on the coffin or the grave is a relic of ancient superstition and idol worship. The early

Christian authorities did their best to stop the custom, but they did not succeed.

The floral wreath is a survival of the belief that it was necessary to provide comforts for the departed. The flowers were also regarded as, literally, a floral offering, a sacrifice to the dead. They were meant to keep them happy, lest, being dissatisfied, they might haunt the mourners. The wreath was a magic circle to keep the dead person's spirit within bounds and away from the sorrowing family and friends.

The ancient Egyptians already used wreaths and kept special gardens to grow flowers for that purpose alone. They crowned mummified bodies with chaplets of flowers or leaves in order to assure them a triumphant and safe passage into the other world.

The wreath for the dead was also a continuation of the Greek and Roman habit of crowning emperors, victorious generals and distinguished athletes with laurels. Their evergreen leaves not only symbolized but ensured eternal life—an existence that would never fade or wither. The wreath was a floral tribute not so much to the dead as to the vegetation spirits which, it was believed, resided in its very flowers.

None of these various early roots are remembered. There is nomagic left in the wreath and to "say it with flowers" has become an established custom in the Western world, though other nations and races still prefer to put small stones on their dear ones' graves.

The Hearse

Originally, the hearse was not a vehicle to transport the dead to their last resting place, but an agricultural implement. Hearse is a French word signifying a harrow and that is exactly what it was in the very beginning: a triangular iron frame to which spikes were attached. The French adopted it from Roman peasants who were the first to use it.

The earliest "harrowing" use (not to be confused with the grievous connotation of the word) is reflected in the modern theatrical term, rehearsal. Like a farmer, the actors harrowed the field of their memory over and over again, until the part they had to play was so deeply ingrained in their minds that they would not stumble over their words.

In the thirteenth century, ingenious peasants discovered that their harrow, when not used to rake the fields, could serve another purpose as well. Turned over, it became a multiple candlestick. The rake's spikes were just right to impale the tapers. The hearse thus took on the additional function of an inverted chandelier, decorating and illuminating the farmer's house. Soon it was found especially useful on religious occasions, particularly at funerals. That is how eventually the hearse was transferred from the home to the church.

With the passing of time, the original, small harrow grew ever larger. With its height extending to 6 feet, it evolved into a magnificent, elaborate construction. Indeed, such was the rake's progress that it became a masterpiece of fine workmanship, worthy of adorning and lighting the burial service of the most noble. Its development did not stop there. From each of the hearse's three corners, supports were erected. These were joined at the top, thus forming a framework. This was draped with black cloth on which mourners and their friends pinned tickets carrying poems and epitaphs composed in honor of the departed. Numerous ornaments were added and the number of candles impaled became so large that the flickering lights were compared to the stars. What followed was almost inevitable. The very width and height of the hearse suggested that the coffin be put on its top, with the whole structure being surrounded by a rail.

The hearse was still stationary, remaining in the church after the body had been removed from it to be carried to the grave. It served as a shrine to honor the dead. The bereaved continued to light votive candles on it in memory of their beloved, long after their remains had been laid to rest. In a further development, the hearse itself, with the dead still reposing on it, was carried to the grave.

Soon wheels were added and the mourners pulled the "harrow" like a cart with the hearse having become a death wagon. In modern times, horses pulled the deceased on their movable bier to their final destination. Then, with the invention of the internal combustion engine, came the motorized hearse, still embodying many remnants and traces of its thousand-years' growth. The hearse has certainly travelled an exceedingly long way since the ancient Roman days when it was but a crude rake.

The Funeral Procession

According to an old belief a corpse must proceed to its grave without stopping or hindrance. The smooth and unhampered progress of a funeral cortege is much in keeping with the solemn occasion. At one time modern traffic authorities suspended some of the regulations in the case of a burial.

A funeral procession should not be split up. Care is taken for a cortege to move at the slowest possible speed.

All this expresses unwillingness, as it were, to part from the loved one, and pays due respect to their mortal remains. Yet, even those sentiments are rationalizations.

Reluctance to impede a funeral procession goes back to ancient superstition. People feared that some dissatisfied spirit, averse to leaving this world, might take advantage of the halt. Seizing the opportunity, it might escape from the body and start haunting and harming the living.

The slow pace of the cortege is not just a mark of respect either. It recalls the earlier days when the deceased was carried by friends on a bier with a cross-bearer heading the solemn procession. The rate of progress was controlled by the mourners' strides, and it is this pedestrian pace that still restricts the hearse's speed.

The Tombstone

The practice of putting a stone on a grave arose not from piety, but from atavistic fear; its origin was not respect for the dead but out of self-protection. Even after all other precautions had been taken, the living were afraid that the dead person might return and act against them. To make absolutely sure the departed stayed in their tomb, they weighted the soil down with a heavy stone.

At first, people were buried anywhere, generally near where they had died or been killed. Graves could therefore be found in the most unexpected places.

Primitive society looked on a dead body as something impure. To touch it or merely to walk over the burial place, defiled the person. It was for this reason that they marked graves with stones. These were meant to be a warning to passers-by to keep well away.

At times, to make the stones stand out more clearly, they were coated with lime. The identical consideration led to the origin of the cemetery. Special fields, removed from human habitation, were set apart to isolate the dead in order to protect the living from contamination.

A later development was the worship of graves. The tombstone was looked upon as an abode of a deity or a spirit. People were then no longer worried about getting defiled, but about the grave being desecrated. Thus they heaped stones on it to prevent animals from digging up the body. Inscriptions on headstones and monuments came later. Initially, they were reserved merely for people of rank, to draw special attention to their last resting-place and to invite passers-by to pray for their soul.

Crocodile Tears

It is said of hypocrites who sham grief that they shed crocodile tears. The picturesque phrase dates back thousands of years to ancient fable and a kind of archaic science fiction. At the time it was believed that crocodiles used guile to trap their prey. Lying camouflaged in slimy water or mud, they spat mouthfuls of water onto the soil near their lair, to make it so slippery that people or animals approaching would miss their footing and fall. Unable to get back onto their feet quickly enough, they would be caught by the crocodile and devoured.

Another interpretation discovered in the (nonexistent) crocodile tears an ingenious ingredient which the reptile itself supplied to add to its daily diet, to make otherwise indigestible parts of its victims soft and palatable! It was thought that the crocodile spurted its tears to soak the skull of its prey, macerating the hard substance and preparing it for a tasty meal!

This piece of folklore was soon embroidered upon. People attributed to the beast evil cunning, believing that it attracted its daily "bread" with bait of a most unethical kind. The myth-makers now alleged that, when hungry, the creature deliberately sobbed and sighed, simulating a human in distress and so luring prey to the slippery river bank. From sobbing and moaning it was only a short step to dreaming up real tears.

To add insult to injury it was further assumed that, whilst

eating its victim, the crocodile continued shedding tears, but now doing so out of pity for the unfortunate fool.

The fact is that crocodiles never shed tears, but they do make peculiar groaning noises. Once upon a time, the crocodile's tears were a traveler's yarn, eagerly lapped up and believed by credulous people. Though nowadays crocodiles no longer cry, even fictitiously, before or during meals, their tears have not completely dried up. They survive among the most civilized people: in their conversation, especially when they talk of the humbug and the hypocrite.

The Grass Widow

In his famous *Dictionary* Dr. Samuel Johnson explains that a grass widow is a corrupted form of a grace widow. But this theory has now been discarded. Certainly, a wife temporarily parted from her husband may be a widow by grace or courtesy but, literally, the term goes down to the grassroots, either of the Indian highlands or the Californian hills.

According to one version, grass widows made their first appearance among Anglo-Indians about the middle of the eighteenth century. British forces were stationed in the coastal plains of India. The sweltering heat during the summer made life there wellnigh unbearable for people who were unaccustomed to such a tropical climate.

To spare their womenfolk unnecessary hardship, the soldiers sent them to the hills during that season. There cool breezes prevailed and, by contrast with the plain's parched earth, the grass was green; indeed, it was the most noticeable feature of the hill country at that time of the year. The men jokingly began to refer to sending their wives "to the grass," and that is how a woman separated from her husband came to be known as a grass widow.

Another less kind and gracious explanation links the grass widow with the Californian gold rushes that took place almost at the same period, though on the other side of the world. Possessed by gold fever, many prospectors felt that their families were an encumbrance. Therefore they boarded their wives in other people's homes. Rather crudely they compared their action to that of a farmer who put a horse out to graze when it was not wanted or useful for work. "I have put my wife to grass!" they laughingly remarked to their mates. Even though those fortune-hunters kept everything they found to themselves, they still, unknowingly, presented the saying as a free gift to the English-speaking world.

CHAPTER 5

Everyday Courtesies

Courtesy is derived from the courtier's custom and used to define a way of living and manners befitting a prince. But this explanation is not correct.

Politeness is not as at first it appears. Behind it is a history of discrimination and terror, of people living in constant mutual suspicion, afraid of attack and assassination. Most customs of courtesy are thus the product of a defense mechanism. Their original purpose was to fortify oneself against attack either from humans or supernatural forces.

Codes of etiquette have varied from time to time and nation to nation. They are geographically conditioned and the outcome of a specific climate of nature and thought.

Anyone belching after a good meal, for instance, would horrify one. Rightly, such a person's behavior would be called rude and crude. However, when one dines as the guest of an Arab, it would insult the host if a hearty belch were not given in approval of the meal.

Courtesy has been described as a lubricant which smoothes human relationships and prevents friction. In fact, good manners are survivals of evil times, as an inquiry into their origin soon reveals.

Etiquette

"Etiquette" is a French word, signifying label or card, which gave birth to the English "ticket." Centuries ago, guests at royal receptions were handed little notes, giving detailed instructions on conduct. These tickets were known as etiquettes. A widening of their application led to the word's modern use.

Another explanation has it that officers in the French forces used to publish their daily orders on small sheets posted around the camp and that these were identified as etiquettes.

A Scot, who had served in the French army, became the chief gardener of King Louis XIV at the Palace of Versailles. In his efforts to lay out a beautiful park, he was continually frustrated by the carelessness of visitors, who walked across new lawns and flower-beds, destroying young plants before they had a chance to take root.

Remembering the "etiquettes" of his army days, he had notices put up all over the grounds directing visitors where to walk and where to keep off the grass. From these small posters at Versailles, it is said, the word found its way into the English language and described the right kind of behavior everywhere.

Shaking Hands

Suspicion and stark fear are the sources of the apparently harmless and polite gesture of shaking hands. People once were haunted by the many dangers which threatened them, both from beasts and other humans. One could trust no one. Thus, in a spirit of self-defense, men moved about well armed. Primitive men carried clubs and more civilized men their swords.

Meeting with a stranger aroused immediate suspicion. Neither man knew the other's intention. Four possible reactions offered themselves. Both men could turn and make their escape without waiting to find out what might happen. They could stand their ground and fight. Grasping their weapon all the more firmly, they could proceed on their way, giving each other the widest berth. Or they could remain peaceful, and perhaps become friends.

To do that, they first had to make sure that there was no possibility of attack: they laid down their weapons or kept their hands well away from them, displaying their empty palms. But to be doubly sure, and to prevent the other man from suddenly grabbing his sword, they clasped hands firmly. The hearty handshake, therefore, in the beginning did not show friendship but distrust. Nor did the customary use of the right hand originate by chance. It was a precaution to immobilize the other man's weapon hand.

Raising One's Hat

The once common custom to raise one's hat to a lady, not inappropriately, dates back to the age of chivalry. Yet its origin was not courtesy, but an assurance of peaceful intentions. Knights in armor lifted the visor on their helmets to indicate they were not afraid of being attacked. Eventually, it became the custom for a knight to stand bareheaded in the presence of a lady.

The doffing of the helmet in a home showed that one relied on the protection of the host, and in a church that one was not afraid of an enemy in the House of God. Friendly knights raised their visors to each other, and the removal of the helmet indicated friendship and utter trust in a hostile world.

Going beyond this chivalrous interpretation, the raising of the hat can be traced to the early days of primitive warfare when captives were stripped. Their nakedness was to proclaim complete subjugation. Gradually, this symbol of serfdom was restricted to the baring of only the upper part of the body, down to the waist. Finally, all that remained of the early stripping was the removal of whatever served as a hat. "I am your obedient servant!" is thus the implicit message from the days of slavery, when silently a man greets a lady by baring his head.

Women have always been exempted from this custom. However, this does not really imply that they have been considered the master. It does not show lack of courtesy on their part either. Perhaps it reflects man's complete trust in the female sex, or his feeling of superiority—that he has nothing to fear from a mere woman.

The Curtsy

The curtsy, as practiced now, is a slight bend of the knee and lowering of the body, a custom reserved for women only. It is the last remnant of the days, not long ago, when woman was considered inferior to man and was expected to bow down in his presence as a sign of subservience.

The curtsy belongs much more to the shameful history of female degradation than to books on etiquette. Perhaps Lewis Carroll was not just being funny when, seeing "through the looking glass," he explained that a woman, while curtsying, may think what to say, which would save time.

"God Bless You" when Sneezing

Nowadays a sneeze is considered merely a symptom of a common cold and nothing to be specially scared of, except as the possible spreader of germs. That was not always so. To primitive races and in biblical and Greek times, a sneeze was regarded as a sign of great personal danger.

Possibly because sneezing had been a frequent occurrence during the great Athenian plague, people assumed it was the first indication that a person had the dreaded disease. Actually, the fear associated with the sneeze seemed widespread. Romans saw in it an evil omen. Parsees felt that the sneeze indicated the threatening presence of evil spirits.

The ancient Hebrews believed that when someone sneezed, they were nearest to death, an erroneous but widely held notion. The soul was considered to be the essence of life. The fact that dead persons never breathed led to the fallacious deduction that their soul must be breath. This was supported by the biblical tale that God, when creating man, fashioned his body out of the dust of the earth but "breathed into his nostrils the breath of life," which made him a living soul.

No one could deny that a sneeze expelled a considerable amount of air. And if air were the substance of the soul and so much of it left so suddenly, was it not understandable that people became afraid that, deprived of this essence of life, death might be inevitable? It is thus not surprising that from the earliest days people learned to respond to a sneeze with apprehension and the fervent wish that God may help and bless the sneezers and preserve their lives.

Somehow in medieval times this early origin of the custom must have been forgotten, because it was Pope Gregory the Great who was credited with having introduced the saying of "God bless you" to anyone who sneezed. During his reign the Roman population was decimated by a plague believed to have been caused by contamination of the air. This, it was thought, made people who sneezed "give up the ghost" immediately. It was then that the Pope prescribed a special form of prayer and the wish for all sneezers that God may keep from them any evil effect.

Hand in Front of the Mouth when Yawning

It is sometimes very difficult to suppress a yawn. However, it can be concealed behind the hand and failure to do this is decried as uncouth and rude.

The fact that people feel so strongly about it indicates that there must be a much more deeply rooted significance in the custom than so-called good manners—a wish to cover up the unpleasant-looking cavern of the mouth and to shut off possibly bad breath.

Primitive people were convinced that an unguarded yawn could make all the difference between life and death, and for two reasons. The human spirit was identified with their breath. This was responsible for the biblical custom of kissing the mouth of a dying person, thereby catching the departing spirit, to transmit it to future generations.

People of some races used to hold the mouth and nose of a dying friend, and in so doing, they imagined, that they prevented the ghost from escaping and thus preserved the person's life. By covering the mouth while yawning was, first of all, a safeguard against the soul's issuing prematurely. Equally, however, a gaping mouth gave access to unwelcome guests. It was, as it were, an open invitation to lurking evil spirits and demons.

CHAPTER 6

Table Manners and Eating Habits

Some people love eating. Mere mention of food is sufficient for their body to begin the process of digestion—the mouth starts watering. Of them it could be truly said that the way to the heart is through the stomach.

Others could not care less about what, when and how much they eat. Percy Bysshe Shelley, the great English poet, could never understand why people wanted more than plain bread. His wife sent meals into his study, but he frequently forgot to eat them. Joining her later, he would inquire, "Mary, have I dined?"

Originally, people gorged themselves like beasts. They ate whenever and as long as they had food. The introduction of regular meal times was one of the great stepping-stones in the history of civilization.

The present generation is highly food-conscious. The right kind of diet, with enough vitamins and not too many calories, is a feature of all menus. Beyond the facts of mere nourishment, early philosophers already appreciated the effect of the food we eat. The "Germans" have a pun, "*Der Mensch ist was er isst*"—"Man is what he eats."

Menus have differed in various ages and they still change from country to country. It has rightly been said that what is one person's meat is another's poison. Every country has its national dish—Irish stew, Italian macaroni, German *Wurst*, Scottish haggis, English roast beef, Australian steak and eggs, and so on.

Thus every age and nation has had its own food fads and taboos, the dishes they craved and abhorred. Few people, however, realize that generally accepted customs have a history set against a background of national traditions and sociological considerations, of irrational superstitions and practical intentions.

73

Three Daily Meals

It is surprising that the basic pattern of three daily meals—breakfast, lunch and dinner—has been established only since 1890. It is the result of a development through many centuries. Meal times have differed in various countries and epochs, the outcome of circumstances such as climate, occupation and working conditions.

Originally, Anglo-Saxon tradition knew of only two meals a day—breakfast and dinner. In the sixteenth century, breakfast was a snack, with no fixed menu. Its only purpose was to break one's fast. Two thousand years later it had become a sumptuous meal, not just for the family, but for plenty of guests as well. It was a social occasion, which commenced at 10 a.m. and often lasted till 1 p.m. Then breakfast began to deteriorate. It became—comparatively—meagre and was taken at a much earlier hour. By 1850 it had retreated to 8 a.m. and shrunk to a family affair. Dinner, however, went the other way. In the sixteenth century it was eaten at 11 a.m. Years afterwards, it moved to the early afternoon, then to 5 p.m. By 1850 it had reached 7 p.m. or 8 p.m.

Lunch is a relatively recent innovation. It first appeared on the timetable as a snack to fill the gap between breakfast and dinner. In his *Dictionary* of 1755, Dr. Johnson defined it as, "as much food as one's hand can hold." The literal meaning of lunch retains its early frugality. It denotes a lump—a piece of whatever one may choose to swallow. As the time of breakfast became ever earlier and dinner later, lunch assumed an important position and developed into a big meal. The division of the working day in the Victorian age into two periods—from 9 a.m. to 1 p.m. and from 2 p.m. to 6 p.m.—finally made luncheon an institution.

That is how the three daily meals, as they are known today, came into existence. It is quite possible that, with ever-shorter working hours, lack of domestic help, calorie-consciousness and popularity of precooked meals, the pattern and rhythm of meal times will change again.

Knife and Fork

Knives have always been used and had a place even in the equipment of stone-age people. Forks are already mentioned in the Bible

and, as excavations have shown, were used by the Anglo-Saxons in
A.D. 796. However, it seems that forks lost their popularity and
disappeared from use.

A book on how good children should behave, written in 1480,
says, "Take your meat with three fingers only and don't put it into
your mouth with both hands. Do not keep your hand too long in
the plate." And yet forks were referred to in Italy long before, in the
eleventh century, and Thomas Becket, Chancellor of England under
Henry II, knew of and introduced them to royal society. Apparently
his innovation died with him as, some 440 years later, in 1611, an
English traveler, Thomas Coryate, observing their use in Italy, was
moved to reintroduce forks into England. But people ridiculed him
and scorned them as finicky and effeminate. Priests condemned
their use as most unsuitable and irreligious. An angry preacher told
his congregation that to eat meat with a fork was to declare impi-
ously that God's creatures were not worthy of being touched by
human hands!

Savages of the South Sea Islands used forks—but only to
devour their enemies. Their religion did not permit them to eat
human flesh with their fingers.

At first, forks were two-pronged. It was only towards the end
of the eighteenth century, when the lower classes also started
adopting them, that the four-pronged fork became standard. Iron
forks were first mass-produced for table use by a German artisan
in 1846.

Crossing the Knife and Fork

The custom of putting the knife and fork crossed or side by side
on the plate on finishing one's food has practical and religious
explanations.

The position of the knife and fork gives a message to those
waiting at tables. If placed parallel it silently tells them that the
diner has finished the course or all they want of it and the plate
can be taken away. Crossed cutlery, on the other hand, indicates
very quietly and politely, that "there is still room for more" and
another "helping" would be welcome.

If crossed, knives and forks can easily fall off when the plate
is removed, which is not so when they are placed next to each

other, a position which also facilitates picking up the cutlery and stacking the dishes. The sign of the cross as a sacred symbol should be reserved for its proper place, which certainly is not a dirty plate. Nor would anyone wish to see as the constituent parts of the cross such menial instruments of eating as a dirty knife and fork.

Chopsticks

The Chinese give much thought to the preparation of their food. It must have perfect flavor, crispness, tenderness and delicacy.

Confucius is said to have divorced his wife because she did not fulfil his expectations as a cook. He demanded that meat should always be served in its proper sauce, be cut perfectly square and have exactly the right color. For him, even the choicest of rice was generally not white enough, and minced meat rarely sufficiently fine.

The Chinese are fastidious, too, in the way food is eaten. Meals, they reason, have to be fully prepared in the kitchen. Once served, they have to be totally ready for eating. To have to cut meat into small pieces at that stage not only would be uncouth, but barbaric. "We sit at table to eat, not to cut up carcasses," is an often-quoted Chinese observation. It was among the cook's duties to dish up the food in convenient size. The process of eating consisted of graciously lifting the morsels from their bowl and transferring them into the mouth. Chopsticks served just that purpose and, if dexterously applied, did so smoothly and at high speed. This is recalled by their name which means "the quick ones." Made of ivory, bone or wood, they obviously had to be used in pairs and, as the Chinese soon discovered, they could also serve as a code between host and guest. Anyone wishing to leave the table, for instance, placed the sticks across the bowl.

According to another explanation of the origin of the chopsticks, initially the Chinese made proper use of cutlery. But one of their emperors, fearing an uprising and assassination, forbade his subjects to own any kind of utensil made of metal. Knives and forks belonged in that category. As the Chinese were loath to eat with their fingers, they invented chopsticks.

The Serviette

For the many centuries when forks were unknown, people used their fingers. This made their hands greasy and dirty. Thus, washing and drying them after the meal, and still at table, became a custom. It was for this purpose that the napkin was introduced and at every meal assumed the practical role of a small towel.

However, once forks were adopted, the napkin became redundant. Nevertheless, it was retained, though with a different objective in mind. It changed from an indispensable adjunct to the dinner table, serving cleanliness, to a decoration. Hosts vied with each other in displaying napkins in fantastic shapes with the various foldings meant to appeal to the diner's aesthetic taste.

Long lists are still in existence which suggest numerous ways to fold the napkin. Instructions of the year 1682, for instance, give twenty-six different shapes. These included serviettes folded in the form of Noah's Ark, a hen and her chickens, a carp, a tortoise, and rabbits!

Today the wheel has turned full circle. The rabbits and tortoises, made of cloth, have disappeared from the dinner table and the napkin, much smaller and less conspicuous, again serves a utilitarian purpose—mostly to protect the diner's clothes from any spilled food.

The Difference between Tea and Coffee Pots

The present-day shapes of tea and coffee pots seem designed to produce the best brew. A low, wide pot provides for the maximum expansion of the tea leaves which, being light, tend to rise in hot water. On the other hand, soon after boiling water has been poured on coffee, the grounds sink to the bottom and pure clean coffee is left in the rest of the pot. Its narrow, high shape thus serves it best.

Originally, however, there was no difference between coffee and tea pots. When first introduced in England, each was circular and tapered towards the top. Only several years later was the tea pot diminished in height and increased in diameter, the only reason being the wish to get a Chinese atmosphere. The new measurements copied the fashionable wide and bulky Chinese porcelain tea pots. Their shape has been maintained since.

The Sundae

A strange mixture of piety, hypocrisy and legal subterfuge make up the Sundae—ice cream with syrup, fruits and nuts. Its name is an obvious and even intentional mis-spelling of Sunday.

One tradition erroneously asserts that it referred to Sunday's left-over ice cream, possibly sold at a cheaper price during the following week. So that a customer would not think that it was freshly made and thus be deceived, it was specially called "Sunday's."

In reality, the first Sundae goes back to the United States of America and the business acumen of a drugstore owner. However, where exactly it was first concocted is still a matter of controversy and of various claims.

Some say that the Sundae was invented in Evanston, Illinois. Others are equally definite that pride of place belongs to Norfolk, Virginia, where to this day people point to a certain store as "the birthplace of the Sundae."

No matter where it was first made, all accounts agree on the reason for it. It was purely a matter of circumventing the law! Sunday, the Lord's day, had to be strictly observed in many, and sometimes peculiar ways. Puritan tradition made it a solemn and somber occasion. Children's swings had to be chained and barred. The reading of books was banned, unless they dealt with a religious theme. Theaters were closed. The "blue law" of Virginia outlawed even soda drinks on the Sabbath!

But people were still thirsty and not satisfied with mere water. An ambitious drugstore proprietor saw his chance, both to give customers a refreshing treat on the Lord's day and to increase his takings to a considerable degree.

If to serve ice cream with soda was illegal, why not offer ice cream with syrup? He began to sell this new and permissible formula every Sunday and no guardian of the law could object. Appropriately, he named his concoction after its birthday—Sunday.

Still, the authorities took exception, not to the "fare" itself but to what it was called. To name it after the Lord's day was sacri-legious, they contended. In consequence, the drugstore owner changed its spelling, for his "Sunday" to become the "Sundae." It still sounded and—most of all—tasted the same. It did not take long for the dessert to become popular all over the world and soon people asked for Sundaes even on weekdays.

Welsh Rabbit

A proverb says that "toasted cheese has no master." The Welsh rabbit has been considered the national dish of Wales and accordingly has been described as "the Welshman's delight" and "Davies' darling."

Many people like Welsh rabbit. It is a simple but tasty dish of toasted bread covered with toasted cheese and smeared with mustard and pepper. People still wonder how the rabbit got into this savory which is completely vegetarian and has not the slightest resemblance to a bunny, in taste or shape.

The appetizing morsel owes its name, and perhaps existence, to human antagonism, the former condescending dislike of the Welsh by the English. At a time when the English looked down on the Welsh and were contemptuous of everything that came from Wales, it was not by chance that the well-known rhyme "Taffy was a Welshman, Taffy was a thief, Taffy came to my house and stole a leg of beef" was coined. The Welsh, so it was thought, were a poor lot in every sense of the word. Their country lacked almost everything, even rabbits which were numerous elsewhere. As they could not afford to buy them from England they were forced to find a pauper's substitute, their own kind of synthetic rabbit. This they made from bread and cheese, the cheapest ingredients available. Disdainfully, the English thus called this national "delicacy" of the Welsh their "rabbit."

An anecdote illustrates this one-time attitude to the Welsh and their (lack of) food. It tells of a bragging Welshman relating how his father entertained twelve guests, employing no fewer than twelve cooks. But the listener would have none of it. Sarcastically he remarked, "Ah, I suppose every man had to toast his own cheese!"

Inevitably Welshmen came to resent deeply all that was associated with their "rabbit." They soon claimed that they themselves had never spoken of a rabbit at all. How could they have done so? Actually, the Welsh "rabbit" was the result of bad enunciation on the part of jealous Englishmen. In reality, the course of melted cheese had nothing to do with the common rabbit but, on the contrary, was a "rare-bit" of delicious food.

Alas, the chronology of philology contradicts this. As attested by the *Oxford Dictionary*, the Welsh *rabbit* was mentioned first in 1725, whilst its refined version, the *rarebit*, came into existence exactly sixty years later, in 1785. Perhaps the change of terminology, after all, was due to some fair-minded Englishmen. Regretful of an earlier generation's bad taste towards a brother race, they may have tried to modify the name by taking the sting out of the rabbit.

Peach Melba

The stage has enriched life in many ways, even in its culinary enjoyment. An Australian prima donna did so by being responsible for the creation of two novel items, which gained wide popularity in their appeal to diners. Years after Dame Nellie Melba's voice has been silent, people still talk of her when they crunch a certain type of thin toast or order a special kind of dessert.

Only the best was good enough for her. "If I'd been a housemaid," she once said, "I'd have been the best in Australia. I couldn't help it . . . It's got to be perfection for me." She wanted to show the world that Australia could produce more than sheep and boomerangs. Even in the choice of Melba as her stage name, she gave worldwide publicity to Melbourne, Victoria's capital, where she was born.

One thing worried her—that not her artistry, but her culinary tastes might be remembered longest. And that is exactly what happened. Melba is still listed among the great sopranos of the world, but her name is spoken most around the dinner table. Peach Melba and Melba Toast immortalized one of Australia's greatest singers to a larger extent than her glorious voice.

Peach Melba, as served now, is a far cry from the original spectacular dessert. A blend of beautiful color, attractive shape and delicious taste, it combined the flavors of raspberry, peach and vanilla. It was devised by George Auguste Escoffier, who has been called the king of chefs. A perfectionist whose principle was that nothing in food should ever be camouflaged, he fought sham and make-believe in the kitchen.

His taste extended beyond the delights of the palate to the world of art. He worshipped Melba, who was one of his patrons. When during 1892–93 she was staying at the Savoy Hotel, London, where he was the chef, he often went to the theater to listen to her, especially in her performance as Elsa in *Lohengrin*. That night at the opera was to him an unforgettable occasion which, somehow, he wished to perpetuate in his own creative way.

He did so when the brilliant singer dined at the hotel on the following day. To surprise her and show his appreciation, he resolved to serve her a completely new dessert created in her honor and recalling her role as Elsa. From a block of ice he shaped two wings of a swan, which he coated with icing sugar with peaches resting on a bed of vanilla ice cream between them. Obviously, the sweet was to recall the most famous scene in *Lohengrin* and, initially, was served as *peches au cygne*— "swanlike peaches."

Later, on the occasion of the opening of London's Carlton Hotel, Escoffier improved the dessert by adding raspberry sauce and, recalling the occasion of its first creation, renamed it by the fitting description it has carried ever since—Peach Melba.

Melba Toast

Melba toast made its debut by mere accident. On one of her visits to London, the Australian coloratura soprano, Dame Nellie Melba, once again stayed at the Savoy Hotel. To control her weight she was keeping to a strict diet and mostly ordered nothing but dry toast.

One day she asked for "the usual." As the head waiter was busy, he left its preparation to one of his helpers. Somehow things went wrong and the toast served was much too thin and dry.

When the chef noticed the error it was too late. Rushing to Melba's table, profusely apologizing, he expected a complaint. To his surprise, Melba did not mind at all. On the contrary, she complimented the chef on the "exquisite toast," the like of which she had never tasted before. The chef was overjoyed and there and then called the toast by her name, continuing to serve the new "invention" as long as Melba was at the Savoy. Soon other guests asked for it and "Melba toast" became a favorite low-calorie delicacy in fashionable restaurants the world over.

The second, much less exciting story, relates Melba toast not to an accident but to yet another of Escoffier's inventions. He created it first not for Melba but for a friend, Madame Ritz, who had complained to him that the usual toast served was much too thick. It so happened that at the time Melba was a guest at the Savoy and known to favor toast which gave Escoffier and his friend the idea to call the toast by the singer's name.

The Adam's Apple

Adam's apple is the popular name given to the odd protrusion in a man's throat, caused by the thyroid cartilage of the larynx. Legend tells that it is a piece of the forbidden fruit Adam ate. It became permanently stuck in his throat, as a constant reminder of man's first sin. As the Bible never identified the "forbidden fruit" as an apple, its description as the "Adam's apple" is all the more surprising. It is due to an early misconception.

To begin with, anatomists named this bulge in the human throat very factually *pomum viri*. *Pomum* was the general Latin description of anything that was rounded in shape and therefore well suited for that "lump." *Vir* (which gave the vocabulary "virility") was the Latin for "man." Its Hebrew and Arab equivalent was *adam* which made early doctors refer to *pomum viri* as *pomum adami*.

As an apple was spherical in shape, it, too, was described as *pomum*. This misled even the learned who, confusing the two, imagined that *pomum adami* meant "Adam's apple." The twice-nonexistent fruit was thus (wrongly) perpetuated in popular anatomy.

To Eat One's Hat

Hunger and curiosity have driven people to eat almost anything. Cannibals ate human flesh. They did so, however, not, as most people think, for the sake of eating. Feeding on humans, they imagined, did not only nourish their bodies but, much more so, their souls! By eating another human being, they believed, they also magically acquired their strength, brains and courage. That was the chief reason for their choice of the inhuman human diet. Aborigines delight in witchetty grubs, whose taste—if raw—is like cream, or—if cooked and rolled in warm ashes—like pork rind.

Frenchmen love horsemeat and those who loathe even the thought of it should know that there is nothing really wrong with it. This distaste stems from the forgotten days when the horse was worshipped and, because of its sanctity, people were afraid to kill and eat it.

In spite of those various and exotic tastes, whoever would think of eating his hat, whether of straw or felt? And rightly so, because the kind of hat spoken of when trying to impress on others one's incredulity and amazement was never the ordinary sort of hat. It is just a confusion between millinery and gastronomy.

This hat's place has always been in the cookery book and not on one's head and is testified by one of the earliest publications of recipes, which relates that "*hattes* are made of eggs, veal, dates, saf - fron, salt, and so forth." The ingredients suggested leave no doubt that a dish of that type would hardly be palatable. Most likely to eat such a hat, or even the wearable kind, would be beyond one's diges- tive capacity.

Pork as Forbidden Food

One of the best-known food prohibitions is that of eating pork. It is strictly observed by Jews and, for that matter, Muslims as well. At times of religious persecution, they preferred martyrdom to par - taking of the flesh of swine.

It is a mistake, however, to assume that the pig was singled out as the only animal forbidden by Jewish law. It is not fit for human consumption, according to Hebrew tradition, because it does not fulfil one of the two requirements of the Bible for an animal to be permissible to be eaten—chewing the cud and having cloven hoofs. Both the cow and the sheep qualify, but not so the pig, as it does not chew the cud.

There must have been other weighty reasons that led the Hebrew people and other groups in the Middle East not only to exclude the pig from their diet but to view it generally with abhorrence. It was a combination of factors that rendered swine unclean to the Jews.

The pig was taboo, at first, for significant religious reasons. It was worshipped by primitive races who also sacrificed it to their idols and ate its flesh in sacred meals. This fact especially, of the pig's association with alien gods and rites, made Jews, in their passion for a monotheist spiritual faith, reject the pig and decry it as unclean.

Although the ancient Egyptians reared and ate pigs, they regarded them as unclean. Herodotus, the Greek historian, recalls how anyone touching a pig had to plunge with his clothes on into a river, and that swineherds, though Egyptian by birth, were the only people excluded from the sanctuary. Socially, they were so ostracized that they had to choose wives from their own class.

It is unlikely that in the initial stages of civilization hygiene prompted the devising of laws and customs. Fear of disease, specifically trichinosis, led the ancient Hebrews wisely to reject pork as part of their diet. Human instinct works in wondrous ways and in many cases anticipates, by centuries, future knowledge. Perhaps that was true of the early banning of pork as well.

A further theory sees in the aversion to the pig, even in pre-Hebrew times, survival of early antipathy of pastoral groups to settled, agricultural races. The nomads thought themselves a better breed and despised people bound to a permanent home and leading a regulated life which seemed to lack adventure. The raising of pigs was part of the early agricultural pattern and pastoral people soon came to regard swine as an expression of a settled existence. Later, they transferred their contempt for a way of life to its symbol, the pig. They decried it as unclean and avoided its flesh.

Finally, totemism has been cited as the earliest cause of rejecting the pig as food. Primitive races recognized in the animal the symbol of their group, indeed their ancestors, and killing and eating it would have been fatal to themselves.

CHAPTER 7

Drinking Customs

Of all the "isms" that threaten the world, one of the most dangerous is alcoholism. Yet spirits, ever since their first appearance, have not only haunted people but helped them to relax, to rejoice and to instill goodwill. Drink makes some jolly and others depressed. It can sharpen the appetite, help digestion, or act as a tranquilizer.

Drink has been used from earliest times as part of communion with gods. Alcohol is mentioned in the Bible 165 times and, it is well to note, in most cases favorably. Wine was served at the Last Supper. Indeed the ancient Hebrews used to bless and thank God for having created the fruit of the vine. On the other hand, some ancients and moderns have decried it as the worst of all evils, a gift of the devil.

Alcohol is one of the most volatile spirits that have roused human passions. In America bootleggers fought the police and prohibitionists fought governments. The teetotaller fought himself. Scots and Irish still fight each other, if for nothing else, for the credit of having invented whisky, whose name derives from Gaelic, meaning so aptly "the water of life." Rum used to be called the motive power of the British navy, but in Australia it became the earliest currency.

Whether drink is good or evil is a matter of degree. It has been pointed out rightly that first the person takes a drink, then the drink takes a drink, and finally the drink takes the person.

A legend relates that when God created the first grapes, He was assisted by three members of the animal kingdom, the lion, the ape and the pig, who, each in turn, sprinkled some of their own spirit on the young plant. That is why up to the present day anyone who drinks just a little grows in strength like a lion; those who imbibe several glasses start resembling strongly their simian ancestors; and those who do not know when to stop eventually lie under the table like a pig.

Host Pouring Wine into His Own Glass First

Ancient and modern, civil and gruesome are the two reasons that account for the custom, which is now etiquette, of a host first tasting the wine. It has nothing to do with the assumption that it is to ensure that the wine is of the best quality and right temperature—thus good enough for his guests.

That, before filling their glasses, he pours a small amount of the drink into his own glass first, nowadays has the obvious purpose of removing any pieces of cork that may have fallen into the bottle whilst it was being opened. This thoughtful gesture, however, goes back to much earlier times, when it was made in different circumstances.

Before the introduction of corks, the Italians used to top the wine with oil, which filled the neck of the bottle. In serving drinks, therefore, it was necessary first to pour off its liquid protection of oil. To make quite sure that none of the guests received in their drink any drops which might still be floating on top of the wine, it was only natural for a considerate host to fill at least part of his own glass first.

The custom leads back still further—to medieval times when conviviality frequently was mixed with assassination, and the drinking of wine offered an occasion to poison one's foes. It was thus not merely as an act of courtesy that the host sipped the offered drink before everyone else, but as a kind of life assurance in its most literal sense. It was to kill all suspicion (and not his "friends"), that he did so. The company was assured they had nothing to fear and could relax. Perhaps this background of the custom explains why Jewish people, for thousands of years, have been using for their toast the wish "For Life," *L'chayim* in Hebrew.

The Toast

Motorists, at one time, learned the value of "additives," said to increase the power of their car when added to the petrol. Long before the invention of the internal combustion engine, people already used to apply additives, in their case to some of their drinks. Thus they put a piece of bread "parched with heat"—

which is the literal meaning of the word "toast"—into a tankard of beer or glass of wine. By doing so, they believed, they improved their flavor. (In fact, "additives" of that kind are still customary at some universities' Loving Cup.)

When the toast was found to be of no value, it was again left out of the drink, without even recollecting its earlier existence. Nevertheless, drinking the health of a person or proposing the success of a cause is still called a toast, after the now vanished piece of parched bread!

Adding an element of romance to the toast, a story tells that, in reality, it originated in Bath at the time of King Charles II. On a public holiday, when spirits were gay, a famous beauty was taking her bath in the public baths of that city. One of her many admirers who was watching her, took a glass of the water in which she was standing and drank her health. Another of the revellers, anxious to outdo him (and, as those who tried to excuse his behavior liked to point out, slightly inebriated perhaps), offered to jump into the bath himself. "I do not like the liquor so much," he explained, "but I should love to have the toast," indicating the lady.

Clinking Glasses

Nowadays the clinking of glasses at toasts is considered a sign of conviviality and friendship. But this has not always been the case. The custom dates back thousands of years, to the superstitious past. People then were afraid that with the drink the devil might enter their body. It was a thought which was not particularly far-fetched, considering the effects of intoxication.

That is why, before actually indulging in the drink, they made a loud noise first. The sound was meant to frighten away the evil spirit.

A modern rationalization of the custom explains it differently and so much more pleasantly. To enjoy one's drink to the utmost, it is not sufficient merely to partake of it. All one's senses must join in the pleasure. One must not only taste the drink, touch, smell and see it, but hear it as well. And it is for this purpose that one clinks glasses.

The Cocktail

America is the home of the cocktail, though no one is sure about the first concoction—either of its name or its ingredients. Cocktail parties have become a social institution the world over, with plenty of people standing or moving about all the time, exchanging lots of senseless gossip and leaving none the wiser but richer in some kind of spirit. Certainly, these parties also frequently serve business interests and the advance of political ambitions. The earliest reference to the cocktail appeared in 1806 in an American periodical, inappropriately called *The Balance*, which defined the drink as "a stimulating liquor, composed of spirits of any kind." Indeed, the cocktail may be a mixture of many things and there is as great a variety of ingredients as there is of explanations as to the origin of this drink.

To start with, people sought for a solution of the mystery of the cocktail in its literal meaning. They tried to fathom any connection—real or imagined—between the cock's tail and the drink. However, the plumage of the rooster in itself did not supply the answer.

It was the dictionary which revealed that at some time a certain type of horse, used mostly for hunting and drawing stagecoaches, had been referred to as a "cocktail." And for an obvious reason. The horse's tail was generally cut so short that it stuck up like a cock's tail. Those horses were never thoroughbreds but a mixture, just as the drink:

"Perhaps it's made of whisky, and perhaps it's made of gin:
Perhaps there's orange bitters and a lemon peel within. . . ."

More likely than horse breeding as the source of the cocktail are certain historic events associated with the Aztecs, the Mexicans and American forces of the Southern states. It is not surprising that the ancient Aztec civilization, renowned for many of its achievements, has been given the distinction of having made the first cocktail as well. An Aztec nobleman, so the story goes, brewed a drink out of the sap of the cactus plant. This he sent as a gift to the emperor by the hand of his daughter, Zochitl, a fact which—no doubt—made it all the more intoxicating. The emperor partook of it and liked the drink and the daughter so much that he acquired both! As it was Zochitl, his newlywed wife, who first introduced him to the world of intoxication, he thought it only fair to call the beverage by her name. Pronounced with the royal Aztec accent, it came to sound like Octel.

All this took place generations before the establishment of the United States and gave the drink time to take root. When, many years later, the American army under General Scott invaded Mexico, they were impressed not only by the country's brave warriors but by their "spirit," which soon conquered the would-be conquerors.

They carried it back to the States as their most potent and lasting booty, assimilating its name into their own tongue by changing Octel into cocktail. Thus a relic of the Mexican war still fights many a battle inside numerous people all over the world.

Another explanation also links the birth of the drink with American soldiery but relates it to the time of the War of Independence. A young widow named Betsy Flanagan then kept a popular tavern close to New York. She called it "The Four Corners" and not without reason, as both French and Americans, coming from all directions, made it their haunt. They were attracted by the friendliness of the inn and the charm of its hostess but—most of all—by its drinks. Patrons spent many hours in the tavern, playing cards and gulping the sparkling liquor, which Betsy herself mixed according to a formula she jealously kept a secret. Mrs. Flanagan's "bracers" became known far and wide, and no other saloon had a chance to compete with them.

It so happened that adjacent to the inn was the property of an Englishman, a loyalist and the soldiers' inveterate foe. He excelled in farming chickens, and his fowls, like Betsy's drinks, had no equal. What a pity that they could not meet—at least inside her guests!

Betsy was a good hostess and a good sport and loved to join in the fun of the soldiers. Soon it became her habit, when the spirit in the tavern reached intoxicating heights, to promise that one day she would serve her guests, free of charge, a meal of fried chicken, stolen from the finest coop in the country, next door.

This became a standing joke, but eventually, it was taken seriously. Officers, visiting the inn, began to inquire when they could expect the promised meal. Then, one day, Betsy made good her promise. To celebrate the occasion (and the theft) Betsy decorated the inn's jars and bottles with the feathers of the roasted roosters.

One of the soldiers, who craved a bracer, noted the decorated bottles and asked for a glass "of those cocktails." His call soon was taken up by others and the trophy of the theft became perpetuated for all time by being linked with Mrs. Flanagan's drink. That same night, a further tradition has it, one of the soldiers, surfeited pleasantly with fowl and drink, remarked, "We are drinking the beverage that offers the palate the same charming sensation as the feathers of the cock's tail offer the eye." Instantly, it is said, a Frenchman proposed a toast, "Long live the cocktail."

That is how from "The Four Corners," from a theft, a war and an early antagonism between British and Americans spread a new name and concoction to the four corners of the earth. At that early stage it showed how British and Americans, though they may differ in some things, by joining forces around the table can create an invincible spirit.

There is yet another interpretation which associates the first cocktail with the American-Mexican war. But this time with its final phase. A truce had been called, and both the commanding general of the Southern armies and King Axolotl VIII had agreed to meet. The negotiations took place in the royal palace. The two men, accompanied by their officers, were seated, ready to commence the talks, when the king, in a convivial mood, suggested as one man to another they first should join in a drink.

The American guest gladly agreed and the king ordered that without delay a drink should be served. In no time a girl of striking beauty appeared, carrying a magnificent golden goblet, which contained a potion of her own brewing.

What had been meant as a friendly gesture, now assumed a critical aspect. A hushed silence fell over the party and it seemed that the fate of the war was in the balance. There was only one cup. Who should drink of it first? Whoever it was, his precedence was bound to insult the other. It was a delicate situation.

The girl quickly assessed the implications of the single cup. With a smile she bowed to her king and the general, and then drained the cup herself. Her presence of mind and female intuition had saved the situation.

Before leaving, the general asked the king who the tactful

young lady was, whose beauty equalled her wisdom. In reality Axolotl had not the slightest idea. He had never seen her before. Nevertheless he told the American that she was his daughter Coctel. On hearing this, the general replied, "I shall see to it, Your Majesty, that your daughter's name will be honored by my army for all time." The general not only kept his promise, but through the American forces "Coctel," now spelled "cocktail," conquered most of the world.

Some people who indulge in drink justify themselves by explaining that they do so for medicinal purposes only. In the case of the cocktail, so yet a further claim asserts, it was actually the medical profession that was responsible for its invention. An American "ancient print," quoted by a New York paper, stated that doctors used to treat certain diseases of the throat with "a pleasant liquid" which they applied by means of the tip of a long feather, plucked from a cock's tail. Patients soon referred to the treatment as that of "the cocktail."

At first only used for painting the throat, the liquid was later prescribed as a gargle, with its original name still clinging to it. Possibly to make its taste more pleasant still, several "appetizers" were added. No wonder that soon the sick swallowed the gargle! Eventually, the cocktail became completely divorced from sore throats and assumed its social function.

Beer

Society began its modern drinking habits with the imbibing of beer, its oldest alcoholic drink. They did not invent it, but discovered it in the process of nature. Possibly some bread crumbs which had fallen into water started to ferment and, tasting the liquid, primitive people rather enjoyed it and, long before the development of their scientific mind, started their research—with intoxicating results!

The history of brewing goes back well over 10,000 years, long before the Egyptians had started building their first pyramid. It almost coincided with the beginning of agriculture and the first making of bread. Indeed, baking and brewing thus went together. Beer not only belonged to people's original diet, but helped them in serving their gods. The very origin of the beverage was considered divine. It was poured onto the ground to appease the gods, for them to bless the fields with fertility. Without this ritual, primitive humans were convinced, nothing would grow.

The brewing of beer was so sacred that among some tribes, men engaged in the task were kept isolated from their womenfolk, as otherwise, it was believed, the magic transformation of corn into spirit would not take place.

One of the most ancient clay tablets in existence, dating back to Babylonian lands and the year 6000 B.C., depicts a crude type of beer-making for sacrificial purposes. Babylonians actually specialized in a bread served for fermentation. By 4000 B.C. they had learned to produce sixteen different types of the beverage. Brewing was a privilege set aside for their kings and restricted to temples. Thus the earliest breweries were places of worship!

The Egyptians attributed the introduction of brewing to Isis, their goddess of nature. Beer became their national drink, as popular with the living as with the gods and the dead. Peasants and workers were allotted a daily allowance of four loaves of bread and two jugs of beer. An ancient hieroglyphic temple-inscription records that Pharaoh Ramses III consecrated 466,303 jugs of beer to the gods.

From Egypt the art of brewing spread to Greece and then to Rome. However, it is quite likely that the people of northern Europe discovered the drink separately. Beer was drunk in Britain already at the time of Christ, to be enjoyed there by the Roman invaders.

Its early religious association lingered on through the ages. Medieval monasteries excelled in making beer and provided different brands for the monks and their guests, each of whom was given a gallon (4 liters) a day.

Churches sold beer to raise funds. It became the most popular drink at weddings, where it was poured by the bride herself. Thus it became known as the *bride's ale*, accounting for the word "bridal."

People soon recognized many qualities in beer. It nourished them and, so they imagined, saved them from the plague. It buoyed up their spirits and relieved fatigue. Water became stagnant and deteriorated on long trips across the seas, whilst beer not only kept its taste but remained wholesome. Beer even made history. It was because their casks were almost empty that the

Pilgrim Fathers, sailing on the *Mayflower*, decided to cut the voyage short and look for a port ahead of schedule: "For we could not take time for further search and consideration, our victuals being much spent, especially beer."

Wine

Wine was already produced in Mesopotamia before the year 3000 B.C. and has been cheering people up ever since. Considered not only a gift of the gods, but part of them, it was drunk as such. Wine was their blood, and with the wine the god was thought to enter the human body. Thus, the drinking of wine initially was a sacred ritual, and intoxication was regarded as the presence of the divine spirit mysteriously working within people. Egyptians saw in the black and purplish grapes, so round and luscious, the divine eyes of Horus.

All evidence points to Asia Minor—and especially to the Caucasus—as the vine's original home. It did not take long to learn to cultivate the wildly growing grapes. The very name of wine stems from that region and at least from the year 1500 B.C. It has been found in cuneiform-script on Hittite clay tablets of that time.

The Bible credits Noah with having planted the first vineyard, relating that he did so almost immediately after the Flood when he had alighted from the Ark. This had landed on the summit of the Ararat mountain range—the highest part of the Caucasus!

Accidents happen and mistakes are made all the time. Sometimes, however, they prove not a bane but a boon. Hence it is quite likely that a Persian legend is correct in its claim that wine was discovered by human error. In fact, at first it was considered a waste of precious grapes and almost poured away as poison.

Grapes were plentiful around the city of Persepolis, whose founder, Jam-Sheed, was exceedingly fond of them. Wanting to enjoy them even when they were out of season, he anticipated modern methods of preservation by having grapes bottled and stored. But one day an accident happened and the grapes were crushed. Their juice duly fermented and its taste was so strange that Jam-Sheed had it poured into a separate jar, which he immediately marked POISON but somehow forgot to throw away.

One of his servants, who had grown tired of life and was determined to commit suicide, by chance saw the labelled jar. It was exactly what she was looking for. Secretly she drank of the juice, with most unexpected results.

When she came to, she drank some more. No one really knows whether she did so imagining that she had taken too small a dose for the poison to do its work properly, or because she was getting the taste of it and rather enjoyed that strange kind of dying. She repeated the procedure until the jar was empty. Far from dying, she had experienced most world-affirming sensations.

She confessed her deed to her master—she had discovered wine. This soon became known all over Persia and was described as "the delightful poison" with its popularity spreading far and wide. In no time the wild vine shoots were cultivated all over the world—climate permitting. The use of wine increased steadily and was glorified in proverbs and hymns.

Champagne

Champagne started with a bang. A bottle of wine burst and a wise monk asked, "Why?" At least that is the traditional tale. Champagne in its name recalls an eastern province of France, famous for its vineyards and generally known as "the Garden of France."

When in 1668 Dom Perignon, a Benedictine, was put in charge of his abbey's cellar, he was not satisfied with just looking after the wine. He tried to improve it. His dream was to blend the best of the grapes growing in the vineyard around him, and for his new creation to surpass everything else in taste, color and fragrance. He spent countless hours experimenting.

One day, so the story goes, there was an accident. One of the bottles of wine exploded. Perhaps it was nature herself who, in her peculiar way, with a loud bang tried to point out what had so far escaped Dom's attention. Investigating the damage, he noticed that strange bubbles were rising in the wine left in the bottle. He immediately assumed that these were somehow related to what had happened. He sipped the wine. Never before had he tasted a drink like it! Excitedly, he called out to his brethren, "I am drinking stars!"

Here was the answer to his quest. All that he needed was to find out what had taken place. Once he had traced the source of the magic bubbles, he would be able to produce the effervescent drink. He reasoned that something inside the bottle must have built up such a pressure that it burst. The bubbles pointed to some kind of secondary fermentation. Soon his research was successful, resulting in the "invention" of champagne.

It may be that all this is just a beautiful story to give additional lustre to the dance of the sparkling atoms. Perhaps the birth of champagne was much more prosaic, yet no less exciting. The fact remains that the world owes champagne to Dom Perignon.

The drink's popularity began with one of the unexpected events which abound in life. At one of his lavish banquets, the Marquis of Sillery wanted to offer his guests something unique. He chose the new champagne. When the party was well in swing, a dozen girls appeared on the floor, dressed in the guise of the drunken revellers who once danced and sang in honor of Bacchus, the Greek god of wine. They carried flower-wreathed bottles whose corks suddenly popped. The champagne, fizzing out, was poured into huge glasses specially made for the occasion. Its taste enchanted the guests who spread the tale of this wondrous drink wherever they went. The court once again set the fashion. Ever since, the serving of sparkling wine has become an indispensable part of all ceremonial occasions throughout the world.

The Champagne Glass

It is said that the saucer shape of a champagne glass, commonly used nowadays, is the result of a love affair. It was modelled on a woman's breast—that of Madame de Pompadour, mistress of King Louis XV of France. The shape, in spite of its alleged romantic association, is the least suitable for the full enjoyment of the drink, in no small measure due to its bubbles. The extended width of the glass contributes to their rapid dissipation and thereby greatly reduces the pleasure. No wonder that the original champagne glass was narrow-brimmed, which gave the bubbles a much longer time to rise.

Another of its conspicuous early features was its hollow stem. It, too, had a practical, though now obsolete reason. When wine was not as refined as it is today, it allowed the dregs to settle in the hollow stem and for people to enjoy a pure drink.

The Teetotaller

The Bible not only gives Noah the credit of having been the first to make wine but, after having tasted the fermented juice of the grape, of becoming drunk and inadvertently exposing himself.

No one could blame or condemn Noah for his drunkenness. How could he have known the effect wine would have on him. Already thousand of years ago, some people therefore decried the use of fermented grape juice, and small groups of men began to dedicate themselves to shun and oppose the drinking of liquor. One of these, the Rechabites, was highly commended by the prophet Jeremiah. Thus prohibitionists and the temperance movement have their roots in the distant past.

The description of those who refrain from taking alcohol as *teetotallers* is of a much more recent date. Nevertheless, this has not prevented a controversy as to the origin of the name. It was first used in 1834 by Richard Turner, a Lancashire workingman, in a speech advocating total abstention from intoxicating drink. Opinions differ as to how he first came to use the term.

Some say that he stuttered and, as is usual in such cases, his impediment showed itself specially badly at moments of nervous tension. Passionately pleading his cause, he wanted to end his address by saying that "nothing but total abstention will do—that or nowt!" Unfortunately Mr. Turner's stammer spoiled it. The audience watched him struggle to articulate and heard him speak haltingly of t-t-total abstention. Opponents immediately made use of the incident. It offered an opportunity of ridiculing both the man and his movement, which they at once named "t-totalism."

Others believed that it was not really a speaker's stammer, but a preference for tea at temperance meetings which was responsible for the new word. Though the spelling itself slightly differs, the sound of tea can unmistakably be heard.

Even a game of chance has been quoted as a possible source of the term, though it can be disregarded as such. The *teetotum* was a small, four-sided, lettered disk or die, spun by a player. The letter which lay uppermost, when it stopped spinning, decided the player's luck. *T* stood for *totum*, signifying that the player had won *all*, the whole lot. Certainly, teetotallers regarded all drink as evil.

Glass

Glass was not invented. Like wine and champagne, it was discovered by accident. No one will ever know by whom, or exactly when. It is one of the many anonymous chance discoveries that have enriched life. Glass has been in use for at least 6,000 years.

Pliny the Elder, the famous first-century Roman writer, claims that it was first "found" on the sandy shores of Palestine. Phoenician sailor-merchants camping there, one night took from their cargo big lumps of carbonate of soda to support their cooking pots over the fire. Next morning, when raking the ashes, they discovered the first glass! It had been created by the melting sand in the presence of the alkali.

Archaeologists, however, have shown that even this early claim was much too conservative. At the site of ancient Babylon Sir Flinders Petrie excavated specimens of glass antedating the Phoenician "invention" by many centuries!

At the beginning, and for a long time, glass was used only as a surface coating or to imitate precious stones and gems. Almost a thousand years passed before the first glass vessels were made. They were in use in Egypt and Mesopotamia in 1500 B.C.

The most common method for making them was the sand-core process. A core of sand was formed in the desired shape of the vessel and tightly wrapped in a cloth, which then was either dipped into, or covered by, a solution of warm, viscous glass. When this had cooled, the inner core was removed and the vessel was ready. Alternatively, glass was pressed into a mould or the vessel was ground out of a cool block of glass.

After another 1,500 years, just around the birth of Christ, and again in Palestine, a new and revolutionary method of making glassware was invented—that of glassblowing, whose essential principle has not changed ever since.

Mystery envelops even this comparatively late invention. Was it the result of ingenuity or again the outcome of chance? Tradition favors the latter view. It says that a glassmaker found a faulty tube—it had been accidentally closed by the hot glass at one end. To remove the obstructing blob, he blew into the tube from the other end. But instead of the tube opening up, the blob of glass became a bubble. Thus the latest method of glassworking was born.

CHAPTER 8

The History of Dress

Biblically, tailoring started in paradise, when Adam and Eve sewed their first dress of fig leaves. Somehow this must have proved unsatisfactory, as soon afterwards the Bible records the first change in fashion, when animal skins supplanted the fig leaves.

Opinions still differ as to what the first dress, at least according to biblical tradition, looked like. Some describe it as a simple girdle. Others suggest that the apron was the first costume. A sixteenth-century translation of Hebrew Scripture erroneously stated that Adam and Eve made themselves breeches!

From the very earliest times, men and women have covered their bodies, and the reasons why have become increasingly complex. Nearly everything people wear has had, at different times through the ages, a definite purpose, although today, in many instances, this has faded into obscurity.

Primarily, clothes protected the human body from the forces of nature. They were needed in order to survive. A sense of modesty was another source. Associating sex with shame, people tried to hide the erogenous zones of their bodies. However, dress was often designed also to impress others and arouse fear, admiration and desire. It is a form of attractive display (like the feathers on birds or the colorful markings on animal skins).

Clothes were introduced to emphasize the difference between the sexes, to stimulate the senses, but to avoid promiscuity. On the other hand, dress was a means to stress distinction. In the nude people are equal. But costumes removed this democracy of the uniformity of naked bodies. An outer skin could make all the difference and thus dress became much more revealing of human character than nakedness. It was the earliest status symbol, proclaiming the wearer's profession, power and social rank.

Always anxious to make the greatest use of anything they

possessed, people soon employed their cloak for numerous other functions as well. It became their blanket, and even their bed. When the Hebrews left Egypt, they wrapped into their garments their kneading troughs and all they contained. Merchants used their robes as counters, on which they displayed their wares, and cloaks served as saddles and carpets as well.

To be properly dressed has meant many things to different ages. What was considered decent to one generation and quite in order, has sometimes shocked and offended another. Fashion certainly is a taste shared by a large number of people for a short time. There have been eras when dress has tried to conceal natural shapes and others when everything possible has been done to display them.

It becomes evident that wardrobes are crowded with intriguing revelations about attitudes and reactions to life, society and the other sex. What applies to dress in general, is equally true of each of its peculiar features, with their contradictions, incredibilities and many surprises.

The leopard cannot change its spots. But people have the power to change their skin. And certainly they have made good use of it. There are few sayings truer than that "clothes make the man."

Trousers

Trousers, first worn by the Nomads of Central Asia possibly 1,000 years B.C. owe their invention to the horse. Originally, people dressed merely by wrapping a piece of cloth or animal skin around their body. The warriors of the Asian steppes found that the wearing of this sort of garment was uncomfortable on horseback and restricted their movement greatly. This gave them the idea to clothe the lower part of their bodies with trousers. Not as drab as nowadays, they were striped, checked and even embroidered.

And when in battle the Nomads clashed with their "civilized" neighbors, these recognized the usefulness of trousers, as their own long flowing garments put them at a disadvantage. They lost no time in adopting the barbarians' attire—not out of fashion but in order to survive in battle. Thus, from Central Asia, through war and the horse, the use of trousers was eventually adopted by the Persians, the Indians and the Chinese to find its way into northern Europe.

When in 55 B.C. Julius Caesar reached Britain, he specially remarked on the brightly colored trousers worn there by the men. It was actually the Romans' conflict with the barbarians of the north that introduced trousers into their empire.

However, at first there was much opposition, and the Romans despised the new garment, called it unworthy of noblemen and fit only for slaves. In spite of it, the trousers' obvious advantage soon made them fashionable, so much so in fact that an imperial edict was issued threatening freemen who wore trousers with loss of property and banishment. But without effect. Trousers had come to stay—at least for a while.

Then, even in northern Europe, they went out of fashion again. In their present form they were reintroduced in England at the end of the eighteenth century, superseding breeches and silk stockings. Still, as late as 1814, the Duke of Wellington was refused admission to his club because he was wearing trousers.

Trinity College issued an order in 1812 that any student who appeared in Hall or Chapel and was clad in trousers should be deemed absent. In Sheffield a special clause appertaining to clergy ruled that "under no circumstances whatever shall any preacher be allowed to occupy the pulpit who wears trousers." Indeed, anyone so attired would not go to heaven!

Modern times rendered the wearing of trousers a matter of life and death. During the French Revolution, they became a political symbol of the equality of people. Former aristocrats put on the blue linen pants of workmen to try to escape the guillotine.

On the other hand, wealthy Englishmen adopted the wearing of trousers for health reasons. Suffering badly from gout, they were convinced that this proletarian (and barbarian) attire would assuage the pain of their swollen legs.

Turn-ups

An immaculate Englishman's concern with his attire on a rainy day in New York is said to have been responsible for the introduction of cuffs on trousers.

People have often wondered why trousers (when it is the prevailing fashion) should have this peculiar fold at the bottom. What purpose did it serve, apart from collecting dirt and dust which, according to clothing experts, amounts to at least one ounce every year.

Some have suggested that tall men invented the cuff because it made them appear shorter and less ill at ease. Others, more commercially minded, assumed that the cuff owes its existence to merchants to whom every centimeter of extra cloth sold meant more profit.

As far as records are available, cuffs on trousers were first seen in New York towards the end of the nineteenth century on the occasion of a big society wedding. This was attended by numerous dandies, as well as by respectable visitors from the Old World. At the time, Americans specially watched their English cousins, whom they then still tried to imitate, at least as far as their outfit was concerned.

One of the overseas guests was late; he had been caught in a downpour which flooded the streets. The ingenious Englishman, so meticulously clad, did not want to get his trousers wet and, to keep them dry, he rolled up their bottoms.

Due to the excitement and his late arrival, he forgot to turn them down again and so, when ascending the church steps, conspicuously displayed his "cuffs." Many took notice of them but, unaware of their real purpose, took them to be the latest English fashion and eagerly copied the "turn-ups."

The Waistcoat

Fashion has had a profound effect upon the waistcoat, a garment that has come and gone many times since its first appearance in the sixteenth century. Its purpose was manifold and equally subject to change.

In its earliest use it was an elaborate and costly apparel of show, lending itself especially to the expression of individual taste. It was worn purely as an ornament and it was most unusual to wear a waistcoat made of the same material as the coat.

Though worn under the jacket, it was meant to be seen and admired and had, therefore, to be—at least partly—visible. This was made all the easier, as at the time the sleeved coat was not fastened at all: its buttons served only a decorative purpose. Indeed, later on, coats were specially cut away in front, so that the waistcoat would show to better advantage.

It was made of the finest materials, often in brocade with silver and gold threads, and in all colors, the gayer the better. Frequently quilted, embroidered and sometimes fringed, the waistcoat was lavishly adorned with delicate handwork.

An inventory of Henry VIII's wardrobe records a waistcoat of "cloth and silver, quilted with black silk" and another of "white satin, with sleeves embroidered with Venice silver." When the Earl of Essex, the unfortunate favorite and victim of Queen Elizabeth I, was led to his execution, he took off his doublet and was seen to wear underneath a scarlet waistcoat.

Even the great Beethoven was anxious to have an elegant waistcoat. In 1793 he wrote to a young lady of whom he was fond, asking her to kindly help him in the realization of his wish that "I may be lucky enough to possess a waistcoat worked by you in goat's wool."

Gradually, however, the waistcoat was not only shortened in length (at first having reached the dimensions of a jacket), but was reduced in status as well. Instead of its original ornamental role, it came to fulfil a strictly utilitarian function. Frenchmen in particular stressed its purpose "to protect chest and stomach from the air" in winter and encourage "a healthy tendency to sweat in the summer."

When medical opinions changed and sweat and the exclusion of fresh air were no longer considered harmful, the waistcoat still served man well. Its multiple pockets were useful for carrying many small items.

Between the two World Wars the waistcoat lost both its aesthetic and practical appeal. Once again, it made a comeback— this time as a unisex garment to brighten up one's clothes.

The Bottom Button on a Waistcoat

Custom decreed that a man should have the bottom button of his waistcoat undone.

One explanation dates this strange fashion back to a member of the British Royal Family who thus attended a public function. Possibly he had dressed in too much of a hurry, or one of his aides had been neglectful in fulfilling his duty. No one could know, or would dare to guess, the reason. So that he should not be embarrassed, all the other men followed suit and the fad caught on. Once again, royalty had set the fashion.

Another theory traces the undone button habit back to the time when dandies were wearing not one waistcoat but two, each of extremely precious and gaudy material, a scarlet one underneath, for instance, and a canary-yellow one on top. By leaving the bottom button of the top waistcoat undone, the wearer was able to show the fact that he had on another beautiful and expensive garment underneath.

Much less glamorous but more practical is a third explanation. Waistcoats were tight, especially so around the waist. Therefore some trendsetter of fashion undid the last button for his own comfort's sake, and everyone followed his lead.

If worn at all, waistcoats have lost their original close fit with tailors remedying the defect of tightness. But, as always in life, customs, once introduced for some valid reason, are accepted to be right for all times and are thoughtlessly continued, even when they have become obsolete.

Buttons on Sleeves

The obvious purpose of a button is to secure a dress for reasons of fit, or warmth and decency. None of these motives, however, seems to explain the small buttons on the sleeves of men's present-day jackets.

Redundant now, they used to serve a definite purpose. Their origin goes back to the early long sleeves. Buttons then were a simple and ingenious means of preventing them from hanging down and impeding movement.

In the seventeenth century, much money was spent on men's coats and, naturally, people tried to avoid anything that would ruin them. Most vulnerable were the sleeves. To keep them out of harm's way, they were turned back. Lest they slip down again, they were fastened with buttons. The buttons, too, could help a man to adjust his attire to prevailing weather conditions. If it was cold and windy, the wide sleeves could be tightened and closed around the wrists.

In centuries past, man was not as drab in his dress as in later years. Like his female partner he also liked to adorn himself and, if possible, to display his wealth by means of his costume. Buttons could serve just that purpose. They were handmade and produced in beautiful shapes and colors. They were both costly and decorative. Their use now was not exclusively to fasten sleeves to keep out the wind and avoid becoming soiled, but much more to boost the ego and attract attention.

The distinctive buttons on military uniforms were said to have found their way there for totally different reasons. At least that is the story usually told. They were the result of a king's displeasure, when he observed some of his men wiping their noses on their sleeves. To make such unseemly behavior impossible, he decreed the fixing of buttons. Any soldier who forgot to use his sneeze-rag and tried to wipe his nose on his sleeves soon desisted in pain.

To "Laugh up One's Sleeve"

To "laugh up one's sleeve" is certainly not a sign of good manners. Worse still, it shows not the best of character. After all, no decent person would laugh at another's expense and do so—cowardly—hiding their amusement.

Altogether the phrase itself seems so absurd. One laughs in front of a person or behind their back. But who would ever laugh up their sleeve? It just does not make sense. Yet what now seems so meaningless an expression was quite intelligible (and possible) in days gone by. To laugh up one's sleeve, indeed, is part of the evolution of people's dress.

The fact is that while costumes changed in shape and dimensions, language lagged behind and was slow to adapt itself. It carried outmoded notions and references to long-discarded fashions. People's sleeves were once not as tight-fitting as they are today. Nor did they extend only to the wrist. They were wide and exceedingly long, so much so that at times they had to be carried over the arm or knotted, so as not to drag along the ground. Ingenious tailors even put holes in the sleeves which enabled the wearers to put their hands and arms through them much higher up—without having to reach down all the way.

In some circles the length of the sleeve indicated the owner's importance, a tradition preserved, like those wide, hanging sleeves themselves, in academic gowns. At Oxford University, for example, an undergraduate's gown lacks sleeves altogether. But those worn by a Master of Arts reach down almost to the ground.

In the days when the phrase was coined, it was quite simple to hide one's smile by lifting and holding the long sleeve in front of the face. It served as a screen and no one could see or guess what one was actually doing behind it.

The Different Way of Buttoning for Men and Women

How to secure one's dress has been a problem ever since humans have worn clothes, which means from the beginning of their existence. Even Adam and Eve must have wondered at first how to fasten their fig leaves!

Whilst the bulk of early clothing merely used to hang down from the shoulders, later on the folds were secured by laces and braces. A further development was the button.

Adopted in the thirteenth century, it first became part of people's dress to serve either practical or decorative purposes, perhaps still hidden away or, on the contrary, conspicuously displayed. In men's clothing it came to play the significant role to help to secure a man's fly, first becoming part of the breeches in the days of King Charles I.

It might be assumed that even though men and women wore different types of clothes, they would at least share the same method of fastening them. Everyone knows that this is not so. Men button their clothes, from pyjamas to everyday jackets, from left to right, while women do exactly the opposite. The origin of this peculiar fashion was not due, as cynics have sometimes suggested, to a woman's stubbornness and her usual way of being contrary—but to the fact that most men and women are right-handed. It was practical, but now forgotten and obsolete considerations that led to this little-noticed but nevertheless marked distinction in buttoning a garment.

Men were always independent, at least in their manner of dressing, which they did mostly without any assistance. Women, however, and noble ladies particularly, were dressed by their maids.

Therefore in their case, it was a convenient process to reverse the sides of the buttons as the maid, who faced her mistress while dressing her, used her right hand and so found it easier to button the garment from right to left. Mothers had to carry a baby, usually supporting it with their left arm. When it became necessary to breastfeed the child in public, which often happened—something not unusual—the left breast was used as being most convenient. To shelter the infant from the wind and the cold while it was feeding, they covered it with the right side of their dress or coat, prompting designers in those days to make women's clothes that would button up from right to left.

Another possible reason for the difference was that medieval man had always to be prepared for a fight and therefore walked about armed. So that he could readily grasp and effectively use his sword, it was essential for him to have his right hand ready for combat and not stiff from cold. To ensure this, he would thrust it into his coat to keep it warm.

To be able to do so, his coat had to open from left to right. In the early days men also wore a loose cloak which they grasped with their left hand, throwing the left side over the right so as to keep the right hand free. This, too, contributed to the introduction of the overlapping from left to right in the case of men's clothes.

None of these motives any longer applies. Yet habits do not die easily, and men and women still carry on the now apparently senseless fashion of buttoning up their garments in opposite ways.

The Slit in the Lapel

Today the slit in the lapel of a man's jacket is only decorative. That is why, according to taste and fashion, its size and shape may differ. However, it was not consideration of elegance that first introduced the "cut." Its origin can be accounted for in two different ways: one rather sentimental and even sorrowful, the other practical and rational.

The ancient Hebrews (and still orthodox Jews of today), as a sign of mourning at the death of a loved one, made a tear in their coat. In the case of parents they never sewed it up again as it was meant to serve as a permanent reminder of their loss. Actually, this custom is merely the last token of an older habit in which the garment was rent altogether at the moment of bereavement. Perhaps it was the manifestation of a psychological mechanism, helping people to overcome their grief by externalizing it.

No matter what the reason, the fact is that the "mournful" tear in one's coat became a widespread custom all over the world. Somehow their Christian neighbors adopted the slit in the lapel and an original mourning rite was continued even at moments of greatest joy. Without knowing it, men began to walk about all the time wearing what is really a gesture of sorrow.

Much more likely is a second explanation. This claims that not sentimental but practical considerations introduced the slit. In olden days collars were very large, mainly because in the wintry cold they could serve as a natural shield. Men just turned them up to protect and keep their throat and neck warm. So that in normal weather the collar could remain flat when turned down, it became essential to insert a slit, which has endured to this day.

The Handkerchief

Poets and dramatists have used the handkerchief both as a beautiful metaphor and a target of vitriolic attack. George Bernard Shaw decried it as a vicious harborer of bacteria, whilst Walt Whitman called grass "the handkerchief of God."

Today a handkerchief seems a very ordinary item. No one would guess its eventful history, full of contradictions, containing an Oriental past and a French corruption. Most disappointing of all, i t got its hand only at the very end, though now this appears as its prefix.

Originally, the handkerchief had no connection at all with the hand. It was a simple piece of cloth used in the East to protect the head from the burning rays of the sun. Probably sailors introduced it from there into France, where it soon became fashionable. With their logical mind, the French called this new kind of garment (which it then was) "a covering for the head"—*couvrir chef*.

The cloth crossed the Channel and the British adopted it and its French name, but in the process corrupted the latter simply to kerchief. It did not take long, however, to become apparent that such a light covering was inadequate to protect the head in the cold English climate. Without doing away completely with the new attire, people removed it from their head, and carried it (often very conspicuously) in their hand! They found the kerchief useful for blowing their noses and wiping away perspiration from the face. They duly acknowledged the new way of carrying the cloth instead of wearing it by adding the hand to its name and thereby creating the monstrous and contradictory word of a hand-headcovering or, in its hybrid English form, hand-kerchief!

A further development took place to add to the confusion. Men put this piece of cloth they had carried in their hands, which originally had covered their heads, into their pockets!

It is a fact that even in the late Middle Ages the handkerchief was still unknown. Priests were then reprimanded by their superiors for using their sacred garments for the blowing of their noses. It was indeed only in the sixteenth century that the handkerchief (just as the word) came into use, though at first only among the aristocracy. Hygiene today has led some people to replace the original cloth by soft paper substitutes. The handkerchief itself has quite largely resumed the role of a decorative accessory.

For a long time France has been recognized as the trendsetter of fashion. Yet who would guess that the world owes the simple square handkerchief to that country as well? It is the result of the logic and pragmatism of a Frenchwoman—Marie Antoinette. In contrast to her weak and dull-witted husband, King Louis XVI, she was not only an ambitious queen but a woman full of ideas and plans to render life more pleasant and enjoyable. Her interests extended even to such trivial items as the handkerchief.

Originally, handkerchiefs were of varied shapes and sizes: triangular, rectangular, oval, round and square. Marie felt that, of all of these, the one cut square was the most useful. Nowadays, royalty may happen to launch a fashion merely by their example. In Marie's day, prior to the Revolution, kings not only reigned but ruled. At the queen's suggestion, Louis XVI issued a law (on June 2, 1785) which instructed his subjects that henceforth "the length of handkerchiefs must be equal to their width through my entire kingdom." The French monarchy fell seven years later. Both the king and the queen were executed.

Whether or not the royal decree was repealed is unknown, but the square handkerchief survived, to become a universal and enduring accessory of dress. Even fickle fashion has not changed it.

The Wig

Wigs have been used for thousands of years. Mummified bodies found in Egyptian graves wore wigs. Men and women alike have used them and did so for various reasons.

Wigs are rooted in superstitious fear and magic make-believe. Hair was considered a source and a symbol of strength and early on people regarded their hair as a seat of the vital spirit of life. The more there was of it, the stronger they imagined themselves (or others) to be. For this reason primitive races refrained from cutting their children's hair for at least the first year of their lives.

People tried not only to protect what hair they had but to add to it by every possible means. For that purpose, first and primarily, wigs were invented. It was thought that—magically—they increased vigor and that the abundance of hair frightened off enemies, real and imaginary. The wig deceived evil forces and threatening foes by emphasizing or simulating towering strength.

A beautiful crown of hair was always treasured. It made people so much more attractive and has been found sexually exciting. Thus it became a significant accessory and weapon in the battle of love.

Sparse hair or, worse still, baldness made people so different. It caused disdain, suspicion and ridicule. Wigs were also devised to hide loss of hair. They served, too, as a useful disguise. They could conceal the wearer's identity and were chosen by spies, fugitives and actors.

As wigs are distinctive and can accentuate social status, they became as well part of one's professional attire. They were worn to proclaim a dignitary's special standing, as they still continue to do in British courts of law and in Parliament. The fashion of wigs, just as their shapes and sizes, has waxed and waned through the centuries. Like the ancient Egyptians and Assyrians, the Romans and Greeks favored false hair.

It was only in the seventeenth century that wigs became firmly established in Europe. A royal example, born of necessity, set the fashion. Louis XIII of France became bald prematurely. He first used a few artificial strands to supplement his own sparse growth, but as his baldness increased he had to don a full wig.

Possibly out of courtesy, if not sympathy, and to make the king's new hairstyle less conspicuous, the courtiers followed suit.

Soon ordinary people, always anxious to ape nobility, copied the *perruque*, as the French called it. It was the word which gave the English language its periwig, eventually to be shortened to the present-day wig.

From France, the wig spread all over Europe, to be adopted in England during the second half of the seventeenth century. Its form changed frequently. Some people wore the "natural" or full-bottomed wig. Others adorned themselves with one of huge dimensions, towering above the forehead in two huge peaks and falling around, and far below, the shoulders.

As a survival of that general fashion it is still worn by the Speaker of the British House of Commons, the Lord Chamberlain, and judges and barristers in the British Commonwealth. Paradoxes and intriguing features became associated with the donning of a wig.

Jewish ecclesiastical authorities made its wearing obligatory for a married woman! Her own hair, considered too seductive to be seen by any man other than her husband, had to be covered up with the artificial creation, meant to render her unattractive, if not ugly. But women soon took their revenge and began to use wigs of the latest color, shape and fashion.

Ostentation, vanity and husbands' fear of losing their wives to other men—they all contributed in making the wig a distinctive feature and playing a part in the course of civilization.

The Fan

Fans were the earliest airconditioners. Among the first of their kind was probably a huge palm leaf, or some other naturally grown means, such as a bird's feathers, swayed by slaves. The artificially created breeze appeared to cool the air, whilst the movement kept away irritating insects. It is a fallacy, however, to assume that a fan lowers the room's temperature. All it does is to swirl the hot air around, thereby helping perspiration to dry faster which, in turn, makes people feel more comfortable and draw the wrong conclusion that the fan has actually cooled the atmosphere.

Hosts in ancient Egypt employed special servants to stand behind their guests with big fans of papyrus with which they created a current of air. Though thus completely utilitarian in origin, it did not take long for the fan to assume other significant functions.

Only the rich and noble could be concerned with their comfort or afford extra servants to carry and sway the then sizable fans. Therefore almost inevitably these became a symbol of the "upper class," of dignity and position. The fan came to indicate superiority and importance, to be used for state and religious purposes, as it is today among Oriental potentates and in Papal processions.

The original, naturally grown fan eventually gave way to new gadgets, cleverly constructed to fold in a small compass and, when expanded, to take the form of a section of a circle. Because of their new small size, servants were no longer needed to carry or sway them. The fan had become an accessory for all people, but especially for women.

Feminine ingenuity soon discovered yet a further and quite unexpected value of the fan: it could rouse passions. Women of primitive races had learned the usefulness of a sham-flight from the men, to be pursued all the more fervently. Their modern successors discovered that by just sitting still behind their fan, in an assumed retreat of modesty, with their eyes peering over its top from time to time, they could lure their prey all the more easily and in comfort. The fan thus assumed the role of a potent weapon in the war of the sexes, with the woman's dignity well preserved.

A Chinese tradition has it that the invention of the fan was one of the pleasant chance discoveries of daily life. A royal princess, participating in the Feast of Lanterns, had her face covered with a mask, as was only proper for a person of her rank. But as the heat and the pressure created by the mask became too much, she lifted it slightly. To cool her brow but at the same time still to conceal her features, she moved the mask quickly to and fro in front of her face. Others, similarly distressed, followed her example and with it introduced what was to become the modern fan.

The Umbrella

Originally, the umbrella served only as a sunshade. Its name is a reminder of this fact. *Umbra* is the Latin for "shade."

Umbrellas were used in the East more than 2,000 years ago. They were known in Mesopotamia, Egypt and China as early as the twelfth century B.C., and were then a mark of nobility. The audience chamber of the king of Siam (the modern Thailand) was furnished with three umbrellas—and nothing else.

Few people could afford an umbrella. No wonder that kings prided themselves on owning one or, luckier still, several, such as the ruler of Ava who signed himself as "the King of the White Elephant and Lord of twenty-four umbrellas."

Umbrellas were not only costly but heavy, and special servants, mostly slaves, carried them. Ancient pictorial representations show dignitaries, kings and priests being accompanied by their umbrella-carriers, whose only duty it was to shelter their master from the sun. Inevitably, the open umbrella, like its rolled descendant in English society in modern days, became a status symbol.

Europe eventually adopted the umbrella, though for a considerable period it remained a guard against the sun only and was reserved for the rich and noble. That is how papal Rome came to use it, and even Italian horsemen in the time of the Renaissance.

Technical advances and the invention of cheaper material in the seventeenth century made the umbrella available to everybody. The traditional leather was replaced by lighter cloths, of which silk became most popular. Whalebone was used for the ribs and the umbrella became so light that the owner could carry it himself. With it, yet another occupation had been made redundant by the progress of science.

It was only then that people began to appreciate the umbrella's usefulness as a protection against rain. The logical French wisely differentiated between its dual functions and, ever since, have continued to speak of the *parasol*—in the case of the sun—and the *parapluie*—in reference to the rain.

Yet the umbrella was still not generally adopted. Opposition arose from various quarters. Men considered it effeminate. Snobbishness, too, made people avoid its use. It was reasoned that only those who could not afford a carriage needed umbrellas. To carry one immediately stamped its owner as a person of little means. The umbrella, once the precious property of wealthy potentates, had thus deteriorated into a cheap substitute for a carriage, appropriate only for the impecunious.

Jonas Hanway (1712–86) made Britain umbrella-conscious. The claim, commonly held, that he actually introduced it there is a slight exaggeration. However, he was the first to display it conspicuously. Because of it, he had to suffer ridicule and almost an assault. The general public, always suspicious of newfangled gadgets, jeered at him whenever they saw him walking about so suitably fortified against the inclement English climate.

Worse still, he angered sedan-chair men and hackney coachmen, who deemed it their monopoly to protect people from rain. They saw a threat to their livelihood in the new contraption. But in spite of all their abuse, Hanway continued to carry his "guard from chilly showers."

Only when his example was followed by one of Britain's famous dandies, popularly known as Beau Macdonald, did the umbrella at last catch on. Though he, too, at first was subjected to ignominy. His own sister refused to be seen with him in public.

Improvements further reduced the umbrella's weight and added to the efficiency of its mechanism. Metal replaced the whalebone and a new frame, first constructed in the 1850s, not only gave the umbrella still less weight and more strength, but earned Samuel Fox, its inventor, large profits.

Of course, people continued to use the umbrella as a sunshade as well. To protect the skin from sunburn was then presumed to be essential for health and a pale face was looked upon as dignified and attractive. Soon after World War I people changed their opinion and came to regard sunshine as health-giving and a sun-tanned face beautiful and desirable. As a protection against rain, the umbrella resumed its initial role of a status symbol, "the acknowledged index of social position." To carry it over one's arm, neatly rolled, came to epitomize the English gentleman.

The umbrella has played a part in many spheres. It has formed the object of affection and inspiration, been an instrument in the psychological interpretation of dreams, and even at a moment of crisis has led one of the modern dictators to draw wrong conclusions.

One woman became so attached to her umbrella that she left instructions in her will that it was to be enclosed with her in the coffin. Sigmund Freud's vivid imagination interpreted the appearance of an umbrella in dreams as an indication of their sexual content. It was a symbol of the phallus.

Neville Chamberlain's umbrella at Munich has become almost

proverbial. The story is told that when Hitler, at that crucial hour of history, saw Britain's Prime Minister alight from his plane, fortified with an umbrella, he had sneered loudly. A nation whose leader was so much concerned with protecting himself from rain at a time when the existence of whole countries was in the balance must lack power of resistance, he reasoned—so wrongly, as he had to find out in the deluge that was to follow.

The Hatband

The color and width of the band around a man's hat may vary according to fashion. But the band itself today is considered as something without which a hat would be incomplete. Its purpose is accepted as merely ornamental, to add a little "color" to an otherwise rather dull male attire.

Yet the origin of the band leads back to man's earliest head-dress. It then served an indispensable practical function. Indeed, it could be said that the band itself was man's first hat. Egyptians, for instance, when travelling, secured their hair (then grown long) with a band around the head. People did not just think of keeping their hair tidy. They were much more concerned with their health. They knew that to walk about bareheaded at times was perilous and could impair their well-being. They had to take notice of the vagaries of the weather and protect the head both from the sun and the cold.

A simple piece of cloth was an obvious device. It is still retained, almost in its original form, in the *Kephiyeh*, worn mainly by desert tribes of the Middle East. A band, a cord or, first of all, strands of camel hair, tied around the crown of the head was essential to keep the "hat" on.

Early specimens of the modern type of hat, which supplanted the primitive cloth, were not made to measure. They fitted loosely and a gust of wind or sudden movement could easily dislodge them. Again, the band was utilized. Tied under the chin, it fastened the hat properly and kept it on. When the sun went down and a headcovering was no longer required, there was no need to take it off and carry it. All that was necessary was to loosen the band and let the hat hang down the back. It was a simple and sensible method of wearing and carrying it, whilst keeping one's hands free.

The making of hats improved and use of new materials and methods at last enabled hatters to take note of individual tastes and measurements. Suddenly, the band had outlived its usefulness. Logically, the band, having thus become obsolete in its original function, could have been discarded forthwith. But people soon forgot its initial purpose. Retaining it, they considered it a "must" for those who wished to be properly dressed. The streamers hanging down at the back of the Scottish cap and children's sailor hats are vestiges of the original hatband. They are just its loose ends.

The Mad Hatter

Only in comparatively recent times has insanity been regarded a sickness. For thousands of years the mentally sick were decried as people possessed by the devil or harmfully affected by the rays of the moon, responsible for them being called lunatics.

To describe a person unbalanced in mind as being "as mad as a hatter" added insult to injury and slandered a respectable occupation. Two explanations proffered for this unfortunate phrase reveal the wretched effect of ignorance. Actually, the observation has nothing to do with a hatter, but refers to the atter, the Anglo-Saxon for an adder or a viper. The word mad, itself used in quite a different sense, described something as being harmful or poisonous. Hence, the phrase originally spoke of a person being "as venomous as an adder."

The alternative version asserts that the words really meant what they said, and that the saying was the result of an early occupational hazard of those who, before the Industrial Revolution, made hats for a living. These were then mostly manufactured from the fur of animals such as the beaver and rabbit, with mercury, more commonly known as quicksilver, being used in the processing. Its harmful qualities were not realized at the time and hatters, through frequent handling of the dangerous metal, slowly absorbed it into their system and poisoned their bodies. The first symptoms of sickness appeared as "the shakes," soon followed by mental aberrations.

Of course, at the time no one even guessed the cause of the illness, and it was not to defame hatters but to acknowledge an unfortunate phenomenon that people began to compare anyone unbalanced in mind with hatters, and that is how the saying first entered English phraseology, to be popularized by William Thackeray and, most of all, Lewis Carroll, in their writings.

To Run the Gauntlet

"Gauntlet" is a word of French origin and refers to a glove. It was worn as part of medieval armor. Being made usually of leather, it was covered with plates of light steel or chain mail.

When speaking of "running the gauntlet" to describe passing through a critical ordeal or being attacked from all sides, that kind of gauntlet has nothing to do with the wearing apparel. Its place there is only because of mistaken identities.

In this phrase gauntlet is derived from a combination of two Swedish words: *gata*, for "a passage" (which actually created the English word "gate"), and *lopp*, meaning "to run" (responsible for "a leap").

The passage referred to was part of a cruel system of punishment of offenders. It consisted of a double row of soldiers, who faced each other and through which the culprit, stripped to his waist, had to run. Each of the soldiers was provided with either a knotted cord, the end of a rope or a stick, with which he had to hit the passing delinquent. It goes without saying that the latter did not amble through this double row of soldiers, but ran as quickly as possible in great leaps to avoid as many blows as he could.

The description dates back to the Thirty Years' War when military authorities first introduced this kind of punishment. Later, it was adopted by American courts of law, the first reference to it being in 1676. American Indians also made use of it, subjecting their captives, of whatever race, red or white, to the ordeal. Scottish regiments applied the same treatment to minor offenders, mostly in order to keep good discipline.

Another, but less likely, explanation is that the phrase comes not from the Swedish but from the Flemings. The gaunt in gauntlet was a corruption of the city of Ghent in Flanders, where the punishment had been invented.

Spectacles

Ancient Nineveh knew spectacles of a kind. They were magnifying lenses which were made not of glass, but of crystal. It was not until the thirteenth century A.D., however, that the first real spectacles appeared. It is now assumed that Roger Bacon was one of the first to make them.

The credit for inventing them has been given to an Italian, whose early spectacles were used by short-sighted monks to read manuscripts. At first, they held the lenses in front of their eyes and the two were joined by some kind of hinge. Eventually, this was made stiff enough to keep them, though very precariously, on the nose.

A long period of trial and error followed during which all kinds of methods of fixing the spectacles to the head were tried out. Long strips of metal were used, leading from the bridge of the nose over the center of the head and down to the neck. It was a complicated and cumbersome way and not very successful.

Further experiments employed chains with little weights at their ends. Straps, not very difficult from present-day motorcycle goggles, were another attempt to solve the problem. Some people even attached their spectacles to their hat. This was not pleasant for indoor studies nor for the citizens obliged to greet superiors in the street.

After many years—the precise date is unknown—someone hit on the idea of fastening the glasses to the ears with sidepieces or "legs." By the end of the fourteenth century spectacles were in common use. They then frequently appeared on paintings and, as they were considered a precious possession, were specially mentioned in inventories. Records show that in 1520 Pope Leo X went hunting wearing spectacles.

Bifocals are not as recent an invention as people imagine. They were known by the end of the eighteenth century. Benjamin Franklin had a pair made so that on his trips he could enjoy both the beautiful scenery and his treasured books. Contact lenses were first applied in France in 1888 for medical reasons. Certain diseases of the eye impaired the vision in such a way that it could not be improved by the use of ordinary glasses. An example at hand is conical cornea.

CHAPTER 9

Beauty Culture

Among the many treasures exhibited by the British Museum in London is the mummified body of an Egyptian woman, at least 5,000 years old. Conspicuously it displays an astonishing feature. It shows that her finger and toe nails had been painted dark red.

Women have used make-up as long as it can be remembered. None of our so-called modern cosmetics is new. They were applied in like manner in ancient Egypt, Babylonia and China. Actually, women today are still lagging behind and have either forgotten or not yet taken up other old-established beauty aids. Apart from shaving off unwanted hair, women of antiquity stained the soles of the feet with henna and touched up the nipples of the breasts with a purple dye.

Make-up has been used on all kinds of occasions. Queen Jezebel of Israel painted her face before looking out of the window to confront Jehu. Pepys proudly wrote in his diary of the black patches worn on her face by his wife.

Throughout history men have tried repeatedly, but with little success, to stop women using cosmetics. Apart from moral or religious reasons, they have done so in self-defense. Clement of Alexandria in the second century A.D. thus encouraged the proclamation of a law to prevent women from tricking husbands into marriage by means of cosmetics. Some 200 years later, John Chrysostomos wrote, "If anyone were painting the ideal body to house the soul of an ideal woman, he would not dream of showing a face that had bloody lips like the mouth of a bear, or sooty eyebrows that look as though they came from a dirty kitchen pot."

In 1770 a Bill was introduced into the British Parliament (but subsequently defeated) which demanded:

That all women of whatever age, rank, degree or profession, whether virgins, maids or widows, who shall from and after such an act impose upon, seduce or betray into matrimony any of His Majesty's subjects, by the scents, paints, cosmetic washes, artificial teeth, false hair, Spanish wool, iron stays, hoops, high-heeled shoes, bolstered hips, shall incur the penalty of the law in force against witchcraft and like misdemeanors, and that the marriage, upon conviction, shall stand null and void.

A century later a disappointed husband sued his father-in-law for the depreciation in his wife's looks after her make-up had been removed. He claimed "compensation suitable to her real, and not her assumed countenance." He pointed out that he had never realized, until the morning after the wedding, what a hag he had chosen to be his spouse.

Millions of dollars are being spent annually on cosmetics. Fortunately, their ingredients no longer include such obnoxious elements as dog's urine, once used by Italian nobility as a tincture against thinning of hair.

Next to the beautifying benefits of cosmetics is their psychological effect. Dry skin, dull eyes and pale lips have depressed many a woman and given her feelings of inferiority. To remedy them, and also any suggestion of ageing, make-up proved a wonderful medicine. Its application led to a cheerful mind, a happy disposition and a sense of well-being. In hospitals the use of lipstick has proved itself a tonic.

Cosmetics have had a place even in the fostering of democracy and the removal of class distinction. They gave every girl a fair chance to shine and be equal.

Make-up thus covers an enormous field. Its range extends to economics, psychology and social living. Women have always found it useful to hide blemishes and to improve natural beauty. They applied it for the attraction of the masculine sex and the envy of their own. Yet originally, cosmetics were a necessity.

Perfume

The sense of smell is one of the most precious gifts. Certain odors immediately call to mind certain people and places. Doctors can identify some diseases by their odor. Even the like or dislike of food is linked not merely with its taste, but with its smell. It can cause both nausea and euphoria. Human beings have their individual smell, a fact of which dogs are well aware.

The history of perfume extends over a period of 5,000 years. It was known to ancient races and has penetrated into almost every aspect of living. When, in 1922, the tomb of Tutankhamen was opened in Egypt, it contained several vases of perfume which, though dating from 1350 B.C., had not yet lost its fragrance. Aesthetically scent is beautiful. Psychologically, it gives women a feeling of well-being and superiority. Erotically, it can excite the senses. In the realm of religion, it has served as a deodorant, a gift to the gods and a stimulant to the faithful, in whom it produced a state of ecstasy. Sorcery and witchcraft employed it because of its "compelling power." Medicine has applied perfume as a curative and a prophylactic. No wonder that the ancient Greeks believed that perfume was created by the gods themselves and called it accordingly "the scent of divinity."

Egyptians were convinced that perfume gave perfection to all parts of the body and that, after death, the soul was wafted to heaven by the smoke of incense. The Bible not only tells that "ointment and perfume rejoice the heart," but supplies instructions for the making of aromatics.

Mohammed admitted that the three things he enjoyed most in this world were women, children and perfume. Not inappropriately, therefore, Islam promised its faithful believers a paradise that was permeated with the finest of scents to arouse their desires and passion. A regulation of the Zoroastrian faith commanded that five times every day "sweet savor" had to be burned on an altar.

The humorous definition of perfume as "any smell which is used to drown a worse one" is not as far-fetched as some people might think. That was, in fact, its first purpose. Perfume originated at sacred shrines. It belonged to religious cults and was the concern of priests and not, as in later times, of beauticians.

Early in history people believed that the best way to serve God was to serve him with meals. These consisted of the burned carcasses of slaughtered beasts, which, it was imagined, was a welcome food for the gods and gained their favor. Altars became the very pivot of worship.

But the burning animal sacrifices were far from pleasant, especially because of the stench that it created. To cover this up, perfume was introduced to become an essential ingredient of the sacrificial service. It still survives in some churches in the form of incense. This early use of perfume is recalled in its name which, derived from the Latin, literally means *through the smoke* (in this case of the burned offerings).

Associated with this earliest religious use of perfume was a belief that it was also a potent agent against evil forces, which were allergic to it and realizing its presence would immediately take their leave. Perfume was even considered a means to exorcise the demon of disease. Greek doctors recommended its health-giving properties, specifically in the prevention of respiratory ills.

People experienced the stimulating effects of perfume. They imagined that its fragrance cleansed the body and cleared the head, not least after their brain had been fuddled by too much drink.

The human body contains more than two million sweat glands and the unpleasant smell of their secretion has been a frequent cause of embarrassment. Perfume was an ever-ready aid to remedy this.

Women realized its sexually exciting qualities. Just as flowers by their scent attracted bees, women, too, could draw near a mate with perfume. Indeed, the choice of the right kind of scent became as much part of a woman's attraction as her voice, her smile and her hair. Rudyard Kipling went so far as to say that "scents are surer than sounds or sights to make your heartstrings crack."

Lipstick

No one can deny that the features of the mouth can reveal character. It explains people speaking of sensuous lips, just as the cupid's bow can easily be recognized. Looking at a person's lips, one may find there affirmations of generosity, self-control and intelligence or of bad temper, hardness and selfishness.

One purpose in painting the lips was thus fear—of giving oneself away. Lipsticks were a perfect means to accentuate a woman's good points and to disguise her bad ones.

Fear and sex are two of the strongest instincts. They aim at self-preservation of both the individual and the race. It was those two forces which most of all were held responsible for the painting of the lips.

One of people's most dangerous zones were thought to be their mouths. It was an invitation to mischievous spirits to enter the body and take possession of it. Red has been universally a protective color, used from time immemorial to stop evil forces, which first prompted people to paint their lips red. Even in the ancient Babylonian "Epic of Creation" it is told that, before engaging in deadly battle against the dragon Tiamat, the god Marduk smeared red ochre on his lips.

Paradoxes abound in life. The same streak of color that was used to repel and frighten demons came to serve also as a force to the opposite sex and arouse their passion.

Nature demands the survival of the species. Anything of help in this aim has been judged right. From the most distant past, women have found a colorful mouth a powerful bait and when the modern girl paints her lips, she does so exactly as her ancestors did 4,000 years earlier. She knows that it helps not only to remedy defects and to enhance her beauty but, most of all, to ensnare a partner.

Shaping Eyebrows

Eyes do not only see but are seen as well. They reveal their owner's thoughts and feelings perhaps more clearly than any other part of the body. A mere glance can convey a message of love or hatred, scorn or encouragement. At times some people "look daggers," while others shoot arrows of love, and everyone knows the person who cannot look one "straight in the eye."

Sight is one of the most precious gifts. Its mystery has fascinated the human mind from earliest days. To preserve and protect the eyes, therefore, has always been a natural instinct. This was once reinforced by the ancient belief that the soul of a person rests in their eyes.

That is how paint and razor were first applied as a supernatural device. A certain shape of the eyebrows and a definite color, so people believed, would ward off evil. When, in the course of the evolution of civilization, paint and razor were no longer used magically, they were employed for medical purposes. The make-up of the eyes was considered efficacious against disease and blindness. People assumed that eye-paint was a defense against insects and infection. It was described as good for sight and a means to stop bleeding.

Only third in importance and chronological order were reasons of beauty. Eventually these outweighed all other considerations. Women realized that the eyes could attract and bewitch the male. They dominated the face and, in no small measure, could render it ugly or enticing. Thus, anything that would enhance its beauty was good and right. Tastes differ and continuously change. What is fashionable and refined to one generation, is decried as cheap and unseemly by the next. However, modes of make-up have repeated themselves time and again.

Eyes have been called the signature of character and it was even believed that fate was written in them for those who were able to decipher it. The appearance of the eyes much depends on the shape of the brows. No wonder, therefore, that these were given special attention. High, eminent and unconcealed, they showed part of the mind within. Soon this was thought to be their only function!

Eyebrows that touched each other, for instance, were once viewed with admiration or fear. Goethe described them as an expression of sensuality. Others saw in them an indication of arrogance and pride. In medieval times, a man whose brows touched each other was marked as a werewolf or vampire, or fated to die a bachelor.

Not surprisingly, women refused to accept their natural brows as final. They examined them and manipulated their shape with razor, tweezers and pencil, in pursuit of the character they wished to show. A little adjustment, paint and powder, they found, could work wonders.

To shave off their eyebrows altogether served an important purpose—it prevented recognition. No one could now see a woman's true thoughts. But then, and not least, it also gave her a sphinxlike appearance, producing an expressionless mask. The very enigma of the face so created, served as a magnet to men who, thus baffled, were anxious to penetrate the screen of inscrutability.

Eyes express individuality. Even if only slightly so, they make women look different. Living in an age of mass production and a love of crowds, individuals count little. To be just like one's neighbor is a commonly held ideal, greatly fostered by commercial interests. To shave off one's eyebrows and replace them with the latest general shape, half-moon or straight, thin or tapering, served well in mass-producing the common woman. This, too, is an expression of character: not only of a person but of an age.

Painting Nails

Women have painted their fingernails for thousands of years. In ancient Egypt, all women used to follow the practice. In Europe they did likewise and enamelling their nails belonged to their beauty culture. It had become a custom so prevalent in Cromwell's days that he denounced and banned it. With the Restoration, when women again won their way, the painting of fingernails also was restored. It was only when, centuries later, Queen Victoria was "not amused" by the habit that the nails again lost their color. But not for long.

Originally, women had thought that the conspicuous color of their nails would repel evil spirits. But then they took up the custom to make themselves more attractive and arouse men's passion. The painting of nails helped equally to cover up small imperfections. The protective cover of varnish, so it was claimed, improved the health of the nails and made them less brittle.

Other significant considerations reinforced the practice in countries as far removed as China, Spain and the United States. Chinese mandarins gilded their nails to indicate their high rank. It was part of their insignia of nobility: not worn in the form of pips and stripes as on a uniform, but painted in distinctive colors on a conspicuous part of their body. As it were, by looking at a person's nails, one would know their position and rank.

It is an unfortunate historic fact that certain races have considered themselves superior to others. They were possessed with the wish of preserving the purity of their blood. Thus anything darker than white was frowned upon. Anyone showing the slightest stain —of "impurity"—was socially ostracized.

Nature, however, was often stronger than convention, and miscegenation took place in numerous cases with laws of segregation being unable to prevent the mixing of whites and the races socially and sexually. The inevitable result were children who bore the mark of their parents' mixed blood.

Sometimes, being "lucky," they took on almost completely the features and color of their white parent and, apparently, did not give away the (to them) unfortunate secret of their dark (prenatal) past. And yet, there was one slight but most visible indication: the pigmentation of their nails. To cover it up and replace it with the "right" kind of color became a necessity, experienced equally by Spaniards with Moorish blood in their veins and American citizens whose parents had not properly observed the line of segregation. They needed the camouflage. Indeed, it was as if the wheel had come full circle and just as in the barbaric past, the paint on their nails was not part of beauty culture but a means of defense: to ward off misfortune, though this time of a different and more tangible kind.

Now mostly a matter of the regrettable past, women have extended the painting of nails from their fingers to their toes, mostly because other women do likewise.

Soap

None of the many industries serving the modern way of life has had as complex and contradictory a past as soap-making. Though soap can be traced into far-distant times, it was not used or known for its real qualities for thousands of years.

The Hittites cleaned their hands with plant ashes dissolved in water, and the early Sumerians in Ur boiled oil with alkali. Possibly first discovered in ancient Egypt, soap was brought by Phoenician seafarers to southern France in 600 B.C. From there it found its way into Germany.

The Bible, at least in its Authorized Version, mentions soap. In spite of this often-quoted evidence, the prophet Jeremiah refers to it only as a cleansing agent for clothes. The passage speaks of washing soda and potash. True soap was unknown in ancient Palestine.

When excavations at Pompeii seemed to have unearthed the oldest soap factory in the world, this, too, was soon proved to be incorrect. Chemical analysis showed that the product found there was Fuller's earth, used for washing clothes, but not the body.

Greeks and Romans loved cleanliness. However, they never used soap. After gymnastic exercises they took hot baths and removed the sweat and dirt by beating their bodies with twigs or scraping themselves with an instrument known as a *strigil*.

Soap is now considered a mark of cultured living. Yet it was unknown to ancient civilizations as a means of cleaning the body. It was invented as such by a "barbarian" people, and it took millennia for it to be adopted as an everyday necessity.

Actually, the first mention of real soap occurs in the writings of Pliny the Elder. He refers to it explicitly as an invention of the barbarian Gauls. They made it from goat's tallow and beech ashes, which were the ancient equivalent of modern palm oil and caustic. They used it not for washing, but as a pomade to give extra sheen to the hair.

When, in the following century, soap at last was used in the bath, it was for medical and not hygienic reasons. Indeed, a Greek doctor in A.D. 160 recommended the use of soap for the treatment of elephantiasis, and a physician in A.D. 383 also recommended it for shampooing.

It was only during the late Middle Ages that, very slowly, soap was accepted for washing the body. As such it was in use in the sixteenth century, though, to start with, only among the aristocracy, because only they could afford to do so. After all, it must be remembered that Queen Elizabeth I had but one monthly bath, whilst lesser folk indulged in this kind of ablution even less, if at all.

For centuries, washing oneself with soap continued to be considered not a necessity but a luxury. Thus it is not surprising that the British used soap—and very effectively—to raise revenue. Soap was taxed from 1712 onwards for almost 150 years and it was only through public pressure that Gladstone, in 1853, was forced to abolish this tax on cleanliness. Probably to make up for the substantial loss, he introduced in the same budget death duties. They and soap are still very much in vogue in some countries.

The Barber's Pole

With its red and white stripes, the barber's pole originated in England. It is a relic from the early days when barbers not only cut hair and trimmed beards, but were also surgeons. Until 1745, in fact, they were members of the Barbers' and Surgeons' Company, practicing blood-letting, tooth-pulling and many other kinds of rough-and-ready surgery.

During the process of blood-letting, which was considered most beneficial, it was customary for the patient to grip a pole tightly in his hand, which made the veins swell and the blood flow freely. In the process it was inevitable for the pole to become bloodstained, which did not encourage squeamish patients and led barbers to paint the entire pole bright red, thereby concealing any actual blood.

When not in use, the pole was hung outside the shop and the barber wound around it the bandages used for tying up the arm. Eventually, one brainy member of the fraternity hit on the idea of replacing the real pole and bandages with a dummy one, painted red with white stripes, which became a fixture and the barber's trademark.

The gilt knob at the end of the pole recalls the brass basin used for the dual purpose of catching the blood and the lather.

The Beard

Hair is one of man's distinctive features and has given him many problems and opportunities. Undoubtedly, it has been a significant factor in the growth of civilization. That nature has provided men and women with hair was, first of all, to act as a means of protection. It can soften blows and, as a nonconductor, insulate the part of the body on which it grows against changes of temperature.

Eyelashes screen the eyes from dust and foreign matter, as well as from too much sun. The eyebrows, at least partially, prevent perspiration from running down the face, while the hair in the nose acts as a filter.

To grow a beard was the natural thing to do, but to cut or shave it off was abnormal. No wonder that the beard became an object of man's anxious concern. Men first cherished a beard for religious reasons. Primitive races were convinced that as hair grew out of a man's body, it was saturated with his personality. Hence it had to be carefully guarded from possible foes.

It was firmly believed that a sympathetic link existed between a man and every part of his body, and that this continued even after the physical connection was broken. Thus, the man himself would suffer from any harm done to the clippings of his hair (or the parings of his nails, or his severed foreskin). This accounts for the centuries-old custom of burning cut hair and nails, thereby preventing them from falling into the hands of an enemy who could use them for nefarious purposes. Indeed, the best course was not to cut the hair at all which was soon regarded as actually sacred and the seat of a god's spirit who, if the hair was cut, would lose his abode and seek revenge. This explains why priests especially, and those dedicated to gods, never cut their hair. The sanctity of the hair made people swear by their beard, as they do now by the Bible.

Thus man's earliest beard was faith-conditioned. Other aspects further increased its importance and value. As women could not grow a beard (or, if they did, were considered witches), the beard was regarded as the special sign, privilege and ornament of manhood. It was seen as God's gift to man, to distinguish him from woman.

Ancient Egyptian and Babylonian monuments display men with full, well-groomed beards, which they tended with meticulous care, using tongs, curling-irons and dyes. On festive occasions, they added scented yellow starch and sprinkled it with gold dust to give it a golden sheen.

Shaving was looked upon as perverted, as it was against nature. If the gods had created man to sprout a beard, surely, to cut it off was against their will. To do so would not only antagonize them, but deprive the man of his dignity and male beauty.

That is why the cutting-off of beards was reserved for the defeated enemy, the dangerously sick and the bereaved. In the treatment of the foe, it was a sign of disgrace—he was thus branded. In the case of a leper, it called public attention to his dreaded disease and kept others away from infection. The mourner who shaved his hair originally did so to sacrifice it, as a vital and sacred part of himself, to the dead.

The growth of civilization soon restricted and regulated the beard's length. A long beard, and not a knighthood, was used to distinguish members of the aristocracy. In the second millennium B.C., beards more than crowns were the sign of royalty, and for that reason kings (and queens) wore false beards, made of metal, and held in place by ribbons or chinstraps.

Continuously growing hair was regarded like blood, as an expression of vitality. The beard was an indication of mature manhood.

Eunuchs and young boys were beardless. It was therefore inevitable that primitive man further reasoned that a beard was not only an indication of virility, but its very source. It was actually the seat of male strength. That is why Samson (and others like him in the mythology of many races), once bereft of his hair, lost all his vigor. It was that reason and not later considerations of vanity that made men cherish their beard and lavish the greatest care on it.

Apart from these earliest superstitions and concepts that lent special meaning and value to a man's beard, its fate often depended on particular circumstances of time and place, and its history is marked by the vanities and vicissitudes of human life.

Alexander the Great, on the other hand, ordered his soldiers to shave off their beards because they presented convenient handles by which their enemies could grasp them.

Parting the Hair

There are reasons for the various partings of hair. Women, in particular, realize that the choice of the "correct" place for the parting can influence their hairstyle and, with it, their facial expressions. The place chosen often depends on the shape of the face and the head. A center parting, for instance, is only advisable in the rare case of a woman having perfectly symmetrical features. However, the decision whether to part the hair on one side or the other is not primarily dependent on considerations of beauty and appearance.

People have often wondered why it is that men as well as women part their hair mostly on the left. It is not out of superstition but the result of purely physiological conditions, namely that for the right-handed it is easiest to part the hair on the left. Most of all, the place of parting is the outcome of the growth of hair and depends almost entirely on the position of the whorl (or crown), which divides the hair naturally.

With the crown being on the left side, as it mostly is, parting is on the left as well. In exceptional cases (fiction claims among the intelligentsia) nature has provided two whorls with the fortunate person being able to part the hair either way.

Hair Standing on End

An obsolete defense mechanism, inherited from the animal kingdom, and a gruesome relic of American-Indian warfare account for all that is "hair-raising." It is claimed that Indians referred to scalping as "lifting the hair" and "hair-raising."

At the first scent of fight, cats and dogs bristle. Their raised hair is meant to frighten the foe, to soften their blows, and to resist their bites. A porcupine's use of its quills is perhaps an even better illustration.

Humans, descended from the beasts, have retained their protective instinct, though in their "civilized" way of fighting this now serves no purpose. Nevertheless, on sudden fright, their hair will stand on end. It is this immediate reaction to danger by a built-in defense mechanism which, by contracting the scalp to erect the hair, creates the sensation of goosebumps and "tingling of the scalp."

The microscope enabled people to detect the muscular tissue attached to the hair that caused it to rise. The only function now left to the *arrector pili*, as it is called, is to keep the shaft of hair in its place.

CHAPTER 10

Animals in Language

Animals are among humans' best friends. Once worshipped and considered sacred, they have fulfilled a significant task in daily life for thousands of years.

Even when technological advances have supplanted animals, they are acknowledged as faithful servants who have left their mark in civilization and culture. That is why, for instance, the force of cars is still reckoned in horsepower. No wonder, therefore, that language is rich in references to animals, used as similes and analogies. Many superstitions attach also to the animal kingdom. The origins of these phrases and beliefs are sometimes much more complex than they appear on the surface.

Animals have the habit of creeping into many places. But no creature excelled in this more than the cat. Perhaps not without reason. After all, it is renowned for its curiosity; everyone knows of the nosey cat. It has found its way even into the loom of language and left its traces there in most diverse ways, the discovery of which is almost a game of "cat and mouse." Everyone likes to be thought the cat's whiskers, and lucky are those able to indulge in a catnap. Though one has to be beware of cat-burglars and of being used as a cat's paw.

It is also good to know that often one has been misled. There are cases when what appears as (part of) an animal is only something else in disguise. Catgut comes from horses or sheep, and the "cat-o'-nine tails" is a frightening instrument of flogging, far removed from a purring feline. A dog watch has nothing to do with the canine species. Elephants do not have a good memory, and bees are not as busy as one may think. They spend most of their time doing nothing.

Humans pride themselves on having tamed wild beasts and having taught animals many a lesson. They forget, however, that they themselves could learn from their dumb friends, who excel them in numerous ways.

131

An owl's eyes, for instance, are sensitive to infrared radiation. Bats in flight have been using their own system of radar for thousands of years. Dogs pick up soundwaves of a frequency up to 100,000 vibrations a second, as compared with a human's limit of a mere 30,000.

Animals, indeed, have been sacrificed numberless times to serve humans, for better or worse, on altars, on menus and for the sake of medicine and civilization.

All this should make one humble if not ashamed. "Why was humankind created only on the sixth day and as the very last of all creatures?" an ancient sage asked. He himself gave the answer, which is still valid. He said, "To be able to tell humans whenever they become overbearing or are swollen with pride, 'Even a flea preceded you in creation!'"

The White Elephant

A white elephant nowadays describes something that is a gift which gives more trouble than joy and is a nuisance. Albinos among elephants are rare and it is little wonder that early generations considered them holy. While ordinary elephants were made to work hard, the albinos were worshipped and fed, and lived in idleness. Though to own a white elephant contributed greatly to the sanctity of one's home, it also added considerably to running expenses, so much so that in not a few cases it bankrupted people.

The ancient rulers of Siam are said to have welcomed this tradition attached to albino elephants. When anxious to get rid of a courtier who had lost his favor or had become too influential or powerful, far from actually dismissing him and thereby gaining his open hostility, the king treated him like the best of friends. He presented him with the most sacred and precious gift—a white elephant.

The courtier had to accept it. He would not dare to refuse the precious beast, or dispose of it later. To do so would imply an insult to His Majesty as much as to divinity. The upkeep of the albino elephant proved so costly that in the end it would bleed the nobleman white, which was exactly what the king intended to happen.

Though the albino's exceptional color (or lack of it) was sufficient reason to account for its early deification, an ancient Chinese
legend gave its own explanation. It associated the animal's high
status with a dream incident in the life of Moye, a mythical
mother figure.

The story goes that one day, whilst walking along a river bank,
a rainbow encircled Moye with the result that, twelve years later,
she gave birth to the hero Fo-Hi. During the sacred time of her
pregnancy she dreamt that the child she was carrying in her womb
was not a human but a white elephant. That is why, so legend has
it, white elephants ever since have been venerated and honored,
addressed as "Lord" and attended by a minister of high rank.
"King of the White Elephants" became the most treasured title of
Siamese royalty.

It is interesting to note, however, that so-called "white
elephants" found in the East are not white at all. Their only distinguishing marks are their pink eyes and a small patch of color
on some part of their anatomy, slightly paler than the rest of
their body.

A Red Rag to a Bull

Widespread and general is the belief that a red rag infuriates a
bull. Therefore to enter a paddock with anything red where there
is a bull would be foolish and dangerous.

The idea is so deeply ingrained in common thought and speech,
that anything that makes one get really angry and excites one's
rage is described as being "like a red rag to a bull."

Equally well known and accepted is the explanation that the
phrase stems from the experience of Spanish bullfighters. To
attract their four-legged adversary's attention and rouse him into
an angry charge, it is said, they flourished their red cloak in front
of the bull's face.

It is true that, from the earliest days of this Spanish pastime, the
torero employed a red cloak. Yet that the bull's anger was roused by
its color is completely fallacious. A bull is not affected by any color.
Like most animals, he is color-blind. It is the motion of the cloth, not
its hue, that annoys the bull. A waving white cape would make him
just as angry. Red was chosen only as a spectacular color.

An ancient but now discontinued presentation in the bullring supports this explanation. In early days a man would stand on a low pedestal in the arena and keep absolutely still. When the bull rushed towards him, he even had to hold his breath. For a while, the animal would gaze at and sometimes even sniff the human statue. Because it lacked all motion, the bull would walk away. But let the frozen figure move ever so slightly and the docile bull would change into a ferocious fighter!

Thus the colorful phrase lacks all foundation in fact and proves once again how some of the most cherished expressions are based on fiction.

To Put a Flea in One's Ear

The flea is Anglo-Saxon, at least in the origin of its name. Very descriptively this recalls one of the insect's outstanding gifts: its ability to "jump." Feeding on the blood of humans and beasts, it can leap thirty times its own height. This fact was first established in Greek days by the philosopher Socrates.

Others have discovered a close affinity between the *flea* and *fleeing*, as this lively creature always seems to be able to get away.

Usually, a flea—like its bite—metaphorically points to something trifling, a thing of really no importance. And yet, to actually put a flea in one's ear can be a serious thing. It becomes most annoying and can drive one almost insane.

Commonly the phrase has been explained as the result of watching a dog with a flea in its ear which makes it so restless that sometimes it flees in terror. However, humans have long been flea victims. As far back as A.D. 700, Saxon nobles complained bitterly of its bites, though only a few of the over 500 different species of fleas choose people as their host.

Fleas became especially aggravating at the time of the medieval knights. Clad in chain mail from head to foot, those valiant men soon discovered that almost more worrying than the adversary they had to face outside was the small glutton that had invaded the inside of their suit of armor, which now shielded the flea as much as its wearer.

To start with, the flea enjoyed a good feed, truly having a field day. Jumping about freely without the knight being able to hinder its progress, it bit him where it pleased. No one could stop it from sucking the man's blood. When, sooner or later, the flea felt that it had had enough of the gentleman, trying to leave its dark prison it just could not find a way out.

In its search for an escape route, it eventually got into the knight's ear, where it settled—sometimes for hours—intermittently biting and jumping, causing the helpless knight unending aggravation. That is how, when speaking of putting a flea in someone's ear, unknowingly those former days of chivalry are recalled, when the knights in shining armor experienced alarm and distress through these wingless insects which unwittingly had become their prisoners.

To Go the Whole Hog

Not all hogs are swine. In the late thirteenth century a hog referred also to a young sheep that was as yet unshorn. Wool has always been a precious commodity. When there was plenty of supply elsewhere, those early "hogs" were left alone. Their fleece was so short that to shear it was quite difficult, and not really worth the trouble. Therefore most farmers used to clip their hogs only superficially, haphazardly and without much care. But there were some who felt that a lot of a little makes much and therefore they "went the whole hog," shearing the lamb closely and all over.

It was this practice by economical herdsmen—changing a hog into a sheep—that eventually was applied, in everyday speech, to anything done thoroughly, without compromise or reservation, going all the way, seeing a thing through to the very end.

The Mad March Hare

Hares have played a sad role in folk history. It was considered unlucky, for instance, if a hare crossed one's way, as witches were said, at some time or other, to transform themselves into the shape of that innocent creature.

Medieval "science" described the hare as a creature that suffered from bouts of depression and tried to cure itself by feeding on special plants. People who ate hare, it was thought, would catch the disease and themselves become melancholy.

It is thus not surprising that in the manner of speech "mad as a March hare" became a common phrase.

The selection of March has its specific reason. It coincided with the hare's mating season and people imagined that during this month, for the benefit of its copulating, the animal displayed itself in peculiar ways which made it appear "off balance."

It has been suggested, too, that the so-called madness of hares had no connection with the month of March or the animal's sex life, and that in reality the phrase was the result of an error. Originally, it did not speak of March, but referred to a marsh. Hares living in marshes were unable to hide themselves because of the lack of bushes and trees, with the result that, driven to desperation in the face of foes, they went insane.

To Let the Cat out of the Bag

Were one to hear the phrase "to let the cat out of the bag" for the first time, one would imagine that, obviously, it gave account of a rescuing act. After all, cats love their freedom and would loathe being imprisoned in a sack.

Of course, the words are used in a completely different sense. They show no concern whatsoever for the cat's fate, its likes and frights. Rather strangely, they tell of a secret coming out, quite suddenly, just as a cat, kept prisoner, would jump out of a bag.

For the origin of the phrase one has to look at marketing methods at the country fairs of old England. Sucking-pigs were frequently sold already wrapped in a sack; tricksters bent on taking advantage of a trusting customer would hand over a sack containing, not a piglet, but a cat, with the deception not being discovered until the purchaser opened the bag at home. The wary buyer who insisted on opening the bag at the fair to examine the nonexistent pig let the cat out of the bag and exposed the scam.

Naval circles suggest another origin of the phrase. It referred, they say, not to an animal but the whip known as the cat-o'-nine-tails. This cruel instrument of punishment was kept in a sack and to "let the cat out of the bag" meant to take out the whip for a flogging. The action certainly left the sailors in no doubt as to their captain's intention.

To Have Kittens

For anyone to confess "nearly to have had kittens" is a dramatic way of admitting how anxious and scared he had been. No one would dream of taking the saying literally, since it is just a metaphor. Yet the phrase goes back to times when women really were worried that, instead of giving birth to a child, they would actually bring forth kittens.

It was an age when people believed in witches and the mysterious influence that cats were deemed to have, which extended even to their sex life. If a black cat, for example, turned up at a wedding it was taken as an omen of good luck and of a fruitful union. A superstition, once prevalent among Scottish people, may be directly responsible for the phrase. This assumed that a woman would conceive kittens, if—unknowingly—she ate any food on which cats had ejected their semen.

In medieval times, women who suffered agonizing pain in their pregnancy were assured by witches that its cause was not the growing child, but kittens inside their womb! A magical potion alone could destroy the brood and thereby alleviate their suffering. As late as 1654, a woman tried in a Scottish court for attempting to procure an abortion pleaded in excuse that she had done so because she had "cats in her bellie. . . ."

The association of cats with humans' reproductive power can be traced to ancient Egyptian days, when the cat was considered not only divine but to have an occult influence on the fertility of both the earth and people. A passionate creature, its couplings and conceptions abounded, especially at periods of the full moon, and it was no wonder that it was thus linked with both Osiris and Bast—the lunar deities.

Apart from its sexual propensities, a cat was equally renowned as a good mother. It was not difficult for people, aware of the animal's strong sexual and maternal instincts, to believe that the cat truly dominated humans and ruled their sex life.

Raining Cats and Dogs

A combination of cats and dogs in itself appears most unnatural. It becomes even more puzzling and extraordinary if people say that it is raining cats and dogs. Of course, they mean to say that it is pouring with rain or, colloquially speaking, "bucketing."

Why, in order to picture such a phenomenal cloudburst, did people couple the names of their canine and feline friends, whose mutual dislike is so well known and who, on most other occasions, strictly adhere to a policy of apartheid?

Greek scholars believe that the mystery can be easily solved. In its original meaning the phrase had nothing to do with cats or dogs. Their presence in the downpour of rain was truly "fantastic," in the literal sense of the word. Human fantasy put them there and not nature.

Catadupa is the Greek (and also obsolete French) word for a "waterfall." According to the historian Pliny, it was the actual name of a cascade of water on the Nile, at a point in Ethiopia where the stream rushed down with a mighty roar. To compare heavy rain with such a waterfall was natural—but eventually people who lacked sufficient geographical knowledge and were not conversant with the Greek tongue imagined that they heard in the sound of the Greek (word for) waterfall—*catadupa*—"cats and dogs."

There is more than one school of thought on the origin of the phrase. An alternative interpretation steers clear of the Nile and its rushing waters and links the saying with ancient Norse mythology and early meteorological misconceptions. Weather prophets of old believed that rainstorms were caused by the nefarious influence of both cats and dogs. Indeed, sometimes sailors said that an exceptionally frisky cat had "a gale of wind in its tail." Again, witches who rode upon the storm were believed to assume the form of a cat.

Dogs, on the other hand, in Nordic myth were the associates of Odin, god of storms. Old German pictures thus frequently show the wind in the form of a dog with a blast issuing from its mouth. As the cat symbolized rain, a combination of those two animals therefore seemed to be an appropriate figure of speech to express lashing rain.

Much more realiztic is a third view. This goes back to seventeenth-century England, where numerous cats and dogs ran wild. After a cloudburst many of them were found drowned, their corpses floating in the filthy torrents that rushed down the streets.

People, seeing the dead animals and unaware of their unfortunate fate, imagined that they had actually come down from the sky with the shower and that—believe it or not—it had rained cats and dogs.

A Cat's Nine Lives

The tradition that a cat has nine lives goes back to the far distant past and to the River Nile. It is linked with both mystical thoughts and very realiztic observations.

One of the most tenacious of creatures, the cat takes good care to guard itself. Suspicious in nature and taught to be cautious, it watches its steps and looks before leaping. It takes no risks and approaches unidentified objects and persons gingerly and with great deliberation. Whilst an expert in catching mice and rats, it certainly knows how to look after itself and to avoid being caught. All these and other varied facts, physiological and psychological in nature, have combined to preserve and lengthen the cat's life. Nevertheless, its longevity and tenacity have been explained by assuming that a cat lives not just once but nine times, a claim based on ancient religious belief.

Nine is a mystical number, composed of three threes, a trinity of trinities. Thought to possess supernatural power and to work as a charm, it was a figure that featured prominently in the myths and traditions of many cultures. Egyptian astronomers taught the existence of nine spheres. The Greek lunar year counted not twelve, but nine months, whilst the River Styx was thought to encircle (the Greek) hell ninefold. Odin, the Teutonic god, gave power to Freya, the goddess of love, over nine worlds. Even Christianity followed this numerical tradition; according to the Gospels, Christ died in the ninth hour.

It is not surprising therefore, that to express the cat's mystical power of life, use was made of that very figure as well. Bast, the cat-headed goddess of Egypt, the country where cats were regarded as divine, was said to possess nine lives, an important factor, no doubt, in the legend of cats' longevity.

As it were, to add further protection to cats, lest their full span of nine lives be diminished, humans have been warned (no one knows by whom first) that they should never attempt to take even one of its lives. If they did, from the beyond the cat would haunt them and devise a particularly nasty revenge. It is one of the most useful cat superstitions—to the cat.

No Room to Swing a Cat

The expression "no room to swing a cat" leads back to early naval days with their harsh punishment for recalcitrant sailors.

The "cat" mentioned is the cat-o'-nine-tails, the thonged instrument used in the British army and navy for disciplinary thrashings. Its link with the cat was forged by the fact that the marks left on the flesh of the unfortunate victim looked much like deep scratches inflicted by a cat's claws.

Sailors to be flogged were usually taken up onto the deck, as in the confined space below there was no room to swing "the cat" (o'-nine-tails) for a proper whipping.

To those worshippers of cats who are loath to see their pet associated—even only "conversationally"—with cruelty of any kind, another, yet less likely, explanation offers itself. This makes the cat a kind of sleeping partner—still within naval circles, though only in a corrupt way.

Sailors used to sleep in swinging hammocks which they called "cots." Ashore they usually dossed in cheap lodging houses, so crowded that they would say that there was no room to swing a cot. In time, through frequent usage and indistinct enunciation, the cot changed into a cat, at least in its sound and spelling.

The Cheshire Cat

Cheshire, one of England's counties, was noted for its independence and famous for its cheese. A combination of these two so diverse distinctions was responsible for one of the versions of the origin of the grinning Cheshire cat.

For almost 500 years after the Norman conquest of England, Cheshire preserved its political independence. It prided itself on its own parliament, courts of law and taxes. Judges appointed by the king of England had no authority or jurisdiction over that part of the land, whose ruling count possessed royal privileges.

This remarkable position, so her people imagined, amused even their cats and made them so proud that they grinned from ear to ear. Though the cat's grin was merely imaginary on the part of its owners, they soon found a way to materialize it: if not on the pet's own face, in the form of cheese!

Cheshire had always produced some of the finest cheeses, that staple food of high nutritional value, enjoyed far beyond the county's borders. It gave the Cheshire people the idea to use their product to tell the world of their proud tradition of freedom, recognized and treasured alike by humans and beasts. That is how, according to this narrative, the people of Cheshire came to sell their cheese in the shape of a cat—with the feline invariably grinning.

Another, totally different explanation sees in the smiling cat the remnant of Caterling of Chester, a feared man. The fact that Cheshire, outside its few cities, was sparsely populated and lacked England's power, attracted fugitives from justice. Soon the large Delamere Forest became a haunt for highwaymen and other criminals. The county itself had neither the means nor the men to enforce the law. Things got out of hand until, under the reign of King Richard III, Caterling became the Forest Warden of Cheshire. Determined to stamp out the evil, his zeal knew no bounds and, within three years of taking the office, he was responsible for the apprehension and hanging of at least a hundred offenders.

Proud of this achievement, Caterling attended each of the executions, sadistically grinning from ear to ear. It was his sneer at the hangings that people remembered and which, in no time, became proverbial all over England. When people saw a smirk on someone's face, they could not help but be immediately reminded of it and accused their friend of grinning "like a Cheshire Caterling."

As time went on, the identity of the man was forgotten and all the horrible circumstances that had given rise to the phrase. As, after all, cats were so much more common than Caterlings, eventually Caterling's grin was shortened into the much more pleasant (but nonexistent) grin of a Cheshire cat.

All this would not make Mr. Caterling a very pleasant individual, in spite of his desire to see justice done. Therefore, and if for nothing else, another story is much more acceptable. It claims that

Caterling himself took up the sword against the many brigands roaming his territory. Fearlessly he confronted them and it was his terrifying facial contortions during the ensuing duels that became famous and were misinterpreted as a grin.

There is a third view, given by Eric Partridge in his *Dictionary of Slang and Unconventional English*. This recalls that a cat, very fond of cheese, was called a "cheeser cat." Hence, when speaking of the grin of a Cheshire cat, people tried to say that they were as pleased as a cheeser cat that had just eaten cheese.

CHAPTER 11

The Story of People's Dwellings

Architecture is the reflection of people, the spirit of the age, the preoccupation of their minds, their hopes and frustrations.

When Heinrich Heine, the great German poet, was asked how it was that people no longer were able to build the awe-inspiring cathedrals of medieval times, he replied, "Men in those days had convictions. We moderns have only opinions. And it requires something more than opinions to build a Gothic cathedral."

Buildings, like human beings, can be honest or deceptive. Some are mainly "facade," whilst others, almost to a frightening degree, are completely functional.

Though much of ancient Egypt's culture has been preserved, hardly any of its homes survive. This was not accidental. Egyptians built their dwellings of perishable materials. All that mattered to them was life after death and thus the home of the dead was their chief concern. The Greeks laughed at the Egyptians' strangely constructed tombs, calling them "wheaten cakes," which gave us the word "pyramid"!

South Africans used to build their banks in the style of Greek temples. Many a modern church is shaped like a supermarket. On the other hand, the United Nations Center in New York has been likened by critics to a king-sized tombstone.

It is told of the famous American architect Frank Lloyd Wright, that he used to sleep all night on the ground under a tree to get the feel of a client's property, before even starting his design. The story emphasizes that building a home means more than putting together bricks and mortar or glass and steel. Churchill in 1944 remarked that first "we shape our dwellings and afterwards our dwellings shape us."

Architecture can be most confusing. It stresses the diversity of people; they frequently change their minds, tastes and values. Americans have turned flats into apartments and lifts have become elevators; they have heightened the traditional ground floor into their first floor.

The exploration of the foundations of everyday architectural terms is fascinating. Bungalow is built around a Hindustani word and records the fact that it comes "from Bengal." Residence goes back, through the French, to Latin. It is a place were one "sits back." Disappointingly, the noble-sounding mansion is most humble in origin. All it meant is an abode "one lives in."

The Palace

Geography has contributed numerous words and expressions to the vocabulary, mostly referring to their place of origin. The province of Burgundy in France, for instance, is recalled both by a wine and a color. However, the use of some words is so widespread that their "geographical" root is completely forgotten. This applies especially to the description of the palace.

Now designating the official residence of a sovereign ruler, its dimensions and costly ornamentation make it a most distinguished dwelling place, with the Roman emperor Nero being credited with having built the very first palace. Actually, its name can be traced to one of Rome's seven hills—the Palantine Hill. At one time the main part of the ancient city, it was indeed the cradle of Roman civilization, where, so tradition has it, Romulus traced the first furrow, around which he built the first wall and, with the city spreading, the Palantine Hill becoming its most fashionable district.

When the Roman Empire was established, it was a foregone conclusion that Augustus, its first ruler, having been born on the Palantine Hill, would choose it as the site for his official residence. His example was followed by nearly all his successors who erected a series of splendid and substantial dwellings there.

With the passing of years, the Roman dominion was accepted and feared all over the then known world. Emperor Nero, in his lust for power and unsurpassed vanity, not satisfied to share the Palantine with others, no matter how noble or aristocratic they were, wanting to have it for himself alone, issued orders that all other private homes adjacent to it should be razed. Once that had been done, he gave instructions to his architect to replace them by a building of unprecedented magnificence. The edifice, the sole residence on Palantine Hill, soon was identified with its name, to become known as the palace. That is how, ever since, royal abodes, as well as their cheap imitations, are called by this name.

The Drawing-room

A drawing-room has nothing to do with lines, designs or art. Its designation is a shortened form of the original *withdrawing*-room, going back to the sixteenth century. Attached then to public rooms, it gave persons of high station an opportunity of finding some privacy away from the crowds.

Two hundred years later the room's function changed by it being reserved for women. They withdrew to it after a dinner party, leaving their menfolk to talk freely and enjoy their port.

The new association gave the withdrawing-room its elegant meaning which it retained even when it was again opened up to both sexes and no longer used for purposes of privacy. Time withered away the word's first syllable and shortened the room, if not in its architectural dimensions, at least in the length of its verbal description, creating the drawing-room.

The Attic

The attic comes from Athens. Though now located at the top of houses, its meaning has come down to an all-time low. The attic, if used at all, nowadays serves menial purposes. For centuries, the poorest of people alone chose this part of the house for their living quarters. Situated immediately under the roof and sometimes within its framework, it could be reached, in most cases, only through a narrow opening.

Yet originally an attic spelt neither poverty nor neglect but an elegant style. In architecture it referred to a special Athenian way of decorating a building and giving it symmetry and refinement. This was achieved mostly by the use of a certain type of facade, enriched by columns and placed above another storey of greater height. When eighteenth-century England revived the ancient classical mode of construction, architects ornamented the top floor of a house in exactly that way. They faced it with the Athenian—

"attic"—kind of pilasters. This made people call the top storey by its conspicuous classical style and refer to it briefly as the "attic." Even when styles changed again and the room under the roof had lost all its Athenian splendor and pillars, the name remained.

The Lumber-room

The lumber-room has come a long way. Its name dates back more than 2,000 years to the Teutonic Lombards, so called by Caesar on one of his campaigns. He chose the name because of their long beards (*longobardi*). When in A.D. 568 they invaded Italy, they settled there in the north-central part of the Po Valley, which was eventually called after them.

They specialized in lending money and did so in large amounts, on terms and for security, with their occupation gradually becoming synonymous with their name. In the Middle Ages some of the Lombards emigrated to England, where they continued their original trade. In fact, they became London's first bankers, settling in the street which to this day is called after them.

Until the reign of Queen Elizabeth I the Lombards held a monopoly for pawnbroking, with the many and miscellaneous pledges they received being kept in a separate part of their establishment, soon to be known as the Lombards Room. As with most foreign words, it did not take long for it to become corrupted and Anglicized into Lumber Room. Though nowadays this no longer stores pledges, it is still reserved for all sorts of odds and ends.

The "W.C."

Many taboos have surrounded bodily functions. To leave evidence of the latter was once regarded as dangerous. It was a source of defilement and had to be carefully removed and hidden away. Worst of all, one's enemy could use it for nefarious, magical purposes. Though the origins of sanitation thus stem from primitive superstitious fears, it might well be that a healthy instinct also played a part.

Those early dreads were responsible for later feelings of shame, and the mere mention of excretion became taboo, though the Bible itself does not shun referring to it, even in relationship to a king. Whilst pursuing David, King Saul felt the need to "cover his feet," as the Hebrew Bible discreetly put it. Its later official Latin translation, the Vulgate, bluntly rendered that passage by the words, "to void his belly." Young David duly took advantage of the situation and, to show the king later how easily he could have killed him, "cut off the skirt of Saul's robe privily."

Society, reluctant to call "the smallest room" in the house by its "proper" name, invented numerous euphemisms to refer to it. Medieval monasteries had their "necessaries" and castles their *garderobes* (literally "to keep the robes"), a forerunner of the modern cloakroom.

Toilet is derived from the French for "little cloth," possibly a towel used to wipe the hands. Lavatories suggested the action of "washing," derived from the Latin *lavare*, which is also the root of the latrine. Privy emphasized isolation. So, too, did *retirade*, used in Dutch-speaking countries.

The multiplicity of words when speaking of the toilet is a record of people's continuous endeavor to circumvent in speech the room's real function. To mention it in as many words was viewed to be improper, if not obscene. And yet, all attempts to do so proved futile. No matter which innocuous word was chosen, after some time, it became soiled by its association. Even the English "water closet," whose abbreviation "W.C." was internationally adopted, suffered the fate of devaluation.

Nowadays men ask where they can "wash their hands," ladies where they can "powder their nose" and pupils to be "excused." Travelers diffidently inquire for the "comfort station" or "rest room." No doubt, these latest terms invented in search of a "bathroom" that does not soil one's speech will also lose their respectability, become unmentionable and thus, in their turn, be in need of replacement.

The toilet dates back to ancient civilizations, which could pride themselves on most modern standards of sanitation. Excavations in Mesopotamia, Crete, Egypt and India have brought to light examples of elaborately constructed and carefully designed water closets and sewerage systems.

Brick-built seat-closets of 2000 B.C. were discovered in the Indus Valley. They were situated on the ground and first floors of private homes. Sloping channels joined them either with an outside receptacle or a sewer. In the fourteenth century B.C., Cretans in Knossos, their island's capital, had closets built over a conduit of running water. The palace of their famous King Minos, which was unearthed by Sir Arthur Evans, contained most up-to-date toilets. The pans, constructed to hold water, were flushed either by rainwater or, if that was not available, by water drawn from a cistern. Residents of Pompeii in Italy, which was destroyed by a volcano's eruption of Mount Vesuvius in A.D. 79, used water-supplied closets hidden in a niche next to the kitchen.

Yet those curiously modern conveniences of ancient days vanished from the daily life of medieval society, which reverted in that part of its habits to almost primitive days. There was no drainage system. Privies were commonly placed over large pits. Worse still, people frequently threw all their refuse, including human excrement, out of the window into the open street, where a gutter served as a sewer.

This is one of the explanations of the British custom for a man always to let the lady walk "inside" along the footpath—away from the road. The upper storeys of houses used to jut out, which protected anyone walking underneath from the contents of slops emptied from windows.

In 1596, during the Elizabethan era, Sir John Harington, a poet and the queen's godson, invented the first modern water closet. He called it "a privy in perfection," of which he installed one in his home near Bath. Its design included a high water tower on top of the house, a hand-operated tap that controlled the flow of water into the pan, and a valve that could be opened and closed to release sewage into a cesspool nearby.

Though the queen had the closet copied in her palace at Richmond, the general public, regarding it as a joke, cold-shouldered it. They continued their usual filthy habits.

Nothing further of a permanent nature then happened to sanitation for almost 200 years till, in 1775, Alexander Cumming, a mathematician and watchmaker, took out the first patent for "a water closet upon a New Construction." Certainly this was an improvement on Harington's design, differing in one significant aspect which, though small in itself, was revolutionary and most beneficial. It has been applied ever since. The soil pipe immediately below the pan was bent, so as "constantly to retain a quantity of water to cut off all communication of smell from below." At long last, the nauseating feature of the toilet had been eliminated. All that followed were merely refinements and comparatively minor advances.

Windows

People's housing problems have always existed. Yet they changed continuously according to the prevalent level of civilization and their peculiar way of life, as well as climatic and geographical circumstances. From earliest times, great ingenuity was shown in devising their dwellings.

A simple windbreak of trees and branches was the most primitive house. And, as is obvious by its very name, the window, too, is linked with the wind. When glass was unknown, windows were mere holes in a wall, covered by shutters or some sort of curtain, with the holes serving a twofold purpose. Like an *eye*, they enabled people inside the house to look out. They also helped to ventilate the interior. Thus window, a combination of Anglo-Saxon words, means "wind's eye."

Gothic Style

The term Gothic suggests an architectural style of great splendor and beauty. But it is a complete misnomer. The Goths themselves never employed it. A Teutonic tribe of the third to fifth century, they have long since vanished. With the Vandals, they destroyed Roman civilization and large parts of southern Europe, for which reason they were looked upon as barbarians, insensitive to beauty and culture. The story of their misdeeds lived on in people's memory, to whom their name became synonymous with all things that were uncouth, primitive and lacking in refinement.

When the generation of the Renaissance revived the classical style, it sneered at the "modern" manner of building as being crude and ugly—in short "Gothic." Thus the name came first into being to throw scorn on an architecture that was misunderstood and abhorred.

Yet, in this case, too, a description intended to be abusive, because of the inherent value of Gothic art, assumed the contrary meaning, and Gothic changed into a term descriptive of priceless, awe-inspiring beauty.

Paradoxically the name, derived from a barbaric, pagan people, was thus identified with the loftiest style of Christian architecture—"the most beautiful of all, and by far the most in harmony with the mysteries of religion." A Gothic cathedral therefore was no longer a contradiction in terms.

Apart from constructional and ornamental considerations, it was religious fervor which, in the twelfth century, actually called Gothic architecture into being. Its soaring style, typified by the pointed arch, expressed in stone people's yearning for the divine. Dissatisfied with the old way of building which seemed so heavy and gloomy, the new shapes reflected the people's lofty ideals with sacred cathedrals pointing heavenwards.

Jerry-built

Anything that is jerry-built does not last. But the word itself, describing impermanent and faulty construction, has been built very well. It has lasted for at least a century. Its foundations have proved exceedingly strong, though the material used is still unidentified, and various theories exist as to the origin of the jerry-builder.

Some authorities suggest that it perpetuates the name of a builder renowned for the poor quality of his work. Nothing he ever built stood the test of time and, consequently, his customers were dissatisfied. That is how Mr. Jerry's name became proverbial, a byword of faulty construction. On any occasion that people wished to stress the frailty of things or ideas, they compared them with Jerry's work, saying that they were jerry-built!

Others have assumed that the word originated not on firm land but on the high seas and as long ago as the seventeenth century. Sailing vessels then had to meet many a trial, worst among them high winds and storms. Masts often snapped, and crews had to rig up a temporary pole to enable the ship to reach the nearest port.

The makeshift mast, used for the emergency and not expected to outlast the trip to the sheltering harbor, was referred to as *jury-built*. It may be that the fact that a jury served on a panel only for a restricted period of time was responsible for the choice of word.

Soon common usage and the slurring of speech changed the jury into jerry. Land-dwellers eventually adopted the word from the sailors, and the jury-built mast became the father of anything jerry-built.

According to yet another theory, "jerry" is the Anglicized form of *jour*, the French word for "day." It claimed that cheaply built houses were so flimsily constructed that they were said to last merely for a (French) day.

Some people like to find in the Bible the answer for everything. Jerry-builders definitely have some claim, and on two counts. It has been suggested, first of all, that jerry is an abbreviation of Jeremiah, that prophet of doom. He foretold so much destruction, of whole people and nations, that his name was most apt to describe all things destined to speedy decay, ruin and impermanence.

Others, however, found in Jericho's walls the origin of the expression. Unstable, they fell at the mere shouting of people and collapsed at the blast of trumpets. Jerry-built thus may stand for Jericho-built. A house constructed in a hurry and with cheap material will be like Jericho's walls, unable to withstand even the sound of people shouting.

CHAPTER 12

Magic

The mysterious has always been fascinating. Anything that is strange, weird and unknown attracts and challenges: doors for which there are no keys and veils through which one cannot see. Myths are the early dreams of people and nations. They express their philosophy of life. Ancient legends, however fantastic, have some background of realizm. They grew out of many strands of experience and belief.

Here are the stories of mysterious and legendary traditions that have assumed worldwide significance: the magic carpet, the witch's broom, the message of the three wise monkeys. Even a New Year's practice, an everyday custom and some simple decoration in people's homes are shown to be rooted in magic—to woo, coerce or avert evil forces and bring good luck.

The "First Footer"

In some regions of the world, particularly in Scotland, people are still concerned as to who enters their house first on New Year's Day. They anxiously hope, or at times even subtly arrange, that it will be a tall, dark-haired man, carrying a gift. To make sure that no one else would precede him—such as a blond person, a woman or, at its worst, a man who is short and cross-eyed—some homes bar their doors till the right "first footer" comes along.

Indeed, everything happening on New Year is believed magically to set the pattern for the ensuing twelve months. The superstition about the luck-bringing "first footer" originated in man's early belief in the magical power of "beginnings." It was therefore thought that whoever entered the home first determined its fate for the rest of the year. Magically, his good looks would make it a pleasant one and his gift—of some essential product, such as a loaf of bread or, in earlier days, a shovel of coal—would ensure that there would be no lack of food or warmth. Certainly, coming events cast their shadows before.

The Door Knocker

Originally, door knockers had a much more significant function than merely to make one's presence known. People believed that evil spirits used to hover around the entrance to their house, anxious to "possess" their home. The loud knock was intended to frighten them off and thus prevent them from getting into the house with the visitor. Identical considerations and fears explain why, frequently, door knockers represent some figure, object or animal, such as a lion's head. Just as in the case of gargoyles, those grotesque carved creatures seen projecting from roof gutters, these fanciful knockers were meant to scare off demons.

Elephant Ornaments

Figures of elephants kept in homes were placed there not merely for decoration but for protection! Powerful creatures in nature, they were thought, even in replica, to serve as magic guardians against evil forces entering or the evil eye crossing the threshold. To be effective, the elephant ornaments had always to face the door, with their trunks pointing upwards to secure the good luck.

"Break a Leg"

To wish an actor prior to his going on stage to "break a leg" is a well-known practice. Germans enlarge on the malediction, wishing him to break his neck as well! Rather a strange wish, actually it is meant magically to bring him luck and make sure that his perform-ance will be a success.

Jealous forces, always present, are only too anxious to spoil any venture. A good luck wish would alert and provoke them to do their nefarious work, whilst a curse will make them turn their attention elsewhere. The underlying principle is the belief that if you wish evil, then good will come.

The Magic Carpet

The legend of the magic flying carpet belongs to the Orient and is found there in numerous miraculous tales. In their simplest form, these tell of a carpet that to all appearances was quite ordinary. However, once a person was sitting on it, their wish to be transported to any other place, no matter how distant, was fulfilled.

The story became so famous and widespread because it was based on Islamic sacred legend and the Koran, the holy scripture of Islam, according to which the carpet had belonged to King Solomon.

It was not the carpet itself, however, that was responsible for the unusual kind of transportation, which was due solely to Solomon's power over the forces of nature. The king commanded the wind to carry the carpet wherever he wished it to go.

Muslim tradition tells that this carpet, woven of green threads, was so huge that it could carry all the king's forces and, like modern aircraft, was permitted to take off only when its load was rightly balanced. Solomon himself supervised the proper placing of cargo and men, grouping them around his throne, which always travelled in the center of the carpet. Men and women had to take their places on the king's right and the spirits on the left. To protect the company from the burning rays of the sun, he had birds fly in formation over the carpet, forming a canopy with their wings.

The Witch's Broom

The broomstick is a simple object, having been used for hundreds of years in every home to sweep it clean. But the moment it was attached to a witch, this household item changed into a complex and puzzling article. Did witches really ride it? And why, of all things, did they choose it and not some other, more suitable carrier?

How did the entire idea of a witch's broomstick first arise? The answer to these questions certainly belongs to the lore of witchcraft, but also relates to as diverse topics as camouflage, defamation, walking aids and ubiquitous sex. Anything a woman (or, for that matter, a man) did, when assumed to be a witch, immediately was subject to suspicion and strange interpretation.

Broomsticks, in times gone by, served not only to sweep the house and yard but, when going out, people (and especially older women) would take their broom with them to help them cross streams or vault over hedges, ditches and other obstacles. Naturally, with the aid of the stick, their progress was much faster. Therefore, in a manner of speaking, they seemed almost to fly on the stick. It was only a short step to seeing the hag not grasping the stick in her hands but actually straddling and riding on it.

Sticks have always played an important part in magic. Magicians would be incomplete without their wands. Like the "pointing finger" out of which the wand evolved, it was thought to be endowed with supernatural power which could either work wonders or play havoc. The stick was very much like the mysterious snake (yet another prototype of the wand) that, instead of remaining coiled up, could suddenly become as stiff as a poker and, striking out, inflict a fatal bite.

Witches certainly would need the stick for their type of work, but they lived dangerously and any object in their home that could give them away was carefully hidden. To discover an actual wand would have led to their inevitable arrest, prosecution, torture and death.

A broomstick was the ideal substitute and an obvious and clever choice. It belonged to everyone's household and was a wonderful camouflage which would never arouse suspicion. Most of all, it was always ready for instant use. Without a moment's notice, a witch could get hold of it, not to sweep the floor but to sweep through the air. Everyone realized that the broomstick itself had no inherent propelling power. This was supplied by the ointment that, prior to the take-off, the witch rubbed not only on herself but onto the stick as well. And it was this secret mixture that served as the fuel.

Everything told and believed about witches riding a stick was reinforced by the recollection of ancient myths. These told of demigods or other supernatural beings that used to travel miraculously through the air on the back of beasts. Thus carried aloft, they pursued their divine or diabolical mission.

Procreation has its prominent place in the world of the occult and witches were alleged to indulge in orgies in which intercourse with the Evil One was the culmination in the celebration of their Sabbats and Black Masses.

Is it any wonder, then, that the broomstick, so tightly gripped between the witch's legs, in reality was the phallus of the devil which she enjoyed riding? The flight itself had its hazards. Both witch and broom could easily be brought down by the ringing of church bells. It was for this reason that witches worked out special routes to avoid passing over churches.

Nevertheless, they were always alert during flight to take immediate evasive action should they inadvertently pass over an uncharted church. They knew that otherwise they would crash. During times when people were obsessed with witch hysteria and afraid of "witchy" air attack, they rang the church bells all night long. It was a noise that lulled them to sleep, sure that this earliest antimissile cover would serve to protect their bodies and souls.

The Three Wise Monkeys

It is a fallacy that the three wise monkeys, who hear no evil, see no evil and speak no evil, are indigenously Japanese. It is true that they have had their domicile there for many centuries. Originally they came from China and were introduced into Japan by a Buddhist monk of the Tendai sect, probably in the eighth century A.D.

At first the monkeys were always associated with the blue-faced deity Vadjra, a fearsome god with three eyes and numerous hands. Their characteristic gestures of covering their ears, eyes and mouths with their paws were a dramatic pictorial way of conveying the command of the god. This shows an early realization of the psychological fact that a striking picture is more impressive and lasting than a spoken message.

Nevertheless, the story has been told in various traditions in prose and poetry. It dates back to at least the seventh century and is part of the teaching of the Vadjra cult that if one does not hear, see or talk evil, one shall be spared all evil. In folk etymology and by a play on words the very names of the monkeys—Mizaru, Kikazaru and Iwazaru—express their three gestures and thus anyone, by merely referring to them, immediately proclaims their message.

In modern times a fourth monkey was added. He covers his genitals with both hands. The gesture was meant to convey the message not to "do evil."

CHAPTER 13

Medicine

There is romance in medical terms. A doctor means "someone who instructs"; a nurse "nourishes" and a hospital is a "guest house." A patient is called so because he "suffers."

Endless in its application and interest is the art of healing. According to biblical writings, the first operation ever performed was the excision of Adam's rib by God. Even then surgery was done under anaesthetic. God first of all "caused a deep sleep to fall upon the man."

The Sumerians called their doctors "those who know water"— an early recognition of the diagnostic value of urine. The ancient Romans already realized the power of the mind over the body. "It is part of the cure to wish to be cured," wrote Seneca almost 2,000 years ago.

Even as objective a craft as that of healing has not remained unstained by national prejudice. A telling example concerns syphilis and the way it has been described by different people. Early English writers used to call it "French pox." The French, in turn, spoke of it as "the Italian disease," whilst Japanese doctors linked it with the Portuguese.

Napoleon liked neither doctors nor medicines. He preferred by far fresh air, water and cleanliness. And yet, a physician is one's best friend. The Chinese were wise when they used to pay their doctors for keeping them well but stopped the fee at once when they became sick.

All this is indicative of medicine's long standing. There is further and perhaps more interesting evidence in the terms and symbols that have been connected with medicine from earliest times.

The Emblem of the Staff and Serpent

Endowed with a magic quality, rods were thought to be able to cure disease. Often they were linked in this special mission with

157

the snake which, when stiff, was so much like a rod. A representation of such a "healing rod," with serpents coiling around it, was discovered going back to the third millennium B.C.

The British and United States Army Medical Corps have retained this very rod as their emblem, known as a caduceus. In ancient myth the latter served as a herald's staff. The messenger carrying it, however, was not an ordinary one but the god Hermes, who used the staff to guide disembodied spirits to the other world and to revive the dead.

Originally, the wand was an olive branch, symbolic of immortality. Its power then was reinforced by the twin serpents. The regular shedding of their skin was seen as representing and magically ensuring rebirth and constant renewal. It explains why, thousands of years later, doctors continue to treasure the rod, and the Masonic Craft uses it in its initiation rites to bring home to the candidate the message of everlasting life.

Surgeons Addressed as "Mr."

Today, all surgeons are doctors. But as at first they had been just barbers, they maintain their original form of address and go on being called "Mister." A present-day courtesy thus leads back to humble beginnings and shows how "titles do not reflect honor on people, but rather people on their titles."

The Caesarean

The delivery of a child by cutting through the wall of the abdomen is generally known as a Caesarean section. First-century Roman author Pliny was one of the earliest writers to refer to it by that name, listing "those (children) who have been cut out of the womb."

One of the oldest operations known, it is mentioned in the mythology of the ancient Romans, Indians and Persians.

The first legendary "Caesarean" section was Apollo's removal of the babe Asklepios (the Greek rendering of Aesculapius) from the womb of the dead Korinis. Bacchus, the Romans' god of wine and fertility, also is said to have been brought into the world in this manner.

Oldest Roman law required that all women dying in an advanced stage of pregnancy should be cut open to save the child— Numa Pompilius, the ruler of Rome, had thus decreed in the eighth century B.C. It was one of the few operations which was whole-heartedly supported by the early Church.

Originally, and for almost 2,000 years, all Caesarean sections were performed on the mother's dead body. That is why the usual explanation—first advanced by Pliny—that the term Caesarean came into existence because Julius Caesar himself was "from his mother's womb untimely ripp'd," is unhistoric and incorrect. Caesar's own letters to his mother Aurelia clearly indicate that she must have survived his birth by many years.

Much more likely is the suggestion that the term was first coined simply because, in the Latin way of speaking, it was an exact description of what was being done. The Latin word for "to cut out" is *caedere*. And because the earliest member of Caesar's family, Scipio Africanus, was born by excising him from his dead mother's body, he was given the name *Caesar*, "the cut-out one."

The first printed illustration of a Caesarean operation appeared not in a medical but in a biographical work, Suetonius's *Lives of the First 12 Caesars*. Written in the second century A.D., its first printed edition appeared in 1506 and included a drawing of the actual surgical delivery, which was used as the frontispiece of the book's second printing.

Dramatic is the first account of a Caesarean operation which the mother survived. It was performed about A.D. 1500, not by a doctor or a midwife but by a husband, to save his wife's life. He was Jacob Nufer of Sigershaufen, who, in great distress, watched his wife's labor going from bad to worse, without her being able to deliver the child. He knew nothing about obstetrics, but was an accomplished sow-gelder. On the spur of the moment he took a razor and with it cut out the child. In later years, his wife was to give birth to six more children.

"Not to be Sneezed at"

Some of the sayings popular today started long ago and in totally different circumstances. A case in point is the phrase "not to be sneezed at." An age that has become very germ-conscious might immediately jump to the conclusion that the words originated as a commendable precaution to avoid catching other people's colds, as "coughs and sneezes spread diseases." But far from it.

People in older times imagined that a sneeze cleared the mind. It certainly gave them a feeling of exhilaration. Suddenly, seventeenth-century Europe caught a craze for sneezing. It was considered the right thing to do in good society. Indeed, the more one sneezed, the more one proved to be a member of the privileged class! No wonder that people made use of every possible way to qualify.

It was soon realized that snuff caused sneezing. Therefore everyone who was someone carried with them a little box, containing a mixture of sneeze-producing herbs or tobacco. By drawing an ample pinch of it into the nostrils, a hearty sneeze resulted in no time.

Of course, only the rich and idle had time to sneeze or could afford snuff. Hence the self-induced sneeze became synonymous with aristocratic living. If you were able to sneeze "on call," you showed audibly your status in society.

One matter had still to be decided. Just to sneeze haphazardly was not good enough. There had to be a special occasion. Soon sneezing became part of conversation. You indulged in it whenever you wanted to show your disapproval of anything said or, even more so, your lack of interest in the matter discussed. A sneeze was an unmistakable way of saying politely "you bore me."

Consequently and logically, anything "not to be sneezed at" was something really worthwhile.

Quarantine

Quarantine as a medical term refers to the isolation for a prescribed period of time of people or animals arriving by sea or air from abroad. The object is to prevent their carrying a contagious disease into the country. Originally, however, quarantine was just a figure, meaning "40." It could describe any period of that duration, whether measured in hours, days, months or years. There are many examples.

In ancient legal tradition, for instance, a quarantine meant the forty days during which a widow had the right to stay in the house of her deceased husband. The privilege of sanctuary equally extended to one quarantine—forty days.

The choice of the figure 40 was not arbitrary or accidental. Once, it was believed that there was magic in figures and the number 40 especially was thought to possess supernatural power. That is why Moses spent forty days and nights on Mount Sinai to receive God's revelation, and the Israelites wandered through the desert for forty years. Both Elijah on his journey to Horeb, and Jesus during his temptation in the wilderness, fasted for forty days. The period of Lent extends over exactly forty days. This caused Italians to call it, simply and appropriately, by that figure—the *quarantena.*

A unit of forty, so it was imagined in early days, could shield people from all kinds of evil. For that reason, widows in primitive tribes had to mourn their husbands for forty days. They did so not in sorrow but out of fear—to ward off any evil from the disembodied spirit of the deceased, effective for that period of time.

Plague was once considered to be brought on by demons. To fight them one needed magic—supplied by forty days! Thus, sailors were first kept in quarantine not out of medical wisdom but in magical superstition. Only forty days exactly could achieve a cure or provide protection. To increase or to reduce that figure instantly broke the spell and subjected the men to the influence of evil forces.

In 1348, at the time of the Black Death, Venetians introduced the quarantine as a magical shield against the disease. England adopted the institution from them. Present-day society still retains the word and the precaution. But it has forgotten how it first started—in the field of magic and through the mystical figure of "40."

CHAPTER 14

Sources of Justice

People have always had a passion for justice. From the beginning of civilization they have felt the urge to see right prevail and wrong punished. At first, the execution of justice was part of religious faith, even in its most primitive forms. It is not accidental that the Five Books of Moses are known as "The Law." The priests were the earliest guardians of justice.

It is a well-known dictum that ignorance of the law is no excuse and it has been generally applied in every country. There should be no excuse either for being ignorant of procedure. To delve into the past and see how it all started provides a wonderful insight both into the workings of the mind and the growth of civilization.

Research shows, for example, that the black cap worn by a judge when passing sentence of death is not a cap. It is a three-cornered piece of black silk, used as a sign of mourning.

Butchers were excluded from serving on juries in medieval times. Obviously, so it was thought, a person whose occupation was the killing of animals was so used to taking life that to them even the death of a human being would mean little.

An eighteenth-century candidate for an important office in the City of London listed eight points as essential for winning a case. They were: a good cause, a good purse, an honest and skilful attorney, good evidence, able counsel, an upright judge, an intelligent jury and, last but not least, good luck.

"Justice is Blind"

One of the most highly treasured possessions of Britain's democracy is the independence of her judges. They are guarded jealously against even the slightest suspicion that their verdicts might be influenced by any personal consideration, prejudice or sympathy. Perhaps one of the best-known statues in the world is the figure of

Justice over London's central Criminal Court—the Old Bailey.

Traditionally she is blindfolded, to prevent her from seeing the scales she is holding in her hand, with the implication that there should be no favoritism and that a judge should be completely impartial, neither intimidated by the mighty and rich nor influenced by pity for the weak and poor. Nothing but the evidence and its right interpretation must guide him in the trial of an action. That Justice should be blind is an ancient principle. It goes back to the old Egyptians, who applied it literally by their Courts of Law meeting in a darkened chamber to make it impossible for a judge to see and recognize the accuser, defendant or witnesses.

The Ordeal

Speaking of an ordeal, one refers to anything that severely tests character or endurance. Use of the term dates back thousands of years to the time when an ordeal was not just a character test, but an actual trial of suspects. The outcome of the trial determined the charged persons' innocence or guilt and thus their life or death. Of Anglo-Saxon origin, the word "ordeal" means "judgment" and that is exactly what an ordeal was assumed to be—God's judgment.

In matters of right and wrong it is of vital necessity to know whether someone is innocent or guilty. That becomes all the more difficult if sufficient evidence is lacking to clear or condemn the accused. Primitive people left the decision to the gods in a trial by ordeal. The question to where truth lay was addressed not to a human judge but to supernatural powers. It was categorically asked, "Is this person guilty or not?" A third possibility was disregarded—that the gods might not reply.

Trials by ordeal were held all over the world. They were known among early Aryan races and examples can be found in the Hebrew Bible. Surprisingly, this kind of judicial inquiry, in which supernatural aid was invoked and relied on in place of evidence, did not disappear with antiquity.

Still in the Middle Ages and all over Europe, both Church and state sanctioned and applied ordeals, with ecclesiastical authorities devising special liturgical formulae to accompany the procedure and law courts approving a variety of such trials. All shared the conviction that God would save the righteous and punish the evildoer. If the accused succumbed to the ordeal, it proved their guilt. If, on the other hand, they passed through it unscathed, God had declared them innocent. Which type of ordeal was chosen depended on the standing of the accused.

There was the "trial by battle," in which the suspects were forced to fight the person who had charged them, believing that victory would go to the party who was in the right. The ordeal was not an appeal to force but to God, who would let the righteous win. It is not difficult to discern how modern warfare among nations goes back to this identical primitive misconception, convinced that not the force of arms but the justice of the cause determined the final outcome.

In the "trial by hot water" the accused had to plunge their hand and arm—up to the elbow—into boiling water. The hand and arm were then bandaged. If, after three days, they showed any injury, it was taken as divine indication of their guilt.

The "trial by fire" was reserved for persons of high rank who could appoint a deputy on their behalf!

The suspects (or those taking their place) were forced to hold in their hand a red-hot iron or, blindfolded and with bare feet, to walk among nine red-hot ploughshares, placed haphazardly on the ground. Passing through the ordeal unharmed was regarded as proof of their innocence.

The "trial by the morsel" had the accused person swallow—in one piece—either bread or cheese weighing one ounce. Being able to do so without ill effect showed their freedom from guilt. But, should the "morsel" get stuck in their throat, that proved their culpability.

In the "trial by water," the suspects, with their hands and feet bound, were thrown into a river. If they sank, it was an intimation by God that they were blameless, but if they floated, the opposite was the case. At first sight and to modern reasoning, such a decision seems paradoxical, and one should have expected it to have been the other way round. The apparent contradiction resolves itself, if it is realized that water was considered the symbol of purity. It rejected the guilty—who therefore floated—but it did not object to receiving the innocent, who hence drowned!

It is one of the peculiar traits of human nature that a custom or institution, having been prevalent for some time, is taken for granted and never questioned. Even when, eventually, it has lost its usefulness or, worse still, has become harmful, people continue to observe it, accepting it as something right and proper. This applies particularly to those features in society which are closely associated with religion and said to be done in the name of God. That is why the cruel and totally misleading "trial by ordeal" kept a hold on the people for so long, who had neither the courage nor the wisdom to rebel against it.

At last, in the second half of the twelfth century, some enlightened people realized the total injustice of a system that, in the determination of a person's innocence or guilt, claimed to listen to the voice of God but, in reality, relied on pure chance. Still, nothing was changed until the Church itself took matters in hand and, in 1212, Pope Innocent III forbade the use of the ordeal, when the Bishop of Strasbourg applied it against heretics.

The Lateran Council of 1215 then decreed that henceforth no priest anywhere would be permitted to participate in a trial of that kind. As the presence of an ecclesiastic on such occasions was indispensable, trials by ordeal could no longer be held. It was one of the significant cases where religion proved itself not as a reactionary force but as a goad to progress. The problem now facing the authorities was who and what should assume the function of the defunct ordeal in determining right and wrong. All agreed that a more rational form was needed. Wisely, the choice fell on the jury.

The Jury

Juries had their beginnings in ancient Greek days and among Teutonic tribes. Many theories have been advanced as to their origin. Equally, there has been much controversy as to whence and how the jury system found its way to England.

Trial by jury is now a proud part of the British judicial system. It is democracy at its best (at least in the opinion of many), as the people themselves are given an opportunity to determine the facts of a trial, though, as is proper, questions of law and punishment are left to the judge.

Formerly, however, a jury served a different purpose. It was used not to foster democracy but to ensure the rights of the king and to enforce his rule. It is generally assumed that the jury system reached England by way of the Norman-French kings. Anxious to establish their power, they used to summon a body of neighbors—the original jury. These were compelled to "take an oath," which is the literal meaning of "jury," stemming from the French, that they would tell the truth and never mislead their royal master.

Through their appointment, the king was able to obtain all essential information for the administration of the district in which they lived.

When William I came to England he, too, was concerned, first of all, to establish the supremacy of the Crown and therefore made equal use of a system of jurors. Summoned by the king's representative, the royal judge, they had to supply him with the correct facts concerning their county. They were obliged to do so by oath. Later, a jury—to be known as a "Grand Jury"—took on another significant role, although still completely divorced from its modern tasks. In 1166 a statute issued by Henry II ordained that twelve "lawful" men out of 100 should be sworn to accuse criminals, so that they might be presented for the ordeal. In 1215, as a direct result of the elimination of the ordeal, the jury itself was called upon to try the accused. It was not until the seventeenth century that the present-day principle, that jurors are merely judges of fact, was firmly established. They no longer took part in the verdict nor could they act as witnesses.

Twelve Jurymen

Originally, juries consisted of a considerable number of men. Eventually this proved too cumbersome for practical purposes. What was needed was a convenient number of jurors, not too big to become unmanageable but still large enough to present a good cross-section of the public. Why twelve men came to be chosen has been explained in various ways. Sources cited were the twelve tribes of israel, the twelve officers appointed by King Solomon (as recorded in 1 Kings 4) and the twelve Apostles.

However, the last claim would be rather unfortunate, as it would imply that there was a Judas on every jury. Subconscious memories of the significance of the figure twelve may have contributed to its selection. Anglo-Saxons appear always to have had an abhorrence of the decimal system and therefore shunned the number ten. Eleven or thirteen, being indivisible, somehow did not seem right either. But the dozen was favorably received. Just as the shilling had twelve pennies, "twelve good men and true" were considered to make up the right value.

The Derrick

A whole gallery of men and women of all ages is hidden away in everyday talk and the dictionaries of all nations. Usage has so camouflaged many words that no one would expect to find behind them someone who, in some way, has enriched the language. This process was without design or intention. The mass of the people, impressed or revolted by a person's behavior, ingenuity or mode of living, seized his or her name and retained it.

Thus Amelia Bloomer's fashion, though now shrunk to shorts, survives, the fourth Earl of Sandwich's hasty meal is still popular, and Adolphe Sax's name is heard whenever the saxophone is played. Similarly, Tsar recalled Caesar, the Count of Sade's sexual degeneration survives in sadism, and Quisling's name has become a byword. Shakespeare, once again, was so right when he said that "the evil that men do lives after them."

The ship's derrick owes its name to Godfrey Derrick, of London, England's public executioner during Queen Elizabeth's reign and responsible for well-nigh 3,000 hangings and beheadings. His most renowned "case" was that of the Earl of Essex.

Derrick did not like the old-fashioned rope method of hanging and felt that he could improve on it. Not lacking opportunities to experiment in this pursuit, he eventually developed the derrick, his new "killing machine," bearing his name. When, not long after his death, a hoisting device was introduced, which in appearance closely resembled Derrick's gallows, people called the novel crane after Derrick as well. That is how a hangman's name lives on. Once used to describe a gadget applied to transport people from this world to the next, it now identifies a harmless mechanical device, moving merely goods into and out of the holds of a vessel.

Derrick served in the Earl of Essex's military expedition against Cadiz, where he was sentenced to death for rape. However, possibly aware of the man's usefulness in his peculiar trade, the

Earl pardoned him, and for a long time afterwards Derrick was able to continue his grim profession.

This would have been a suitable finish to any story. Unfortunately it did not end there. However grateful Derrick had cause to be to the Earl for saving his life, the day came when he was called upon to take the life of his own benefactor. Having committed treason, Queen Elizabeth condemned Essex to death, and it was Derrick who had to execute the sentence!

Being of noble blood saved the traitor from the usual method of hanging, reserved for common offenders. Beheading with an axe was considered more appropriate for Essex's status. Derrick certainly did not like the job or the occasion. Politely apologizing to his former friend for what he was about to do, he explained that he was merely obeying orders. But then things went wrong. Inexperienced in this type of execution, Derrick botched the job and had to apply the axe three times before severing the head.

This enraged the vast crowd of the Earl's admirers who had come to witness his sad departure. They seized Derrick, and would have killed him had not soldiers come to his rescue. Thus, for the second time, his life was spared in order to end the lives of others. Notorious as "the hangman of Tyburn," in people's minds his name became synonymous with the gallows. Thus are linked a man, a gibbet and a crane.

Lynching

At least four men named Lynch have been cited as the possible originator of the term describing mob-law. The word itself was first recorded as late as 1817.

Best known is the Irish claim to have been the home of the original Lynch, whose story was full of personal tragedy. He was James Lynch Fitz-Stephen, the highly respected Mayor of Galway. About 1493, he had sent his son to Spain to purchase a cargo of wine. But losing his father's money at gambling, the young man bought the wine on credit, assuring the merchant it would be paid for in due course. The Spaniard, anxious to see the debt paid and perhaps suspicious of the young man, sent his nephew with Lynch back to Ireland to collect the amount owing.

During the voyage, Lynch, to avoid being found out, killed

him, throwing his body into the sea. Lynch's father soon discovered the crime. As Mayor, he had to conduct the trial of his son, and according to the law pronounced the death sentence.

Everyone was shocked by the great tragedy that had befallen a citizen so well thought of and loved, and no one was prepared to carry out the execution. Old Lynch, however, was determined to see justice done, though it meant the death of his own son, and so he hanged him from a window in their home!

Courts of justice are most assiduous to establish the true facts of a case. But when popular feelings run riot, the result can only be much confusion. This certainly applies to lynch law and the many attempts at explaining the origin of its name. Even the story of the Mayor of Galway has two versions. The second tale, though still relating to the same year and the identical persons, differs in all other aspects.

According to this tradition, James Lynch Fitz-Stephen, anxious to improve trade relations between his country and far-off Spain, himself undertook the arduous journey, and successfully carried out the mission. Having done so and ready to return home, he invited his Spanish host's son to sail with him to Ireland, to stay there as his guest, which he was only too happy to do.

Back in Galway, things went well and everyone seemed happy, till one day the Mayor's son became suspicious. He imagined, or perhaps it was not just mere fancy, that his father's guest was paying too much attention to his own sweetheart and, overcome with jealousy, stabbed him to death.

The rest of the story—more or less—follows the pattern of the first. Lynch, as the head of the guard, seized the murderer and, as Mayor, according to the law, passed sentence of death. But the people of Galway felt for the young lover. Wishing to protect him, in spite of what he had done, a riotous mob tried to rescue him. However, Mayor Lynch, forcing his way through the crowd, and when all others refused to inflict the punishment, himself hanged his son. Having done so, he returned to his home, never to be seen again.

Other claims to having originated the term lynch law belong to the American scene. Charles Lynch (1736–96), a Virginian planter and a colonel in the army of General Green, during the American Revolution, was concerned to keep order in the Staunton River district where he lived. With two of his friends he set out to protect the region from marauders, though some have suggested that this protective union was against political opponents.

Taking the law into their hands, Lynch and his associates punished all those breaking the peace of the realm (or not sharing their views!) by creating their own—extralegal—court. They punished lawlessness (or political disagreement?) either by flogging the offenders or expelling them from the district. However, so different from what lynch law came to mean in later years, no one was ever killed. Eventually—in 1782—Lynch was apprehended and accused before the Virginian Assembly, for his unlawful execution of justice. Wisely, however, the judges indemnified him. Other authorities attribute this type of unauthorized tribunal and its name not to Charles but to his brother John Lynch, the founder of Lynchhurg in Virginia.

Early editions of *Webster's Dictionary* quote yet another American, James Lynch. A farmer at Piedmont in Virginia, he was highly respected and as the nearest court was a considerable distance away, neighbors elected him to try and pass sentence on accused persons at Piedmont.

Boycott

Boycott as a word and policy was the result of the struggle between the Irish and the English and a landlord's refusal to take note of his tenants' poverty and distress.

In the late 1870s, crop failures in Ireland were disastrous and there was a great famine. Thousands of farmers were unable to pay their rent to the absentee English landlords, and suggested paying as much as they could. In many cases landlords reduced the rent. But not so Lord Erne, who owned big estates in the county of Mayo. He instructed Captain Charles Cunningham Boycott, his local agent, to use any measure he deemed essential to get the money. Though some 3,000 people were affected, Boycott showed them no mercy.

He had reckoned without the Irish temper and the people's determination to throw off the English yoke once and for all. Far from being intimidated by Boycott, the farmers now refused to pay any rent. Going even further they stopped reaping the harvest, such as it was, and, joining forces, formed the Irish Land League. Thus organized, they decided to have no dealings of any kind with the captain and intensified their campaign against him. Servants were forced to leave his employ. Boycott's mail was intercepted and attempts were made to cut off his food supply.

In retaliation, fifty Orangemen from the north of Ireland, protected by 900 soldiers, were sent to Mayo. They not only harvested what remained of the crop, but managed to rescue Boycott who fled to England, where he died, seventeen years later, in 1897. In next to no time, his name was adopted everywhere as a new word describing the very treatment meted out to him by those he had victimized.

With Boycott's fate still fresh in his mind, J. Dillon, one of the vigorous young Irish members of Parliament, expounded to his countrymen the new policy as a bloodless safeguard against their rapacious and avaricious masters. He did so in a speech he delivered to the Land League in 1881.

"Let every man's door be closed against him; and make him feel himself a stranger and a castaway in his own neighborhood," he said.

The Guillotine

The French Revolution, with its thousands of executions, inherited from the monarchy a carefully graded system of death. Different methods were used, according to the condemned person's crime, as well as their position in the community.

Under King Louis XIV heretics were burned, traitors quartered, and assassins and highwaymen broken on the wheel. Others who had committed any of 115 capital offenses were treated with class distinction. If they were of the common people, their fate was hanging. But if they belonged to the aristocracy, they had the privilege of being beheaded, which was a method less cruel and not so prolonged in its agony.

Dr. Joseph-Ignace Guillotin, a true son of the Revolution, did not question the actual putting to death, but he was horrified at the differentiation in the means of execution. He demanded that the new spirit of fraternity and sameness should reach to the scaffold and that decapitation should be extended to the masses!

Therefore, on humane grounds and with a passion for equality, he took up his cause in the French Chamber. Eloquently he pleaded it, demanding a gadget which was more merciful. It should be applied to all and sundry, "whatever the rank and status of the guilty party."

The press enthusiastically echoed his feelings and recommended "the humane sentiments which breathed in the Guillotin proposal." Commentators referred to the need for some machine which would be "worthy of the new order into which we are about to enter."

Although Guillotin had urged the necessity of such a device, he did not invent it himself. Another medical practitioner, a Dr. Louis, adapted earlier mechanisms of a similar type and constructed the first modern beheading machine, which was soon introduced all over France. Because its adoption was due solely to Dr. Guillotin's indefatigable agitation, people gave it his, and not Dr. Louis's name, and despite Guillotin's strong objection, his name stuck.

A story has it that he himself died by means of his "invention." Actually, Guillotin passed away at the age of seventy-six from a carbuncle in a shoulder. After his death, his children petitioned the government, out of deference to their father and for their own sake, to change the name of the guillotine. Their request was rejected, but they were permitted to change their own name instead!

Psychologists have been at pains to explain why Guillotin devoted so much time to the question of humane execution. Some of them felt that the reason was Guillotin's own premature birth. While his mother was pregnant with the future Joseph-Ignace, she unexpectedly witnessed a criminal being tortured to death on a wheel. The experience so shocked her that she gave birth to her son before it was due. Thus the guillotine may have been envisaged through prenatal influence!

The Scapegoat

Throughout history the goat appears to have been identified with fools and sin. Though the medieval tradition that represented the devil in the shape of a goat is now obsolete, people are still rebuked for "acting the goat." Those blamed or punished for the misdeeds of others are known as scapegoats. Not a mere metaphor, this description is based on an ancient sacred rite.

Mosaic law decreed that on the Day of Atonement, the holiest day of the Jewish year, two goats had to be brought to the altar of the Tabernacle for the High Priest, by casting lots, to choose one of them to be sacrificed on the spot, whilst the other was sent into the wilderness to escape there, symbolically carrying with it all the sins of the people. An early mysterious rite thus still survives in an everyday expression. The omission of a single letter, which once prefixed the word, altered its original meaning. The escape goat became the scapegoat!

With its roots so far back in history, it is strange to realize that the word "scapegoat" was first coined as late as 1530, when William Tyndale translated the Hebrew Bible into English. It was his attempt to render adequately the mysterious Azazel as it appears in the Book of Leviticus. In his version, Tyndale spoke of "the goose on which the lotte fell to scape."

CHAPTER 15

Parliamentary Procedure and Royal Regalia

Parliament is the very heart of democracy. Its growth in British lands reflects the maturing of a nation's desire to rule itself in the most effective and reliable manner. Every detail of parliamentary tradition and procedure was evolved in the pursuit of that ideal. Added to this was a determination to stop any government from becoming an autocratic force.

Parliament goes back to 1258. In that year, in opposition to King Henry III, the Earl of Leicester convened an assembly at Oxford. He ordered two knights from each shire and representatives from certain boroughs to meet selected barons and members of the clergy there. However, what has been called the Model Parliament dates back to 1295, when "Commoners" were first elected—and not just appointed—to represent the people.

Rules of courtesy permeate all parliamentary procedure. Members must stand up to speak. They are expected to do so without reference to notes. Maiden speeches are treated with special consideration. Tradition demands that a member of the opposing party shall congratulate the speakers on their effort.

Even in the heat of debate, everything that might hurt or insult a member must be avoided. No one in Parliament can be accused of having lied. That is why Churchill, when trying to point out how a member had made an untruthful statement, was unable to do so in so many words. Instead, in his ingenious way of coining new phrases, he suggested that the person had been guilty of "a terminological inexactitude."

Parliament has taught that democracy means not "I am equal to you" but that "You are equal to me."

The Chamber

A fourteenth-century chapel, which was destroyed by fire in 1834, was the earliest Chamber, serving as a place of assembly for members of the legislature. It still is the prototype of Houses of Parliament within the British Commonwealth throughout the world. Continuing its original rectangular shape, its altar has been replaced by the canopied Speaker's Chair, whilst its pews survive in the members' benches, which explains why, up to this day, those sitting in Parliament do not occupy individual seats.

The comparative smallness of the Chamber gives all debates dignity and intimacy. It also creates an atmosphere of friendship even among opponents who, though far removed in political views, sit close together. Furthermore, as was pointed out at the rebuilding of the House of Commons in London, after its destruction by enemy action during World War II, a crowded small Chamber is much more advantageous than a large one, depressing by being mostly half empty.

The arrangement of benches along two sides, following the example of the ancient church, fostered the two-party system. British tradition taught members to respect their opponents' opinion. Thus the Opposition is officially known as "Her Majesty's Opposition," with its implied suggestion that the "Opposition" is as much a part of "Her Majesty" as is the Government. The remuneration of its leader is not far behind that received by the Prime Minister. To pay someone to oppose is a telling example of British democracy.

The Speaker

The Speaker is one of the most important persons in Parliament. His (or her) word is law and those who dare act against it are duly punished. Presiding over the House, he controls its debates.

Tradition demands that he be nominated and selected by backbenchers. This is done to stress his duty to protect minorities, and to express his complete impartiality. Invested with royal prerogative, in Parliament itself the Speaker ranks superior to the Crown. Anyone who wishes to approach or address him must pay due deference to his standing. Like a king, he is distinguished by regalia: the Mace is his scepter, the Chair his throne, and the wig his crown.

Today a coveted position of the highest honor, the Speaker's office at first was least desired. Its duties, at times, were perilous and unrewarding. His very title preserves his original function. The Speaker spoke on behalf of the Commons, expressing their majority view to the king.

This all goes back to the time when Parliament, in the literal sense of its name, "talked" (from the French *parler*) about matters of state to ascertain the wish and opinion of the greatest number of its members. At first, these discussions were held in unofficial meetings behind closed doors. The only right of the "Commons" then was not to direct the king, but to address humble petitions to him. The man chosen to convey to the Crown the wish and desire of the House thus acted as their mouthpiece—their "Speaker." It was an unenviable task, especially when the views of king and people clashed. The Speaker had then to bear the brunt of the sovereign's wrath and, at times, pay with his life. At least nine Speakers are known to have died a violent death.

Sir Peter de la Mare is said to have been one of the first to be called upon to act as the Speaker of the House, and his thankless mission illustrates the origin of the office. Dame Alice Perrers was a "lady to the bedchamber" to Philippa, the Queen of Edward III. However, far from being satisfied with her appointed duties, she showed much greater interest in the king himself, who reciprocated her feelings. It was a most remunerative relationship for Alice. She amassed a truly royal fortune, which included a grant of land, jewelry worth hundreds of pounds, and the guardianship of wealthy orphans. When Queen Philippa died in 1373, her death further enriched Alice.

But her appetite grew all the time on what it was feeding, whilst the king, certainly, was eating out of her hand. Wealth alone no longer satisfied her. She wished to wield power as well, and started to meddle in affairs of state. Becoming ever more arrogant in her demeanor, Alice in 1376 dared to enter Westminster Hall trying to instruct Parliament's presiding judge on how to act.

For a long time the Commons had watched with anxiety and exasperation Alice's mischievous influence on the king. But now she had gone to the very limit. Something had to be done and done quickly. Somebody had to be sent to the king, telling him how they felt and that, once and for all, he had to break up the affair and put Alice in her place.

Sir Peter de la Mare was elected to go and speak on their behalf. That is how he became the Commons' first Speaker, an office whose birth, at least according to this tradition, is due to a woman of doubtful morals and scandalous behavior. However, the actual title of Speaker was bestowed first on Sir Thomas Hungerford who, in 1377, was officially appointed to that office.

The Mace

The mace has come a long way. Now associated with the Speaker of Parliament as his staff of authority, and symbolically representing the head of state (and until recent times, specifically the king), it stems from the Orient. Originally it was not a sign of sovereignty, but a most effective and feared weapon. It was used long before swords and consisted of a heavy, spiked metal club hanging from a horseman's saddle. Its blows, though not capable of severing the adversary's head, could crack it, and its spikes were able to pierce the heaviest armor.

The mace was a weapon specially welcomed in later years by hypocritical clergy who, in spite of their calling, were anxious to participate in battle. According to the Bible, they could not shed blood, but by adopting the mace they still could kill people— bloodlessly. It was a pitiable piece of casuistry on the part of ecclesiastics.

Even after the introduction of the sword, when the mace became redundant as a weapon, it was not abolished altogether. Its antiquity gave it special value and it was thus retained by kings and noblemen. They no longer carried it for the purpose of individual combat, but as a sign of their status and might.

The next step was obvious. For royalty to encumber themselves with a heavy iron ball was no longer considered the proper thing. Hence, this office was delegated to a trusted knight, the king's champion. He preceded his royal master on all state occasions, carrying the mace on his behalf.

As the spikes had lost their practical purpose they were removed, and the mace, now silver and gilt, was richly ornamented and decorated with a crown. Ever since, it has been the symbol of the king or head of state. No longer actually protecting the person, it came to symbolically take their place. Wherever the mace could be seen, people felt the sovereign's presence, though he might be miles away.

Thus the mace found its way into Parliament as the visible sign of royalty. It is ceremoniously borne in front of the Speaker and, during debates, conspicuously displayed, resting on two hooks on the table in front of the Speaker. In his absence, when the House "sits in committee" (which originally meant free from the king's supervision), the mace is removed and concealed under the table.

The word mace has its roots in the ancient language of Sanskrit, but reached the West through the Greek. It described an aromatic spice, once rare and highly prized. Bulblike, it was similar in shape to the iron club which for that reason was named after it.

The Whips

Each party elects its Whip whose duty it is to watch over the activities of members and enforce discipline whenever necessary. When divisions are about to take place, he rounds up all those belonging to his party to ensure they vote on a question, lest their absence defeat a cause. Most of all, the Whip sees to it that members "toe the (party) line."

The Whip's power was illustrated by the traditional circular sent out before a motion in the House of Commons. This gave notice to the member that his presence was *earnestly* required. The number of lines—in red ink—under the word "earnestly" indicated the degree of urgency of the request. One line meant that he was *expected* to come and four lines that, if he stayed away, he did so *at his own peril*.

The Whip's manifold responsibilities and the power he wields prove the appropriateness of the choice of his name. An abbreviated form of the word Whipper-in, this was borrowed from the eighteenth-century vocabulary of fox-hunters, who were mostly English squires. The whipper-in was a hunter's assistant and his task was to keep the hounds from straying by driving them back to the pack with a whip. The parliamentary whip lives up to the original meaning of his title. Though wielding his whip merely metaphorically, in the final result it is no less effective.

"Hear! Hear!"

The usual way of applauding a speech or performance is to clap hands. This goes back to the Roman stage. Actors then did not take any chances. At the end of a play, they asked their audience to show their gratitude and approval in "the usual manner." "Clap your hands!" they requested, and in most cases the audience obliged.

This Roman custom of "giving a hand" spread all over the world and, from the theater, to other occasions and institutions which demanded an audible sign of compliment and acclaim. University students and their like, however, devised a different way to show their approval and appreciation. Possibly to keep their hands free to take down notes uninterruptedly, they started to stamp their feet instead. Others again neither clapped nor "stamped" but just rapped the desk.

British parliamentary institutions, however, created a totally different type of applause. This was not directed to the speaker, but to those who ought to listen to what he was saying. "Hear him! Hear him!" became their traditional call. It was meant to underline a statement and to draw all members' attention (and especially those whose minds had wandered elsewhere) to a voiced opinion. It was a procedure so much more dignified and appropriate in "the House" and altogether a much more logical way of showing acclaim. Eventually, possibly for the sake of brevity and so as not to interrupt the speech for too long, the "him" was dropped and "Hear! Hear!" became the traditional and accepted way of showing approbation.

Yet this method of voicing consent goes back to even earlier times, when to make oneself heard was not as easy as nowadays. Present-day rules require proper decorum in Parliament, commensurate with the dignity of the nation's representative body. Technically, members must not leave their place or wander about in the Chamber while a debate is in progress, nor are they permitted to read a newspaper or to carry on a private conversation. Those who catch the Speaker's eye are not only given a chance to say their piece but, no less essential, to be heard as well. And if, at times, tempers run high and there is a commotion, it is the Speaker's right, if not duty, to call the House to order and remove anyone disobeying.

Parliament used to be—and in some countries still is—a rowdy place with much noise and lack of attention and the voices of speakers frequently drowned in uproar. Gladstone and Disraeli used to write letters to the Queen while the House was in session and a member was making a speech. Contemporaneous reports speak of "a sound of drone-like humming, having almost the sound of a distant hand-organ or bagpipes, coughing, sneezing and ingeniously extended yawning." If members considered a speaker boring or uninteresting, they made so much noise "that the speaker scarcely could distinguish his own words."

It was not surprising, therefore, that friends who wished people to listen to what someone was saying, tried to stop the noise by calling out to others, "Hear him! Hear him!" As it was assumed that silence was demanded for a statement of special significance and value, this call soon came to be associated with actual applause. That, most likely, is how the call of "Hear him! Hear him!" became the parliamentary type of applauding.

The Coronation Stone

A king (etymologically) is one of his kin (and kind) and therefore (was assumed to be) blood-related to the people he ruled. The Kaiser's and Tsar's titles recall Julius Caesar.

The splendor of royal regalia and the solemnity of the ceremonial of coronation are rooted in most ancient and sacred traditions, going back to pre-Christian days and the rim of a hat, the branch of a tree, a magical potion and a stone, said to have been used as a pillow.

Stones have played a significant part in the history of religion, not least those which seemed to have come down from heaven and which are now recognized as meteorites. Held to be sacred and the abode of supernatural forces, they were believed to be able to act as a safeguard from evil.

In his flight from Esau's wrath, Jacob "by chance" had chosen such a stone for a pillow. His subsequent dream of the ladder linking heaven and earth convinced him of the sanctity of the site and the stone, which he thus set up as a pillar and anointed with oil. There is no doubt that it became the most sacred object in the later Sanctuary. If not divine itself, the stone was "the House of God," or, as the original Hebrew has it, a *Beth El*. Had not the stone proved itself, as it were, to be heaven's gate, through which the divine descended to earth? As God's anointed, a king, most of all, was in need of this stone, which could act as a special protector and continuous source of divine power.

That is how the Coronation Chair, made by order of King Edward I and in use at Westminster Abbey for a considerable time, was specially designed to enclose this very stone, believed to be Jacob's pillow. The story of how the stone found its place in the chair is full of mystery and associated with strange legends that proliferated through the centuries.

When in 586 B.C., Nebuchadnezzar of Babylon had destroyed the ancient Temple, Israelite refugees are said to have carried the stone with them to Ireland. Recognized as the Stone of Destiny, the Irish used it at the coronation of their chieftains, initially, when one of them married an Israelite princess.

More than a thousand years later, about A.D. 850, the stone reached Scotland. There, at Scone, 2 miles north of Perth, it was enclosed in a wooden chair which served at the coronation of Scottish kings.

Still, its destiny was not settled yet. Once again, in 1296, Jacob's (alleged) pillow was carried away, as the Stone of Scone, by Edward I. For centuries it was to form part of the throne of England, though from time to time Scottish patriots have tried, either by force or an Act of Parliament, to remove it to what they considered its rightful place. Finally, in the late 1990s the English returned it to Scotland.

The Anointment

Christ—from the Greek (*Christos*)—means "the anointed" and is the literal translation of the Hebrew *Mashi'ach* (Messiah). It was an obvious choice for a name for Jesus by those who considered him "The King," which led the Roman executioners to superscribe his cross with the words, "Jesus, the King (*Rex*) of the Jews."

From earliest days, anointment has been an essential feature of a coronation. At times, British monarchs themselves wondered what, apart from its symbolism, the purpose of anointment was. In 1246, for instance, King Henry III, in a letter to the Bishop of Lincoln, asked for an explanation of the rite. He was told that the sacrament of unction conferred on a king the sevenfold gift of the holy spirit, the better to help him serve his people.

Actually, the anointment of a king was the result of several deeply rooted beliefs and practices which, by many years, anticipated the anointment of Saul, the first Jewish king, by Samuel, the prophet, who took a vial of oil and poured it upon his head, and kissed him and said, "Is it not that the Lord has anointed you to be prince over His inheritance."

The primary motivating force in anointment can be traced to the tradition that kings were divine. The sacred unction ceremoniously bestowed on them not merely symbolically, but actually, that distinction.

Primitive races imagined that certain types of organic matter were charged with mystical power and divine spirit. Its potency varied according to the substance. It was believed that people, particularly the elect, could absorb this sacred essence into their bodies by actually eating the flesh or drinking the blood, a practice which thus became a sacramental rite.

Fat, above all, was regarded as saturated with the divine. Thought to be the very seat of life, it was too holy, and hence too dangerous, to be eaten. It therefore was applied externally and, because of its highly potent sanctity, mere contact was sufficient to transfer its gift of supernatural power. At first, the king's whole body was rubbed with fat. Subsequently, fat was replaced by oil, in which the king was bathed. Ultimately, oil was poured on his head.

It was also believed that the sacred unguent permanently immunized the king from the influence of harmful spirits. It served as a magical, protective armor against any kind of evil forces. Hedging the king with an invisible fence of sanctity, it rendered him invulnerable in the execution of his so dangerous office.

Lastly, it must be remembered that anointment was practiced generally by the noble and rich of ancient races, especially on festive occasions. It was part of their toilet and a mark of honor. It refreshed the body, creating a feeling of comfort and personal well-being. Most of all, however, the extra sheen it gave to the skin lent that air of distinction and shining presence to the anointed so fitting to the supreme moment of a monarch's enthronement.

The Crown

The crown has uppermost importance in the royal regalia. Its very name has become synonymous with sovereigns, and their investiture is referred to as their coronation. The crown, indeed, came to symbolize power, prosperity, victory and glory. It can be traced back in history more than 5,000 years, when it was worn both by kings and gods.

The practice of displaying an individual's special status in the community by a symbol belonged already to the lifestyle of primitive races. Those of higher rank were distinguished by their headdress, especially at celebrations. Chiefs, priests and medicine men dressed their hair most elaborately, ornamenting it with all kinds of material, such as feathers, teeth, bones, shells and leaves. To stop the hair from falling into the face, a band or skin was wound around the head and it was this "rimless hat" that became the earliest crown.

A sovereign's authority implied superiority. This could be expressed most conspicuously by giving him greater height, easily attained by wearing a tall hat—the crown. It made the ruler stand out above all other people, who thus were constantly reminded of the supremacy of their royal leader.

Kings, looked upon as divine, claimed direct descent from the gods and it was believed that the crown surrounded the head with the radiant nimbus of the sun-god. The crown was his aureole, and a living, powerful being itself. In ancient Egypt, it was identified with the god's burning eyes, a flame protecting the king, a Uraeus, a sacred serpent which spat fire at the monarch's foes.

The crown might also have evolved from the garland worn by victors and gods in early times. Initially made of the flowers and leaves of sacred plants and trees, it was "great in magic." Serving rulers as an instrument of divination, people tried to propitiate its occult power by singing hymns to it.

Thus, the crowning of sovereigns was at first a magical, ritual act. It set them apart from all other people as being singled out by divinity as the ruler of their people and, if not gods themselves, as divinely anointed.

The Scepter

The scepter has served as a sovereign's badge of office from most ancient days, though its shape has varied with time and place. Frequently mentioned in biblical writings, it was part of the regalia of Oriental monarchs and appeared in the representation of Greek gods.

Behind its present-day, merely symbolic use, a totally different past lies hidden. Though views still differ as to its original purpose, all agree that at first the staff provided a potent means of exerting authority over both nature and people.

Taking the place of an ancient magical wand, the scepter was said to have been a branch from a sacred tree, if not the tree of life itself, which gave those wielding it supernatural power to control the world.

It has also been suggested that the scepter grew out of the *lituus*, which Roman augurs employed in their acts of divination. Similarly, priests engaged in the ritual of rain-making used such a mystical branch from the sacred oak tree.

Others have seen in the scepter the original shepherd's staff, indispensable to him for keeping his sheep together. Later, the staff proved itself as an all-purpose utensil which also could be used effectively as a weapon, a tool to help break the soil and, in the case of overseers, an instrument for the punishment of idle slaves. Small wonder that, ultimately, the staff became a symbol of authority.

In primitive wars the victors were always anxious to appropriate the foe's weapons, not only to disarm the enemy but magically to secure for themselves his former strength. They thus kept and carried with them captured weapons, especially spears, as a continuous source of extra power. Eventually, the spears became the badge of victory, a telling sign of the victor's invincibility.

The captured spear lost its usefulness as a weapon and gradually was transformed into a ruler's emblem. As such it was richly embellished and finally the camouflage was so complete that the last traces of the scepter's original role—in war—were lost.

CHAPTER 16

Symbols of Nationhood

A barbarian, originally from the Greek, meant a stammerer. It was a word used to describe (and decry) the foreigner, whose language could not be understood.

Idiots, on the other hand, were persons disinterested in politics and public affairs. Literally, they were someone "private," who shunned civic responsibility, living completely "on their own."

Service to the community and patriotism have been part of national life from earliest days. Flags and anthems not only expressed and fostered national feelings and differentiation but, in their origin, reveal a people's soul and fundamental beliefs.

The Flag

Opinions differ on how the flag originated. Many trace its beginnings to a carved pole carried by primitive people in battle or before chiefs, displaying the tribal totem at its top.

The ancient Egyptians are said to have crowned a staff or spear with the figure of the animal they held most sacred. The Greeks carried a pole on the end of which were pieces of armor or a single letter. American Indians had pikes bedecked with feathers from eagles' wings. The Vikings made use of a raven and the Saxons of a white horse. Romans had shafts ornamented with circles and discs and surmounted at first by holy beasts and then, from 100 B.C., by the figure of an eagle.

This original kind of "flag" has its basis in totemism, one of the very early primitive forms of religion. The pole symbolized and, it was believed, actually carried into battle the people's ancestral spirits, their totem and god, just as the ancient Israelites had done with the Ark, the seat of their God. Its presence was a source of power and an aid to victory, giving courage to the warriors fighting under it and putting fear into their enemy.

185

Viewed with awe and considered sacred, held aloft the staff identified the forces, marked the position of their leader and served as a rallying point. Whilst its role remained the same, gradually it developed into a more elaborate banner or standard, with colors added to the totem figure.

Finally, streamers or tassels tied to the banner, not, as may be imagined, as an ornament, but, fluttering in the wind, were meant to indicate the divine presence. It is thought that from this bunting the present-day flag developed.

The story of how a piece of colored cloth came to represent a nation begins with the ancient belief in omens and magical practice. The wind mystified primitive people. Its power evaded their grasp in every sense. Those who dared the open sea in their light craft learned to fear its force which could either hasten their advance or spell disaster. Anxiously, therefore, they watched the wind and tried to detect in its direction an omen for good or evil. But as the wind was invisible, this was an almost impossible task—until they realized that the smoke of fire could expose it to view.

People began to observe the smoke with awe and to imagine that the way it moved indicated, and then actually effected, the will of the gods. If the smoke blew towards the foe, it was an augury of their imminent flight and defeat. Significantly, the Welsh word for a bonfire means "sure omens."

Some ingenious mind then realized that far superior to smoke was a piece of cloth, fluttering in the breeze from a pole, to show which way the wind was blowing. After a time, the cloth was regarded as a magical means of determining the outcome of a battle. Activated by the wind, it symbolized and could bring victory. For that reason it was carefully guarded and became the first target of attack. Its capture or fall caused confusion, if not defeat. Flags in their present form were invented by the Chinese. It is known that the founder of the Chou dynasty in the twelfth century B.C. had a white flag carried in front of him. Yet national flags did not appear in Europe till the twelfth century A.D. They were introduced by the Crusaders on their return from the Holy Land, where they probably had adopted them from their Saracen foes who, in turn, had copied them from the Indians. No doubt, they had appropriated them from China.

As one huge Christian army, the Crusaders found a banner most useful in identifying themselves from their heathen opponents. Fighting in the name of Christ, their choice of the cross as an emblem was a foregone conclusion. But coming from every country of Christendom, they also had need to distinguish themselves from each other. For that purpose the Knights employed the various forms of the cross, linked with their individual patron saint, and a combination of contrasting colors. From the Knights who had fought in the Holy War, their countries took over and then developed the flag as a national emblem.

The Union Jack

Britain's Union flag—usually wrongly called the Union Jack—records in its name and fusion of three different emblems the growth of one kingdom out of the successive union of three crowns.

The original English flag was white and bore the plain red cross of St. George, the country's patron saint. He was a third-century Christian soldier who had preferred death by beheading to denouncing his faith. The red cross recalled his martyrdom by Roman hands at Lydda, in Palestine. When the English knights joined in the Crusades, they identified themselves by the saint's symbol. On their return, the religious emblem eventually became the national flag.

The choice of St. George as a patron has been linked with the tradition that during the Crusades the saint's apparition rescued the English from the fury of their Muslim foes. His sudden appearance on the battlefield threw the Muslims into confusion and flight. Thus the English recognized and acknowledged him as their patron. King Edward III adopted his name as a battle cry, and his emblem became the English flag.

St. Andrew was one of the twelve Apostles. A simple fisherman, he, too, suffered martyrdom. The story is told that because he had converted a Roman consul's wife to Christianity, her husband had him flogged and, subsequently, crucified. The cross used for the execution was shaped like the letter X, which explains how this became the saint's symbol and is still called St. Andrew's cross.

His association with Scotland dates back to the tradition that in A.D. 368 a monk transferred some of his relics from Constantinople to Scotland, to be buried there on the east coast, on the very spot where the city of St. Andrew's now stands.

The story is further told that when the Picts and Scots were attacked by the Saxons, they called on St. Andrew for help. Looking up, they noticed a strange formation of clouds. It seemed as if their white vapor had formed itself into the shape of a cross backed by the blue sky. The anxious watchers saw in it a manifestation of the saint and an assurance of victory. Spurred on, they joined in battle and defeated the foe. After their victory, they adopted St. Andrew's cross as their emblem, with the specific colors of cloud and sky. It was the birth of the Scottish flag.

When, in 1603, James Stuart came from Scotland to ascend the English throne as James I, the two kingdoms were united. The immediate problem was which flag to hoist on the king's ships. English sailors resented the Scottish colors and the Scots scorned the cross of St. George.

A compromise was the answer: the creation of the first Union Flag. In 1606, a royal decree declared that the ships of the Kingdom of Great Britain "shall bear on their maintops the red cross, commonly called St. George's cross, and the white cross, commonly called St. Andrew's cross." After the Act of Union of England and Scotland in 1707, Queen Anne sanctioned this combination.

The white border which surrounds St. George's cross is not due to aesthetic or decorative reasons, but was meant to express deference to both original flags. Even in their union, they were to remain distinct. The rules of heraldry demanded that two colors must never be placed on top of or touch each other. They must be separated by a strip, no matter how narrow.

Neither the exact year nor place of St. Patrick's birth is known. It was towards the end of the fourth century somewhere in Britain or Gaul. Pirates captured him when a youth of sixteen, to sell him as a slave to Ireland. After serving there for six years, he managed to escape to France. However, a vision, so it is said, made him return to the island to rid it of snakes and convert its pagan people to the Christian faith. In pursuit of his task, he miraculously overcame the magic and cunning opposition of the Druids.

Because he died an old man from natural causes, no cross was linked with his name at first. The red saltire on a white ground, which eventually became his emblem, dates only from the twelfth century and was adopted from the heraldic device of an Irish family.

When in 1801 the Parliament of Ireland was joined with that of Great Britain, what was then recognized as the cross of St. Patrick was incorporated in the Union Flag. Its distinctive markings and colors recollect the inspiring stories of three great saints and the traditions of three ancient races which, step by step, grew into one United Kingdom.

The popular but erroneous description of Britain's flag as the Union Jack can be traced back either to naval tradition or to the historic union of Scotland and England.

James I was the first common ruler of the two kingdoms. He signed his name the French way, Jacques, which, spelled phonetically in its English pronunciation, was Jack. Colloquially, people nicknamed his new flag the Union "Jack." The term therefore perpetuates the name of a specific king and one of the great moments in British history.

Correctly, however, a jack relates only to the sea. It is a small flag used by naval vessels for signalling. It received its name because it was hoisted on a mast known as the jackstaff. Thus, in the view of some, the Union Jack refers merely to a flag of comparatively small dimensions, used at sea.

The Australian Flag

When the first navigators reached the southern hemisphere, they felt greatly bewildered. A completely different world seemed to encompass them. There were strange beasts and birds. Instead of the familiar stars, totally unknown constellations looked down on them. Among them, with great rejoicing, they recognized a cross.

They were now convinced they were still sailing under the guidance of their faith, whose very symbol was watching over them. They had nothing to fear. A sign from heaven had shown them that, however far they proceeded, they could never leave the realm of divine care. That is how the southern cross assumed a significance far beyond that of a new constellation. It stood for promise and assurance.

From earliest times Australia was thus linked with a group of stars apparently proclaiming the Christian faith and it was a foregone conclusion that if Australians were to choose a national emblem, the southern cross would be part of it.

Moreover, was not Australia's very name coupled with the religion symbolized by the cross? When, in 1606, in search of "another Indies," de Quiros thought he had sighted the country, he called it Terra Australis del Espiritu Santu, "the Great South Land of the Holy Spirit." To select a cross for the flag of such territory, from this point of view as well, was appropriate.

On several occasions, long before the need of a national flag, Australians made use of the southern cross to symbolize ideals for which they were fighting. It was included in the flag of the Anti-transportation League, which proudly displayed it for the first time in Hobart in July 1851. Again, the cross was conspicuous in the crudely designed banner flown at the Eureka Stockade at the time of the miners' uprising on the Ballarat goldfields in December 1854.

When, in 1770, Cook landed at Botany Bay, he naturally raised the British flag. Under its colors the original penal settlement grew into a nation. But with the establishment of the Commonwealth of Australia, the need of a new national flag was felt. A number of private firms, supported by the Federal Government, were invited to suggest a design for it.

Thirty thousand entries were received. They were displayed at a special exhibition in Melbourne in September 1901. Five of them were considered of equal merit and, therefore, the first prize was shared by five people, among them three youths, living in Perth, Melbourne, Sydney and—Auckland, New Zealand. A huge flag, incorporating all the features suggested by the five winners, was hoisted over the Melbourne Exhibition Building on the day the awards were announced.

This was the birth of the first Australian flag which, with slight adjustments, has remained the same for more than 100 years. As a symbol of the British settlement, it made use of the Union Jack, in the form of the British Blue Ensign, but conspicuously it also displayed the five stars of the southern cross! An additional large white star was placed in the hoist. This corresponded to nothing in the sky. Purely symbolic of the Australian Commonwealth, its seven points represented the six states and the territories.

It is wrong therefore to say that Australia owes her first flag to one individual. Like so much in her life, it is the result of a joint effort, of cooperation, competition and, in no small measure, the work of young people who, in the years to come, were to play an ever greater part in the building up of the nation.

The Stars and Stripes

Officially, the first flag of the United States was adopted by the American Continental Congress in Philadelphia on June 14, 1777. It was based on the report of a special committee, submitted by John Adams. Congress then resolved—

- that the flag of the United States be thirteen stripes, alternately red and white;
- that the Union be thirteen stars, white in a blue field, representing a new constellation.

George Washington explained the flag's features to the people in stirring words. He said, "We take the stars from heaven, the red from our mother country, separating it by white stripes, thus showing that we have separated from her, and the white stripes shall go down to posterity representing liberty."

There are various views on the flag's beginnings and to whom the credit should go for its final design. Not even the names of members of the committee have been preserved. In spite of sworn affidavits as to the accuracy of one claim, this has now been accepted as a legend.

Probably several people were responsible for the new flag, although Francis Hopkinson, a delegate to Congress and signatory to the Declaration of Independence, considered himself entitled to a reward as the originator. His claim was rejected because, as was pointed out to him, he "was not the only person consulted."

The fact is that the American flag is the result of a long evolution and each of its parts has its own story.

What was regarded as the first distinctly American flag was flown on Prospect Hill on January 1, 1776, by the American forces besieging Boston. Unmistakably, it was meant to proclaim by thirteen red and white stripes the union of that number of seceding colonies, yet paradoxically, it still carried in the canton the British crosses of St. George and St. Andrew.

It was a strange combination. While the thirteen stripes told the world of the colonies' united revolt against the mother country, the inclusion of the Union Jack reminded the people of their allegiance to Britain. Indeed, it took almost a whole year after the Declaration of Independence to remove any obvious likeness to the British flag. The two crosses in the canton were replaced by thirteen stars.

Several theories have been brought forward as to the origin of the stars. They were preceded, so it is said, by the picture of a rattlesnake with thirteen rattles and the motto, "Don't tread on me!" No one knows whether the stars were taken from the flag of Rhode Island or from the coat of arms of the Washington family.

The story is told that in June 1776, George Washington with two other men called on Betsy Ross, a widowed seamstress renowned for her needlework, at her upholstery shop in Philadelphia. They showed her a rough draft of the suggested flag and inquired whether she could make one.

Betsy convinced her callers that it was advisable to use five-pointed stars instead of the proposed six-pointed ones, because these could easily be made by a single clip of the scissors. Washington is said to have suggested that the stars should be arranged in a circle, to emphasize the full equality of the states.

Actually, there was no definite rule about the arrangement of the stars at first. Earliest samples show a circle of twelve stars, with the thirteenth star occupying the center. After the preliminary discussion, a sketch of the new model, prepared by an artist, was submitted to Betsy who, in no time, sewed America's first national flag. No contemporaneous independent report supports the claim which was made only by Mrs. Ross herself to her family. Though her descendants repeated the assertion and even supplied sworn statements, many now regard the claim as only a legend. Nevertheless, the house of Betsy Ross at 239 Arch Street in Philadelphia has become a national shrine to her memory.

Originally, it was intended to add a new stripe and star for each state joining the initial thirteen. By 1818, their number had grown to twenty, and it became obvious that the method proposed was impractical. Consequently, Congress resolved to revert to the original thirteen stripes, but to indicate the admission of new states by adding a star for each. That procedure has been followed ever since.

The Israeli Flag

Religious symbols make up the flag of the modern state of Israel. The Star of David, its centerpiece, both leads back to Jewry's glorious past and points to a Messianic future.

The prayer shawl, in which pious Jews wrap themselves during worship, suggests the flag's blue and white colors. In the synagogue, those hues reminded the faithful of a pure life and a God-centered existence. Blue, by its association with the sky, immediately suggested heaven.

There was no difficulty in reinterpreting those colors for a national flag. The white was to be symbolic of the purity of the new life the Jewish people, when returning to their ancient homeland, were meant to lead—a life of social justice, unsullied by arrogant nationalism. The blue was to point out to the new citizens, and to those whom they chose as leaders, that their country should be based on God's law and be worthy of a people called into existence with one aim in mind—to serve God.

The Israeli flag was designed before the establishment of the state. Theodor Herzl, Zionism's greatest dreamer, who wrote the blueprint of the new state, already had felt the need for a flag. "We need one," he wrote in 1895. "If we desire to lead people, we must raise a symbol above their heads." He claimed that with a piece of cloth as a banner, even if fixed to a mere broomstick, he would be able to lead the Jewish people back into the Holy Land.

In 1897, the first World Zionist Congress met in Basle. Among the 240 delegates present, who came from many countries, was David Wolffsohn. He was responsible for the arrangements and it was also he who designed the first Israeli flag. "Let us take the praying shawl from its bag and unfold it before the eyes of all nations," he said. When the congress met, it did so under the sign of the new banner. Quickly this captured the imagination of Jewish people everywhere and came to express their aspirations to return to the Holy Land.

When in 1944, during World War II, Nazi armies theatened the Middle East, a Jewish fighting force was created in Palestine. On the occasion, Winston Churchill suggested consulting the king, as, "I cannot conceive that this martyred race, scattered about the world and suffering as no other race has done at this juncture, should be denied the satisfaction of having a flag." Two months later, Churchill was able to announce to the British Parliament the formation of the Jewish Brigade Group. With it, for the first time in history, the flag gained official recognition.

When the State of Israel was born in 1948, as everyone had expected, the Zionist banner was proclaimed Israel's official flag.

The Red Flag

There were, of course, red flags long before Soviet Russia or Communism were thought of. Red is the color of blood and since time immemorial has been associated with danger and bloodshed. A red flag was thus the signal for battle among the ancient Romans—their call to arms and war. The distinctiveness of the color, which made it visible from long distances, added further significance to its choice.

In the eighteenth century, the ancient red flag was adopted by modern revolutionaries as a symbol of defiance and rebellion. In France the struggle was not between nations, but classes, and the red flag became a political badge. It meant to express the people's challenge, violent if need be, to the established order.

In 1792 the French National Assembly decreed that the Paris Municipal authorities were to show a red flag at the principal window of the Town Hall whenever there was a sign of riot. It is said that it was from that moment onward that the red flag became finally identified with revolution. As such it was flown again on the barricades of a rebellious Europe in 1848.

It was almost inevitable that Communists would take over this revolutionary symbol. Another intriguing factor might have reinforced their choice and lent it special importance. Russians consider red the color of beauty. They do so not accidentally. It is not just the result of a peculiar national aesthetic sense but the effect of a linguistic connection between "red" and "beauty." The Russian word for "red" is *krasny* and for "beauty"—*krasivy*.

National Anthems

How is a National Anthem created? Is it decreed by government order and given birth to in a cabinet room? Should a referendum "sense" people's opinion and a competition call for suggestions? Should a country adopt a popular song, so that the National Anthem truly arises out of the people, as at one time Australians unofficially seemed to have done with "Waltzing Matilda"? National Anthems—at least in their text if not their music—differ from country to country. And rightly so. After all, they are meant to express the character of a nation and to stir its soul.

The British pray for their monarch. Germans used to praise their country "above everything in the world," whilst Americans visualize their Star-spangled Banner.

Few anthems have been specially written or were the result of a poet laureate's appointed task. Most of them were born out of some particular event of war or revolution. Written then, on the spur of the moment, for that one occasion, they have survived ever since. It was the people themselves who made them their own, whilst governments only (sometimes after years) acknowledged tune and words as the authoritative National Anthem.

As most anthems go far back in nations' histories, the origin is often difficult to trace.

"God Save the Queen"

Mystery and romance surround Britain's national anthem. It was never written or composed as such, but just grew out of the people. First mentioned in the sixteenth century, its text—originally in Latin—has frequently been changed and added to. In their anthem Britons express loyalty to their country, not with an exciting marching song or a martial hymn, but a humble prayer for the health, long life and prosperity of their sovereign. No wonder that its most essential words stem from the Bible in which the phrase "God save the King" occurs three times.

No one is certain who composed the anthem and wrote its final words but by 1545 "God save the King" had become a watchword of the British navy, to be responded to by "Long to reign over us."

An old prayer, nominated by the Church for the anniversary of the Gunpowder Plot—November 5, 1605—may well be the original source of part of its second verse. This ancient supplication contains the lines "Scatter our enemies . . . assuage their malice and confound their devices."

No doubt, the anthem is a combination of such loyal phrases brought together at a moment of grave national crisis—though which crisis is still a matter of controversy.

Obviously, for the people to ask God to save their king implied that his life was endangered. That is why one tradition ascribes the origin of the hymn to 1688, "when the Prince of Orange was hovering over the coast," threatening the ruling dynasty. This claim says it was written as a Latin chorus for the private Catholic Chapel of James II. Concerned with their monarch's fate, people soon sang it in London's playhouses and on the streets. Various composers have been credited with its original tune. The best known (and least likely) claim to authorship of the British anthem is that of the man who wrote the original "Sally in our Alley," Henry Carey, son of the Marquis of Halifax. This unfortunate man, who ended his life by his own hand, is said to have written and sung it first at a London tavern dinner-party he gave in 1740 to celebrate Admiral Vernon's victory at Portobello the year before.

Others attribute both words and music to a Dr. John Bull, once a choirboy at the Chapel Royal of Elizabeth I and later its organist. Indeed, his tune, still preserved in the early manuscript of a copyist dating back to 1619, is similar to the present "God save the Queen."

It certainly would be a pleasing coincidence if a man whose name was to become a symbol of Britain was also the author of the national anthem. The song's simplicity and sincerity endeared it to people's hearts, and they joined in it on all patriotic occasions. It did not take long for other nations to appropriate the tune, so that this typical and original English air was used, at some time or other, by at least twelve other countries, including the United States and Germany.

Composers, too, admired the tune enough to incorporate it in their own works—Haydn in his "Emperor's Hymn" and Brahms in the "Triumphal Song." Beethoven was so deeply moved by it that he published seven variations on its theme and wrote in his diary, "I must show the English what a blessing they have in 'God save the King.'"

"Waltzing Matilda"

"Waltzing Matilda," Australia's most popular song, is based on a poem by "Banjo" Paterson, whose ballads express so vividly the early bushman's spirit.

Though of such comparatively recent date, "Waltzing Matilda" already shares with Britain's National Anthem uncertainty as to its real beginnings. Even its title has been a source of bewilderment and of various interpretations.

The poem is now a well-known description of the carrying of a swag. Yet in the earliest known use of the phrase, this did not speak of waltzing Matilda at all, but of walking Matilda. "Waltzing" is American slang and Mark Twain used it in the sense of a verb that meant to "carry" and to "transport."

Matilda, obviously, is a woman's name. No one knows why it was chosen to identify the swagman's bundle. This contained his sparse belongings and it is perhaps because of it that he called it endearingly by a personal name. Some, with lots of imagination, recognized in its outlines the shape of a woman. This fancy and the fact that he used to sleep with his swag may jointly account for the eventual choice of Matilda as the name of his portable luggage and sleeping companion.

Views differ as well as to what gave Paterson the inspiration to write his famous poem. Whilst he was staying at a friend's station near Winton in central Queensland, his host's daughter, Christine Macpherson, to pass the time, was playing her autoharp. Among the tunes was a very catchy one, which immediately caught "Banjo's" attention.

She had heard it at a Victorian race meeting, though actually it was an air with a long tradition. The melody of an old Scottish ballad, it had been adapted from a song, popular at the time of Marlborough among Kentish soldiers. Its words had been forgotten.

Paterson wanted to give the tune a new lease of life. All it needed was the right kind of lyric, appropriate for the Australian scene.

In search of a theme, he recalled an incident of the early 1890s. With two mounted police and an Aborigine, he had surprised a swagman camping under a coolabah tree beside a waterhole. The man, who had killed a sheep and wasted much of its carcass, was taken aback and feared arrest. Fully clad, he jumped into the hole, trying to escape. Unable to swim across, his water-soaked clothes dragged him down and he drowned.

Here was Paterson's opportunity to perpetuate the incident in song. A chance remark by the station overseer while "Banjo" was contemplating the new verses seemed to fit in. He told "Banjo" he had seen "a couple of men waltzing Matilda down at the billabong."

That is how the song, according to one tradition, took shape in Paterson's mind. It was first sung in public at the North Gregory Hotel at Winton, as a plaque there still testifies. It quickly caught the people's imagination and "Waltzing Matilda" became a favorite number of many bush singers. In 1903 Paterson sold the poem, together with other ballads he contemptuously described as "a lot of junk," to the firm of Angus and Robertson, and its eventual publication made the song popular throughout Australia.

The fact that it was being sung by Australian soldiers during the two World Wars on almost every battle front gave it world fame. Soon people of many countries came to identify "Waltzing Matilda" as Australia's National Anthem! This, of course, is incorrect. Australia's National Anthem is "Advance Australia Fair."

Another account also associates the creation of the song with Paterson's visit to his old friend at Dagworth Station. Driving into Winton with Macpherson's sister and a drover, they passed a man carrying a swag. "That's what we call Waltzing Matilda in these parts," Macpherson explained. The phrase so intrigued "Banjo" that, there and then, he jotted down his verses.

On their return to the property, Macpherson's sister, a musician, wrote the tune. And on that same night all of the company joined in the song which, ever since, has reverberated in the hearts of Australians.

"The Star-spangled Banner"

Few people realize that 117 years after its words had been written—on March 3, 1931—did an Act of Congress officially recognize "The Star-spangled Banner" as the nation's anthem.

Its story began in August 1814, when the British fleet was

anchored off Baltimore with William Beanes, an old doctor of Marlborough, Maryland, a prisoner in the flagship *Surprise*, which was commanded by General Ross. Francis Scott Key, his friend, a young lawyer and patriotic American, felt it his duty to come to the doctor's rescue.

Reaching the British fleet in a sloop, his passionate appeal for Beanes did not fall on deaf ears. General Ross acceded to his request. He could take his friend home—but not yet. The British were about to shell Fort McHenry, hoping to reduce it in no time. Therefore for Key's party to return to the mainland immediately might jeopardize the action, as naturally they would give due warning to their people. They would have to stay under guard on the sloop till the fortress had been captured.

Thus they were compelled to witness from afar the terrific bombardment. Anxiously throughout the day they watched the "Stars and Stripes" flying on top of the fortress, sometimes obscured by mist, drizzle and smoke. During the night, they continued to look for it, happy to recognize it whenever lit up by the burst of shells or the flash of guns.

When at last dawn came, with grateful hearts they could see that the flag was still flying. Obviously, the attack had failed, in spite of the boast by the English. Stirred to the very depths of his heart, it was then—on September 14, 1814—that Key composed the poem, writing down its words on the back of an envelope.

When the fleet was about to withdraw, Key and his party were allowed at long last to go ashore. He took his new poem with him. No wonder that it was immediately read by his friends who, equally deeply moved, had it printed at once and distributed as a handbill. Baltimore's daily paper printed it in its first issue after the city's liberation.

Still, it was merely a poem and not a song. But when Key wrote it on that glorious morning after a fearful night, he must have anticipated its tune. He certainly chose the right meter, fitting for an air that was then most popular. It belonged to a song which had come from England, where it had been used for the opening hymn at meetings of music lovers who had established clubs known as Anacreontic Societies. American soldiers celebrating their victory were joined in a city tavern by Francis Key who, exhilarated, read them his poem. An actor who was present got up on a chair and, on the spur of the moment, led them in song, choosing the melody Key had envisaged.

Within four days all Baltimore was singing it. It spread throughout the land. The original manuscript of the poem was sold for $24,000 at an auction in New York in 1933.

The Israeli Hymn

Though Israel can be regarded as one of the young modern nations, its national anthem preceded the new state by almost seventy years. It was written by an Austrian Jew who dedicated it—with other poems—to a Christian English friend.

Its words express the eternal Jewish hope of the fulfilment of ancient prophecy: the return of a rehabilitated and rejuvenated Jewish people to their ancestors' land. That is why, appropriately, the very title chosen for Israel's anthem is "The Hope."

The hymn was written by Naphtali Herz Imber, born in Galicia in 1856. At fourteen, he won a government prize for a Hebrew poem on a patriotic Austrian theme. Four years later he migrated to Vienna, but he did not stay there for long.

Always restive, he led the life of a wanderer, travelling through Hungary, Rumania and all over the Balkans, finally reaching Constantinople, where he met Laurence Oliphant, one of the most outstanding non-Jewish Zionists. Born of Scottish parents in South Africa, Oliphant became a member of the British House of Commons, a diplomat by profession and a successful novelist. However, the idea that dominated his life was the wish to re-establish the Jewish people in the Holy Land.

Imber and Oliphant became intimate friends, fervently sharing the Zionist dream. Together—in 1878—they went to Palestine. There Imber was greatly inspired by the early Jewish settlers who, in the midst of malaria-ridden swamps, had founded their first colonies, one of which they had called—quoting the prophet Hosea—"The Gate of Hope."

The name gave Imber the title and message for his poem. In nine stanzas he expressed the eternal longing of the Jewish heart: to dwell once again in the city where David had put his camp, to become "a free nation in Zion and Jerusalem."

A young pioneer in an adjacent colony set it to music and, in no time, it became the people's hymn. Its tune is that of both an old Spanish and Slav folk song, which can also be found in Smetana's tone poem *Die Moldau*. Spanish and Portuguese Jews had used the melody for one of their ancient Hebrew prayers, a supplication for dew.

Imber did not stay in Palestine either. When, in 1888, Oliphant died, after a sojourn in Britain, he proceeded to the United States. Associating with mystics there, he became interested in the Theosophical movement.

However successful Imber was in his literary work, there was no real happiness in his personal life. Eventually he took to drink. Taverns became his haunt. Rarely sober, drink did not make him amiable but quarrelsome with the result that even his friends could not bear with him any longer, making him still more bitter and cynical.

Typical was the incident at a Zionist meeting from which Imber, obstreperously drunk, had to be forcibly removed. When from outside the hall at the meeting's end, he heard the crowd join in his song, the cast-out drunkard, with shaking but triumphant voice, exclaimed, "They may kick me out, but they must sing my song."

Lonely and embittered, he died in 1909, aged fifty-three, in a New York hospital. He had a pauper's funeral, but the hymn did not die with him. It circled the world. First sung by the colonists in the Holy Land, it soon became the fervent expression of Jewish national aspiration in every country.

The fact that "Our Hope" *(ha-tikvah)* was sung by the world delegates attending the Sixth World Zionist Congress held in 1903 at Basle, Switzerland, gave the hymn official recognition. It was a foregone conclusion that at the declaration of Independence of the State of Israel, forty-five years later—in 1948—this Zionist song was to become the national anthem.

The Passport

The very name of the passport explains its (at least initial) purpose. It was issued to facilitate travelers' progress by helping them to pass safely through a port on their journey.

Passports go back to the most ancient civilizations. It has been suggested that even the Bible implied their existence in its story of

Abraham, when he sent Eliezer, his servant, to Mesopotamia to find there a wife for Isaac, his son.

Originally a passport was not a written document but a precious ring with the ruler's seal. Its possession secured the travelers' protection. Thus the Pharaohs of Egypt, likewise, gave their messengers a cartouche, an oval figure engraved with their royal name in hieroglyphic script.

The document was first given as a "Letter of Confidence" to subjects travelling on behalf of the king. It was actually referred to by his name as testified in a Greco-Roman papyrus of the second century B.C.

Roman Emperor Caesar Augustus is said to have furnished Potamon, a philosopher, with a certificate for safe conduct which did not mince its words. It read: "If there be anyone on land or sea hardy enough to wage war with Caesar." The wording thus anticipates by 2,000 years its modern text. Though couched in more diplomatic terms, a passport still serves the same purpose and requests and requires "all those whom it may concern to allow the bearer to PASS freely, without lack or hindrance, and to afford him (or her) every assistance and protection of which he (or she) may stand in need."

Rulers throughout the world (as far back as China over 1,000 years ago) deemed it their duty to control and protect the movement of their subjects. They also claimed, when necessary, the right to exclude other nationals from their territory. Eleventh-century King Canute is said to have been the first potentate to have issued documents to pilgrims en route to the tombs of St. Peter and St. Paul in Rome, with the express purpose of securing their safe passage through the many countries they had to traverse before reaching their destination. Copies of this early passport are still in existence.

That by 1215 passports must have been generally adopted in Britain is obvious from a clause of the Magna Carta, which provided that certain categories of persons might leave the country without such a document. This plainly implied that all others could not do so. This passport, a royal instrument, had, still in the days of Charles II, to be signed by the king himself. Yet eventually, and generally until World War I (excepting periods of unrest), passports were no longer needed for foreign travel. They were just helpful to establish a person's identity and nationality.

A Texan likened them to a pistol: "You didn't want it often, but when you did want it, you wanted it very badly."

The year 1914 changed all that. Passports became compulsory for going abroad, and in that same year photographs were first added to the British version. After the war passports remained essential. For centuries the passport was merely a thin sheet of paper, sometimes torn from a roll and still showing perforation marks at top and bottom. In 1921 the League of Nations introduced a uniform document which was adopted by almost every country. The ancient ring had become a booklet of thirty-two pages.

CHAPTER 17

Naval Customs

The tradition of the sea has widely and deeply influenced the English way of life, and nautical terms and customs abound in everyday talk and habits.

People who try "to make both ends meet" most probably do not realize that they are speaking in nautical terms. Many centuries ago, some frugal owners of sailing vessels were unwilling to replace broken ropes. They had the torn ends pulled together and spliced. Thus, by making both (of their) ends meet, they saved money.

Many people wonder why a ship is referred to as a "she." The explanation is that it was customary in early days to dedicate a new ship to a goddess, under whose protection she sailed. The ship carried the deity's carved image on her bow not as a decoration, as later generations imagined, but as an aid to finding the way.

Many customs and phrases "sail under false colors." Beneath their present meaning they hide surprising facts. It is well, therefore, "to know the ropes" (once, there were hundreds of them on board ship) and to "fathom" how it all started.

Consider the pilot. Navigating vessels safely into port, he received his name from the fact that he did so without use of the *peil-loth,* the lead-line.

Christening Ships

In spite of its apparent Christian association, the christening of a ship dates back to pre-Christian centuries and a pagan way of life. It is a relic of a rite of propitiation, when anxious sailors, afraid of the vagaries of the sea, tried to influence the divine powers controlling the oceans, to protect their ship and keep them safe.

To buy their goodwill, so to speak, the mariners bought the gods a drink. In ancient days, when a ship was completed, she was garlanded with flowers and the sailors wore floral crowns. And then, accompanied by loud acclamation to the gods, a pagan priest officiated at a ceremony. Equipped with a lighted torch, an egg and brimstone, he poured wine and oil on an altar erected on the ship, and dedicated her to the goddess whose carved image she was to carry.

Though no one believes in idols any longer and "divine figure-heads" have ceased to adorn and protect ships, the ancient libation is still carried on in the form of the christening ceremony. Some researchers have suggested that the modern way of shattering a bottle of champagne over the bow of a new ship has a link with the days when the Vikings and South Sea races invoked the protection of the sea gods on launching war galleys.

They did this by making a human sacrifice! Victims were bound to rollers over which the ship was launched, and blood from the broken bodies of the sacrificed spattered the ship. It explains why in civilized times blood-red wine preceded champagne as the christening beverage.

Modern authorities have vehemently decried as obnoxious and offensive the custom to call the naming of a ship her "christening." After all, to christen implied to make Christian, and the use of a bottle of wine for this purpose appeared like a parody of baptismal water.

Tattooing

Fascinating is the manifold and often odd use made of tattoo marks. On occasion they can be gruesome. A man once had a dotted circle tattooed around his neck with the inscription "Cut along the dotted line."

During World War I some "Tommies" expressed their aversion to the German emperor by having his image tattooed on their buttocks. A wealthy businessman in the United States ordered a tattooist to imprint hinges on all his joints. A famous doctor had his skin tattooed solely because the vibration of the needles soothed his nerves!

Perhaps the most ghastly tattoos of modern times were those with which Nazis branded their victims in concentration camps.

Tattoo is one of the few Polynesian words that have become part of the English language. The explorer Captain Cook introduced it in 1796 from the Tahitian language, in which it was used in the form of *tatau* to describe any kind of mark.

It has nothing to do with a military tattoo. In that use the word is derived from the Dutch *taptoe*, meaning "to turn off the tap of a cask." Tattooing by means of gashes or, in the modern technique, with small punctures filled with pigment, is an ancient and widespread custom. Fear of the unknown and of evil forces may have accounted for its first appearance. Tattoo marks were a kind of magic to protect people from the evil eye and sickness. Just as the ancient Britons painted their bodies with woad to strike fear into their foes, so tattoo marks were used to ward off intangible dangers.

However, many other and less frightening reasons were soon superimposed. They rendered the custom a permanent feature, continued even when people had outgrown their primitive superstitions and dreads.

Sex has dominated the human mind at all times. Therefore, it is no wonder that tattooing was soon believed to serve as a potent means to increase virility and sexual attraction.

Tattoos were used as well as tribal markings or professional emblems, as a sign of rank or caste and to indicate whether a man or woman was married or not. Sometimes tattoo marks served as a badge of courage, reminding both observer and "owner" of the pains suffered at the hands of the tattooer.

Again, some parents tattooed their children with the sign of a god to ensure his protection. Humans have always possessed an aesthetic sense. This urged them to add beauty (or what they considered as such) to life as they found it. Instead of looking for stones and trees to impose on them their artistic creations, did not their own bodies provide a readily available canvas? That is how in one culture tattooing became a form of artistic expression, a favorite way of bodily decoration.

People's innate desire to show off and impress others further fostered the custom. To have their etchings and paintings on constant exhibition made the "art" all the more popular. This way people could carry their masterpiece with them wherever they went—in fair weather and foul—and it was no burden at all!

Weighty utilitarian reasons as well were responsible, if not for the creation at least for the retention of those early tattoo marks. They were a lasting identification in time of war, so frequent in the annals of history. By their tattoo marks combatants could be easily recognized on the battlefield—whether dead or alive. They were the earliest type of uniform and surpass those of today in one respect at least—they never wore out. Traitors and fugitives could not disguise their identity as the marks labelled them permanently.

Going even further, the scars' special significance extended from this world to the next. The Hindus of Bengal, for instance, regarded tattoo marks in a vastly different light. They believed that a person without them would find it hard to enter heaven.

Though biblical legislation expressly stated that "you shall not make any cuttings in your flesh for the dead, nor print any marks upon you," tattooing became fashionable among Christian nations, including their sovereigns.

That sailors are fond of being tattooed (even King George V had himself tattooed as a young midshipman) has several reasons. Sailors are renowned for their superstitions and their love of the ladies. They maintained the ancient belief that tattoo marks made them all the more desirable and assisted them in their amorous adventures, especially so if their bodies depicted suitable subjects and legends.

Sailors first introduced the art of tattooing into the Western world from China, Burma and India. It is not surprising therefore, that they themselves preserved their new discovery. Finally, there was the constant but secret fear among mariners that one day they might be drowned and their bodies washed ashore beyond the possibility of recognition. Tattoo marks, which were always individualized, were a wise precaution to ensure identification in such unfortunate circumstance. The custom was fostered all the more by the additional superstition that the mere fact of being prepared for such ill luck would keep it away.

The Sailor's Bib

Most parts of the sailor's uniform have their interesting story, with their blue-and-white colors having a romantic association. It was chosen as the result of a king's admiration for a pretty horse-woman whose riding outfit was of those colors.

Contrary to popular belief, the three stripes of the sailor's collar (which itself served as a kind of antimacassar to keep his uniform from getting soiled by his greasy pigtail) are only decorative. They definitely were not meant, as frequently suggested, to mark a trio of famous victories by Admiral Lord Nelson.

The sailor's bib has been linked with Queen Victoria, her aesthetic sense and human susceptibility. It is said that when she inspected the Fleet at Spithead for the first time, she was deeply impressed—and said so. However, in her own private circle she later confessed that there had been one feature of the review which had rather upset her, namely the men's hairy chests. This criticism came to the ears of the Admiralty and when next she inspected the Fleet, the sailors' chests were covered by bibs. They have continued to be so ever since, with the bib having become an essential part of the naval uniform.

There is another and much more likely, though less colorful, explanation. Sailors were always expected to look spick and span. To have any part of their uniform sullied carried a penalty. On the other hand, in more distant days, clothes could be washed aboard ship only at certain stated hours, and these were few and far between. To add to the sailors' hardship, the frequent drill with greasy rifles inevitably soiled the men's uniforms, particularly their shirts.

Therefore, whatever they did, they could not do right. If they washed their shirts outside laundry hours, they were guilty. But if they did not do so and were seen dirty, they were punished as well.

They solved the shirt-washing problem by making a dicky. This was detachable from the rest of the uniform and could be washed, clandestinely, in a small basin.

It did not take long to detect the ruse. Wearing a dicky was made a punishable offense and some ships even introduced searches for dickies. Those found were confiscated and subsequently destroyed. In modern times as well, the navy did not recognize the dicky as part of a sailor's correct uniform. Thus, a man going on shore leave and found to be wearing a bib was dismissed from the shore-going party and made to replace his dicky with a shirt.

The Blue Peter

The Blue Peter, a blue flag with a white central square, is hoisted as a signal that a ship is about to sail.

Of the many and diverse explanations given as to its origin, only one—the most unlikely of all—assumes that Peter actually represents the name of a person. Admiral Sir Peter Parker was Chief of Command of the British navy between 1793 and 1799. Convoys used to sail from St. Helens, but they were not given the order to leave until the wind was fair. It was only then that, from Portsmouth, the Admiralty gave the signal. As it was known that Sir Peter himself issued the command for the hoisting of the blue flag, it was only natural that his name was coupled with it and sailors have referred to it as the Blue Peter ever since.

Others, however, detect in the Blue Peter a corrupted French word and a telling example of the British practice of assimilating foreign words to their own way of speaking. According to this tradition, Peter is not a name, but the Anglicized form of the French verb *partir*, for "to leave."

A further interpretation discovered in the flag a relic of the Old English portmanteau for a cloak bag. The signal was hoisted to inform all naval personnel that, as the sailing of their ship was imminent, they were to go aboard at once with all their baggage— their portmanteaus.

Slovenly speech among sailors was yet another reason given for the Blue Peter. Its name did not refer to admirals, mispronounced French expressions or ancient obsolete English words, but was a commonly used good English phrase. Once the signal of departure had been given by the admiral, it had to be repeated by all the ships under sailing orders, a procedure applied to every kind of naval signal. By swallowing just a small syllable, the Blue Repeater soon came to sound like Blue Peter.

The most likely explanation, however, belongs to the 1750s. On taking command, admirals used to issue instructions for their captains, detailing the various signals and flags to be employed. A flag book published by Sir Edward Hawke in 1756 listed a blue flag with six white balls.

Practical experience soon showed that this was a very unsatisfactory arrangement, as it was impossible to distinguish the six balls from a distance. This led Hawke to replace the flag with one which he described as "blue pierced with white."

Once again, it was said, lack of clear enunciation on the part of the naval men led to the corruption of the Blue Pierced into Blue Peter.

Some authorities suggested an intermediate stage, when the Blue Pierced was briefly referred to as the Blue P. Some sailors, ignorant of the real identity of the letter *P*, imagined it stood for Peter, which they spelled out.

Fathom

It was only natural that when people began to take the measure of things, they used their own body for comparison. With the foot they could step out any distance. The inch simply referred to the twelfth part of the foot's length. A cubit equalled the distance between the elbow and the tip of the middle finger. Whilst these units of measurement were factual and unexciting, it was left to the sailors to bring romance into the realm of calculations.

The fathom is the nautical measure of depth, now ruled to be exactly 6 feet. The well-known term comes from the Old English *faethm*, meaning "to embrace." Since an embrace of his sweetheart involved the whole length of a sailor's arms, averaging 6 feet , an Act of Parliament decreed that this fathom should become the standard measure for gauging the depth of the ocean!

A further development took place. As the extension of "a swain's arms around the object of his affections" (the actual words of the early statute) was now used to assess the depth of the sea, in an extension of meaning "to fathom" came to express, too, the desire to get to the bottom of things.

The Ship's Bell

A ship's bell is looked upon with almost reverential awe and considered so precious that it is preserved even after the ship has been broken up. This suggests that the bell once had a purpose beyond that of merely sounding the hour and calling sailors out of their bunks to duty.

This assumption is reinforced by the fact that, after all, the bell could not be heard in the bowels of a ship nor could it be imagined that sailors would wake up each time the bell was sounded, assiduously to count the number of its strokes, to ascertain whether their turn had come to go on watch. Actually, they are called on deck by word of mouth or a whistle.

Originally, the bell was used to repel nefarious forces of the ocean which followed ships, according to popular belief waiting for an opportunity to harm or destroy them. But they could not endure a loud clanging noise. Hearing it, they would scatter far and wide. Horsebells and those that once were attached to the hem of the High Priest's cloak initially served the same purpose— to scare away demons.

The Dog Watch

A sailor welcomes cats on board ship, as their diet of mice and rats suits both parties concerned. Dogs really have no place at sea. Nevertheless one speaks of a "dog watch."

However, there is nothing canine about the expression. The dog crept into it only by linguistic corruption. Members of the crew were divided into two watches—the starboard and the port. They went on duty alternately for four hours each. Soon it was realized that this division of time and service was neither practical nor fair. It could easily happen that the same men had the identical four-hour period every day.

To avoid this, the watch from four to eight in the late afternoon and early evening was halved into two short watches of two hours each, one from four to six and the other from six to eight. Thus the number of daily watches was increased from six to seven, an uneven number, which ensured a just rotation of duties.

For men to be called upon to do the same duty at the same time on the following day was now impossible. And as each watch would *dodge* a watch, it was called the dodge watch. Somehow its original purpose and meaning were forgotten, and the men came to speak of it as the dog watch.

No one likes to be associated, even in a manner of speaking, with dodging work. Sailors on guard might have found an affinity, and not merely a play on words, between a watch dog, in which capacity they really served, and a dog watch.

Crossing the Line

"Crossing the line" offers the modern tourist plenty of fun. A mock baptism, unique of its kind, awaits those who cross the equator for the first time. The ceremonial includes a court, held by Neptune, the ruler of the seas, and the victim's lathering, shaving and ducking. On conclusion a "baptismal certificate" records that the person in question has been duly initiated and, therefore, never again need undergo the ordeal.

Everything appertaining to the event is now part of the social program arranged on board ship to keep passengers busy and amused. And yet, it all started—centuries ago—as a most serious occasion.

Crossing the "line" was an auspicious event, not for the passengers but for the crew. The first description of the ceremony belongs to French sources and the year 1529, when the brothers Parmentier crossed the equator on a French ship.

Many important factors contributed to the introduction of the ceremony and its paraphernalia. Sailing was not safe at the time. Storms and calms alike were a constant threat to the lives and health of those manning ships. Sailing south of the equator presented additional hazards caused by the tropical climate, scarcity of drinking water, and stale food. It was a big event for any sailor who had never travelled so far before. First of all, therefore, the occasion was marked by a solemn service in which the men asked for divine protection in those insecure and still little-known regions. At the conclusion of the voyage, having safely arrived at their destination, they thanked God for having guarded them.

Though invisible in the ocean, the "line" was conspicuously marked on all maps. It played an important role in the mind of a sailor, as it showed where he entered the southern hemisphere. The fact that the equator could not be seen in the water, but was an imaginary line, gave its crossing an even more mysterious and mystical meaning.

Superstition and fear, always present in a sailor's life, soon attached themselves to the event. Somehow the equator's spirit had to be placated. To achieve this, sailors were ready to suffer ignominy, ridicule and even pain. They paid with them, as it were, for their safe passage.

Passing from the northern to the southern hemisphere was like entering a new world. Therefore, it was considered a sailor's graduation and attainment of maturity. Small wonder that he adopted a kind of initiation rite, as practiced in other trades and crafts. The baptism, like the christening of a child, signified his being admitted into the company of fully qualified seamen.

The rough and sometimes merciless (horse)play that accompanied the baptism belonged to all initiation rites. It was a test. The young and inexperienced sailor was "on trial" and had to prove his power of endurance, his courage and his indifference to physical and mental pain.

That is why, in early days, apart from the shaving and general humiliation, the ritual also included bodily chastisement and the throwing of the sailor from the deck into the sea. Having passed the ordeal, this test of manhood, he was presented with a certificate, stating that "it gives the god of the ocean particular pleasure to be able to say that during baptism he bore himself as a brave tar should."

The initiation soon came to serve other purposes as well. Voyages were protracted and could become boring, which did not exactly improve the morale of the crew. The rites of the crossing offered a welcome break from monotony and served, too, as a safety valve for the sailors, to let off steam. Discipline was rigid. The cat-o'-nine-tails was not just a figure of speech. It left its deep mark on many a sailor's body and mind. It was good, therefore, to create a temporary make-believe world where things were topsy-turvy and members of the crew could imagine for once that they were the masters and ruled the waves.

Paradoxically, the ceremony reinforced discipline. Every member of the crew had to conform. However ridiculous or meaningless the ritual appeared to him, he was not permitted to exclude himself from it. Whether he liked it or not, he could not break the tradition of the group to which he belonged.

Travelers entering a new country have to obey strict health regulations in order to keep out disease and infection. Before entering the southern hemisphere, sailors equally had to cross an—invisible—border, the equator. But, first of all, they had to be cleansed of all impurities, both physical and spiritual, and from the dirt of the north. Only then were they allowed to proceed.

Even the shaving part of the ceremony originally was not meant to be hilarious. To remove all of one's hair has always been part of initiation rites, on land and at sea. There was another significant factor. A youth who started sprouting a beard, and therefore needed a shave, had "grown up," just as a sailor who had crossed the "line."

Neptune with his trident (or a fishing spear) now belongs to the festive occasion. Actually he is a comparatively recent (English) newcomer. He was preceded by a French figure, whose duties he first shared and in later times appropriated. Neptune was the ancient Roman god of the water, identified with the older Poseidon, the Greek deity of the sea. He was, therefore, a most fitting figure to participate in the event. Yet, his first appearance was the result of the need to personify the invisible line of the equator. People just cannot live with an abstract idea. They need its symbolic expression in something tangible, such as a picture, an icon or, as here, a figure of flesh and blood.

The presentation of a certificate, also, had a practical purpose. To undergo the whole treatment was not pleasant. Once was sufficient. But how could anyone prove that he had been baptized before? He could do so only by producing documentary evidence. Hence sailors treasured and always carried with them their baptismal form. The document's frequent use wore out the paper and therefore only a few of the original copies have survived.

The Albatross

The albatross has been the companion of sailors on the high seas far back into history. When all other birds had left off following a ship, this largest of web-footed birds kept on circling it, now and then alighting on the ocean, perhaps dropping back for a while, but always reappearing. In a sense, it became a member of the crew, who regarded it with superstitious fondness.

Anxiously they looked out for its presence. This alone could explain the objection to killing the albatross. It was such a steady and loyal friend, whose company helped to relieve the monotony of sailing.

Imagination runs high on the lonely watches at sea. It is not known who the sailor was who first began to fancy that there was something mysterious about the way the bird clung to the company of a ship and showed such stupendous power, flying long distances against the wind, apparently without ever using its wings as a means of propulsion. From his musing sprang the haunting legend that the bird embodied the soul of a drowned sailor, clinging close to his own kind. From there it was only a logical step to believing that the killing of an albatross was unlucky. Perhaps, after all, thoughts of mere self-preservation could account for the superstition among sailors. The bird was so strong that tales were soon current that it had lifted up ship-wrecked sailors out of the sea and brought them to safety. To kill a potential rescuer was tantamount to suicide.

Making use of the tradition, the English poet Samuel Taylor Coleridge (1772–1834) in 1798 wrote a poem entitled "The Rime of the Ancient Mariner." It relates how, whilst at sea, one of the crew, the "old mariner," killed one of the great birds. Shortly afterwards, the ship became becalmed and ran out of drinking water before being able to reach port. Blaming the sailor, greatly angered, the rest of the crew punished him by hanging the dead bird around his neck.

The account of the incident led to the custom of referring to anything that causes trouble or worry, as well as a problem that is difficult to solve, as "having an albatross around one's neck."

"Tell it to the Marines"

To express disbelief in a claim or a statement, the informant is asked to "tell it to the marines." People have often wondered how it came that these valiant men, specially praised by Rudyard Kipling, should be considered so gullible.

Most probably, it all started as a natural dislike of experienced sailors for newcomers—troops serving on board ship. These might excel on dry land, but seemed completely out of their depth at sea.

Britain led the way in stationing groups of soldiers aboard ship. These were soon referred to as the Royal Marines. They represented a new and significant development in military strategy, though to start with, sailors resented them.

Proud of their own tradition of service and knowledge of the sea, they looked down on the marines as landlubbers. What did they know of the hazards of the ocean? They could be told anything and, in their credulity and lack of experience, would believe it. Naive in matters of sailing, they would swallow any tale.

That is how empty bottles were nicknamed "marines." To the sailor, often keen on his drink, they served no purpose. They only took up precious space. Another explanation is much kinder, though equally old. It goes back to Samuel Pepys, the famous diarist, who also served under Charles II as Secretary of the Admiralty.

One day he told the king about a naval captain who had alleged that, on a cruise through the Red Sea, he had brought up with his anchor a wheel of one of Pharaoh's chariots, sunk there in Moses's time. He also claimed that, while sailing in the southern seas, he had frequently met with shoals of fish "flying in the air."

The king laughed heartily. It was just unbelievable. Who had ever heard of flying fish? It so happened that during this conversation between King Charles and Pepys, an officer of the newly raised Maritime Regiment of Foot was standing nearby. The king called him over, asking his opinion. "What do you say, Colonel, to a man who swears he had seen fishes fly in the air?" he inquired.

The sea-soldier was not at all surprised. His reply confirmed what the captain had said. "I should say, sir," he answered, "the man has sailed in the southern seas. For when Your Majesty's business carried me thither of late, I did frequently observe more flying fish in one hour than the hairs on my head in number."

Having listened to the marine confirming the story, the king, now convinced that there were flying fish, addressed Pepys again. "From the very nature of their calling, no class of our subjects can have so wide a knowledge of seas and lands as the officers and men of our loyal Marine Regiment. Henceforth, ere ever we cast doubt upon a tale that lacketh likelihood, we will first tell it to the Marines."

That is how, according to this version, the phrase was first introduced by none other than Charles II. Obviously, it was then meant not as a slur at all. On the contrary, the king intended to convey by it that, if his marines would believe a story, he could do so as well. After all, they had served in all parts of the world and observed there many strange sights unknown to anyone else.

The "Senior Service"

The Royal Navy is known as the Senior Service. Most people imagine, wrongly, that the expression highlights the fact that the navy preceded both the army and the air force.

Actually, the term first became current in the seventeenth century during the rise of the East India Company. Many of the Company's trading ships not only were better than those of the Royal Navy, but offered much higher pay. As a result, a number of officers relinquished their commission in the navy and joined East India Company vessels which, for many years, were the finest even among merchant ships.

Nevertheless, compared with the Royal Navy, the East India Company's fleet was a mere newcomer. It was in recognition of this fact that the Royal Navy was spoken of first as the "Senior Service."

CHAPTER 18

In the Army

Churchill said that "the story of the human race is war. Except for brief and precarious interludes, there has never been peace in the world."

As long as can be remembered, people have fought for their lives, property and country. The earliest monuments celebrate victories. History, to a large degree, is nothing but a record of innumerable battles, defeats and conquests.

Military traditions and customs are the pride of every army and country. They express and reinforce the spirit and discipline of a nation and have contributed in great measure to the whole pattern of life—to the vocabulary, phrases, customs and even dress. However, in most cases the original influence was exerted so far away and so long ago that nowadays it is concealed in a perfect kind of camouflage.

Etymologically speaking, all soldiers are mercenaries. Their name recalls the (Latin) "money" or, originally, "salt," paid them for their services. Privates owe their (verbal) existence to the ancient Romans as well. They were men "deprived" of rank or office.

The modern tank is camouflaged, even in its name, which was specially chosen in December 1915 during World War I to mislead the enemy and make them believe that the oblong monsters, then being manufactured and assembled, were innocuous water containers.

The Chinese have a keen sense of humor. They invented gunpowder and found its best use in making firecrackers to celebrate their grandfathers' birthdays. Similarly, nitroglycerine was introduced by a French chemist in 1847, not as an explosive but as a remedy for headache!

Nothing is too costly for war. The latest inventions are first applied for defense and attack. Yet in its martial aspect, modern war shows its primitive roots and its link with ancient superstitions, polytheism and astrology. The term "martial" itself is derived from Mars, the Roman god of war.

Khaki

Khaki is a Hindustani word meaning "dust." The very name of Britain's earliest uniforms thus points to the scene of their origin. They were first used during the Indian Mutiny (1857–58). An irregular corps of Guides raised at Meerut adopted the color and was appropriately referred to as "the Khaki (dust) Squadron."

To protect themselves against native snipers, who excelled as marksmen, the soldiers dyed their white drill with curry powder or the mud and dust (*khak*), available in huge quantities at the site of action. It was soon realized, however, that this primitive kind of "khaki" was not colorfast or weatherproof. It also spoiled the spotless white uniforms and wasted a lot of time, as the process of dyeing had to be carried out repeatedly with officers feeling the urgent need for ready-made battledress in khaki color.

When, in 1883, a Mr. Leeman, as the representative of a Manchester cotton firm, went to India to sell cloth, he met a Colonel Kinlock who related to him his problems, suggesting that if he could find a way to produce cotton cloth of khaki color that was fadeproof and resistant to frequent washing and weather changes, he would profit both the army and himself.

On his return to England, Leeman and F. A. Gatty, a Lancashire dyer, began experiments, with his wife's kitchen serving as their laboratory. They boiled samples of khaki cloth in Mrs. Leeman's copper pans, but somehow none of their efforts was successful. Though the color was all right, it faded when exposed to the sun for any length of time.

Chance eventually led to success. On one occasion Mrs. Leeman was cooking dinner, with all the pots being used. Not prepared to wait till at least one of them would be available, the two men boiled a piece of cloth in a rusty old pan. The dye they used, oxide of chromium, was fixed by the oxide of the iron from the rusty pan.

From then on khaki had come to stay. The two friends formed the firm of F. A. Gatty and Co. which for more than fifty years enjoyed a monopoly in supplying the British forces with their khaki battledress. The cloth was no longer used in India alone, but in many places throughout the empire, wherever British soldiers were sent to keep the peace or to restore order. It was not until the Boer War in 1899, however, that the khaki battledress was universally adopted.

The Baton

Several traditions account for the officer's baton. Today a symbol of authority, practical considerations were responsible for its use first of all.

The baton was an aid to the good manners expected in army leaders. Carrying the stick prevented the officer from uncouthly putting his hands into his pockets. As to point with the finger was impolite, especially for an officer, to do so with a stick was deemed becoming. In addition, grasping the baton prevented him from fidgeting with his hands—commonly decried as bad taste. Just as in some countries modern policemen may carry truncheons for use at close range, so the baton served also as a weapon of defense.

All these explanations are of comparatively recent date. Actually, the baton recalls much earlier times, when it was an ever-present means of enforcing discipline. A General Order of 1702 prescribed "swagger sticks" for the British officer. Equipped with them, he could administer on-the-spot punishment to any recalcitrant soldier. Up to twelve strokes were inflicted for minor offenses, which included such violations of regulations as "giving officers a cross look," "sneezing in the ranks" or "scratching one's head."

Authorities agree that the baton developed from an ordinary bludgeon, carried by Teutonic races, and that, going back even further, it is a survival of the sacrificial axe of prehistoric man.

The Drum-major's Staff

Bands have accompanied armies for centuries, their music meant to raise the men's spirits and make them march all the better and always in step.

Though music has been used from earliest times in the service of war and soldiers, it was only in the seventeenth and eighteenth centuries that military bands were properly organized. The drum-major's ornate staff has a conspicuous place in an army's life in the way it is used in the role it plays. People have always admired the deft way it is whirled, tossed into the air and caught. The staff, too, goes back at least to the eighteenth century. Napoleon's drum-majors particularly were renowned for their spectacular use of it. No one should imagine, however, that it was employed merely to give a grandiose display to onlookers. It came into being for important, practical considerations.

The band had to be properly conducted, but to do so in the usual way was out of the question. On the march, the men had to see the conductor's directions. He certainly could not move along with them raised on a platform or march backwards in order to face the musicians.

Thus the staff originated as a sort of extended baton, whose flights and air-acrobatics were essential to conduct the band's playing. Its travelling through the air was not haphazard and followed well-thought-out courses. It controlled starts, halts and stops, and the rhythm and volume of the music.

There was an even more significant purpose the staff fulfilled. The loud music made it impossible for the men to hear any given command. A shouted "right wheel," for instance, would go unheard and unheeded. Therefore, the staff's further function was to convey all marching orders visually.

The Busby

A high fur cap of cylindrical shape, with a bag of colored cloth hanging from the top and often coming down to the right shoulder, made up the original busby which ultimately was reserved for purely military wear. Its early beginnings lead back to much less martial associations.

No one really knows the derivation of its name, which has been linked with various places and people. A village in Yorkshire, England, called Busby led people to assume that the famous hat was conceived there. On the other hand, as a Dr. Richard Busby, who served as Master at Westminster School from 1606–95, has been credited with the invention of the hat, it was thought that in acknowledgment it was given his name. Yet another suggestion linked the term with a family of that name and renowned as hatters about the time the conspicuous headdress was first introduced.

Actually, the busby is Hungarian by birth. Originally worn there as a peasant's cap, it was made almost exclusively of red cloth with its only furry part being a band around the edge. In time the furry rim was rendered wider and bigger, until it reached the height of the modern busby. Inevitably this reduced the space that would be allotted to the cloth until there was no room left for it except as a covering of the top, a last reminder of the original busby.

The Hungarian army adopted the peasant's cap, but reserved it for its most illustrious forces and it became the badge of Hungary's cavalry regiment, known as the Hussars. From them the British took it over.

The little flap which hangs from the busby is not, as might appear, merely decorative. Formerly it was attached to the Hussar's right shoulder and padded with cotton, meant to act as an effective buffer against sword cuts.

Medals on the Left Side

With few exceptions, medals are worn on the left breast. Today, this regulation aims, first, at uniformity and trimness.

Obviously the fact that this military tradition is observed by the armies of every nation points to a common origin. This can be traced to the Crusaders who treasured the emblem of the Order in whose name they fought and, therefore, wore it nearest the heart.

Practical considerations as well influenced the choice of position. The left arm carried the fighter's shield which thus guarded the heart and kept the right arm free to wield a weapon. To protect the badge of honor, this was placed behind the shield—on the left side of the soldier.

The White Feather

Linguistically the effect of cockfighting extends to terms relating to weapons and to concepts such as cowardice and bravery. To "show the white feather" thus became identified with faint-heartedness and proving oneself a coward.

During World War I patriotic women used to present men staying away from the fighting front with a white feather. Everyone knew what it meant, though an alternative theory suggests a different origin.

The best fighting cocks were of a pure breed and had coats of black and red feathers. Inferior birds, which lacked courage, were of mixed blood. This could be recognized by a white feather in their tail. No matter which explanation is correct, both agree that the white feather as a symbol of weakness and lack of daring comes from the cockpit.

The Emblem of the Rising Sun

It is an interesting fact that the Rising Sun, symbol of the Australian forces, originally had nothing to do with either the rising or, as some disgruntled soldiers would have it, the setting sun. This eliminates the otherwise surprising paradox that Australians should have chosen as their military symbol a motif traditionally Japanese.

The customary interpretation that the badge was meant to represent the young nation as rising out of the Southern Seas, however beautiful and patriotic, is equally incorrect. In reality, the apparent rays of the sun are the blades of swords and bayonets, and the solar body originally was a stained piece of wood.

When the first Commonwealth contingent was about to be formed, in 1902, for service in South Africa, the military commander, General Sir Edward Hutton, felt that a distinctive badge should be chosen for the battalion. He invited his staff to submit ideas. Most of the suggestions made use of the Australian flora and fauna. But Sir Edward deemed the proposed emus and kangaroos, waratahs and wattles unsuitable, as they lacked martial significance. Rejecting the designs, he pointed to a trophy of arms over the doorway of his office in Melbourne's Victoria Barracks. It consisted of a semicircular red board, which carried a crown and half-circle of bayonets and swords. Something like that would be much better, he said. His advice was regarded as an order, and a Melbourne engraver was commissioned to design an emblem embodying the general's suggestion. Duly executed and approved by the military authorities, it was produced in sufficient numbers for all the men of the First Battalion. The emblem has become a motif of Australian valor, though under an erroneous name.

The Digger

It is surprising how the origin of even modern traditions and usages is sometimes doubtful and shrouded in mystery. That applies to the Australian term "digger."

It is commonly accepted that it first referred to the miners on the goldfields of the 1850s. English people then generally regarded all Australians as diggers for gold and rolling in wealth. That the word became the description of the Australian soldier has been linked with the South African War, though no record confirms this. Much more feasible and widely accepted now is the claim by Charles Everitt of Birdgrove (NSW), that he introduced the term in its modern connotation. However, gold diggers were then furthest from his mind. He was stationed with the 17th Battalion at Gundagai Post on the Sinai Peninsula. "All we did," he recalled, "was dig trenches."

Drifting sand made the work almost futile and again and again they had to dig the same trenches. "We aren't soldiers, we're diggers!" he complained. Use of the term soon became common throughout the Middle East and the soldiers of the AIF adopted it as the proud title now emblazoned in the annals of Australian history.

The Slouch Hat

Uniforms were introduced as a means of identification. In the heat of battle, they helped those fighting to distinguish between friend and foe. Psychologically, they created a sense of belonging and greatly assisted in the discipline of an army. As time went on, further practical considerations were responsible for innovations and developments in the soldiers' dress. The slouch hat and its peculiar way of being turned up on the left side owes it origin to that purpose.

Now a conspicuous part of the Australian uniform, "diggers" wore it years earlier in the South African War. It is said to have originated in Burma.

The turned-up side is due not to any kind of affectation or the wish to appear smart. It dates back at least to the 1880s and the Victorian Mounted Rifles. Their headgear, however, was turned up on the right. To them, this was essential for effective combat.

The rifles then used—of the Marini-Henry type—were very cumbersome and, when soldiers were shouldering arms, the muzzle usually caught the brim of the hat. To avoid this, the obvious thing to do was to wear it with that side turned up. Rifles and muzzles today are streamlined. Yet the turned-up slouch hat of the Australian soldier remains in service and recalls an early precaution in military drill.

ANZAC

ANZAC is one of Australia's most sacred words, expressing a spirit of heroic values and sacrifice. Yet few of the very men who landed on Gallipoli had ever heard the word, which their actions were to immortalize. According to one claim, it was not even an Australian, but an Englishman who coined it.

There was no emotional quality or military glory attached to the expression when it was first introduced. It was born as a mere code-word, to replace the cumbersome title of the Australian and New Zealand Army Corps.

Soon after the outbreak of World War I, Australia's special volunteer army for overseas service was formed. Named by General Bridges "the Australian Imperial Force," it is best known by its initials as the (First) AIF.

It was sent to Egypt, where Poona-born General Birdwood was appointed to establish and command a joint Army Corps of Australian and New Zealand troops. He intended to call it the AAC, standing for Australian Army Corps, but then agreed, as was only fair, to include New Zealand's name. Thus the title Australian and New Zealand Army Corps came into existence, with its printed stationery headed A & NZ Army Corps.

The new name became even more familiar to those who frequented headquarters at Cairo's famous Shepheard's Hotel, as numerous boxes stored outside the clerks' room carried the Corps' title. Those in charge of communications soon realized how tedious it was to use the long string of words. To register correspondence, therefore, two sergeants cut out a rubber stamp bearing just the initials A.&N.Z.A.C. In no time the clerks started referring to it as their ANZAC stamp.

There are other suggestions as to how the abbreviation came about. One morning Major Wagstaff had called at the office and asked the men whether they could think of how suitably to shorten the extended title of the Corps. Sergeant K. M. Little, trying to recollect in later years what happened, asserted, "We all had a shot and *I* suggested ANZAC."

His claim was contradicted by Lieutenant A. T. White, a member of the English Army Service Corps. With equal sincerity he alleged that it was he, also a clerk in the office when Major Wagstaff made his request, who—with the rubber stamp in mind—had called out, "How about ANZAC?"

No matter to whom the merit really belongs, New Zealander or Englishman, sergeant or lieutenant, the fact is that the major immediately took a liking to the new word. He passed it on, in January 1915, to his superior, General Birdwood, who approved of its choice and ANZAC was thus adopted as the Corps' official code-name, though no one at the time could guess the part it was going to play in the destiny and history of the Australian people.

Anzac Day

To prolong the weekend period of rest and recreation, Australians move most public holidays to a Monday. Not so Anzac Day, which is always celebrated on April 25, and with good reason. The day commemorates the first great action of the AIF—the Gallipoli landing—and has become symbolic of Australians and their way of life.

Anzac Day was celebrated for the first time in 1916, the first anniversary of the landing, and by those very troops whose valor made Anzac Day a date not to be forgotten.

The celebration took place not in Australia but at Serapeum in the Suez Canal Defense Zone, where the forces, returned from

Gallipoli, were stationed. General (Sir) John Monash himself participated in the organization of the festivities that marked the first Anzac Day.

The event had been looked forward to with much anticipation. Manning of the Canal's defenses could not be neglected and there was much disappointment among units and officers allotted this task. The rest of the troops, however, made it a real holiday.

Whoever had served on Gallipoli wore a blue ribbon on the right breast and those who had taken part in the historic landing a red ribbon as well. Writing home, Monash regretfully noted, "Alas, how few of us are left who are entitled to wear both."

A short, dignified service was followed by "The Dead March in Saul," played by massed bands, after which all bugles joined in "The Last Post." The rest of the day was free and all work ceased.

The morning was spent at cricket or in other amusements. In the afternoon the whole division went down to the Canal to swim and participate in a great aquatic carnival. From the Serapeum pontoon bridge, both sloping banks of the Suez Canal, for about a mile, were a teeming mass of naked humanity. At times, there were more than 15,000 men in the water.

Championship events commenced at 15:00 hours. A special program for the occasion was printed in Cairo. This listed a race across the canal (about 100 yards) followed by plunges and underwater swimming, as well as a competition on the greasy pole and relay races.

A fifth event was entitled "The Bellman." A man with a bell or whistle dived into the water. Competitors were blindfolded and had to swim after the sound of the bell or whistle. Whoever caught the bellman first, won. If no one was able to get hold of him within sixty seconds, he himself received the prize.

Later in the afternoon the Prince of Wales joined the soldiers and enjoyed the fun so much that he stayed for more than an hour. Concerts concluded the celebrations and wishes were exchanged that there would be other opportunities of "enjoying many happy returns of this famous day—OUR DAY."

This wish came true. What took place in 1916 as almost a spontaneous commemoration, subsequently was given official standing. Eventually, April 25 was set aside as a public holiday and a solemn Day of Remembrance not only for those who fought and fell at Gallipoli, but for all who gave their lives in the two World Wars and subsequent clashes of arms.

Three Volleys over the Grave

Fear of haunting originally led to the firing of volleys over a soldier's grave. People were afraid that an evil spirit might attach itself to the dead person. Only the loudest possible noise would frighten it away. The identical explanation applies to the tolling of a bell at funerals.

Material virtues soon rationalized and militarized the ancient superstition. Soldiers were used to the sounds of battle. To fight for their country and hear the booming of guns represented to them the essence of life. To fall in battle was a glorious end. Thus, the last volleys tried to re-create an atmosphere of war and to convey an impression that the dead soldier was going to a life beyond on an occasion of battle, that to the very end he was doing his duty.

Belief in the Holy Trinity is responsible for the actual number of volleys fired. Just as a child the soldier had been baptized in the name of the Father, the Son and the Holy Ghost, so now at his death he was blessed by the symbol of Trinity, this time expressed not in words but by their military equivalent. The firing takes place after the solemn words: "Earth to earth, ashes to ashes and dust to dust."

CHAPTER 19

The Origin of Sporting Terms and Pastimes

People have had their hobbies from earliest times and even Adam is said to have dug in his garden as a pastime. They do not merely extend far back into history, they reach into human nature and may serve as an indication of character. To know what someone is really like, one has only to observe what they are doing when they have nothing to do.

Civilization has been rightly defined as what people do with their leisure time. A nation's or individual's hobbies reveal their culture, education and refinement—or their lack. They range from bull-baiting, cock-fighting and horse-racing to reading, mountain-climbing and chasing after (nonexistent) leprechauns.

In his *Conquest of Happiness* Bertrand Russell described the ability to fill leisure hours intelligently as the very best product of civilization. Unfortunately, however, progress has led to the development of more and more machines providing more and more people with more and more leisure time in which to be bored.

As games and sports have always been part of life, they have enriched language in numerous ways. From the cockpit arose not only "showing the white feather" but also "crestfallen." To "throw in the sponge" comes straight from the boxing ring. Similarly, "beating about the bush" and "running riot" are originally hunting terms.

Of all hobbies one of the most fascinating and entertaining is the pursuit of their origin.

Chess

Chess has been called "the game of kings" and, indeed, its name comes from the French *eches*, in turn derived from the Arabic *shah*, for "king." Today chess is considered a game for the most peaceful of people. In fact, monastic orders introduced it to break the monotony of their life. However, it was invented in India in the seventh century A.D. as a game of war: to illustrate and rehearse army movements. It is thus not surprising that at one time, and not so long ago, the playing of chess was regarded a valuable pursuit in the training of Russian soldiers.

Even the name retains its martial beginnings, as it has been linked with the Indian *Chaturanga*, meaning "consisting of four divisions." These were the four kinds of troop formations that made up the traditional Indian army: infantry, cavalry, chariots, and elephants. Added to them, as was only to be expected, was the supreme commander in the person of the king, and his minister.

The names of the pieces, as they are known now, hardly remind one of the field of battle. This is not the result of intentional camouflage of the soldiers but due to the development of language and the moves of chess through many lands.

Persia took over the game from India. When the Arabs conquered Iran, they made chess part of their life to carry it wherever they went. That is how, with the spread of Islam, chess came to extend as far west as Spain, as far north as Turkestan, as far east as the Malayan Islands, and as far south as Zanzibar. It did not take long to advance from the Muslim countries into those of Christian Europe. Italians, the French and the English adopted many of the original terms for the pieces. Whenever they knew their meaning, they simply translated them into their own tongue. But if the meaning was obscure to them, they retained the foreign words, which might still baffle the uninitiated. The pawn, the piece of smallest size and value, may well represent the infantry. The medieval French word for the footsoldier, it is derived from the Hindu description of an attendant. The rook, on the other hand, literally recalls the ancient Persian armed chariot.

The Italians determined to change the battlefield into a model state. For that purpose they did not even desist from changing sex—at least on the chessboard. The minister was made the queen of today. Then, perhaps remembering how thick-skinned politicians must be, they converted the original Oriental elephant into an elder of state, not inappropriate in ecclesiastic Italy, represented by a bishop.

Of all the terms of the chessboard, checkmate—the declaration of final victory—is the most interesting. It has become part of everyday speech, expressing the thwarting of effort and the foiling or outwitting of others. "Checkmate" is the traditional exclamation by which a player announces having put the opponent's king into a position from which he cannot escape from being captured. The word could not be more explicit, if it is realized that it retains (though in Anglicized form) the original Arab victory cry "The King is Dead," check being the corrupted Arab title for a king—*Shah*—and mate the Arab's description of all that is "dead"—*mat*.

There are other, and much earlier, claims about the invention of chess. Some give the credit to the ancient Egyptians, doing so by an interpretation of early wall paintings from the time of one of the Pharaohs called Ramses II. A further suggestion has it that, as in so many other things, the Chinese first enriched the world with this game of skill. They designed it to help their soldiers pass the time in their winter quarters. Perhaps because of his proverbial wisdom, King Solomon is asserted to have been the first chess player, just as Aristotle, the Greek luminary in the field of philosophy, has been called the father of chess.

Dice

One of the root causes of gambling is the innate love of taking a chance. The modern fruit machine is the latest robot to serve an urge that has possessed people from the beginning of history. Even the Bible tells of the drawing of lots to determine human fate.

People gamble not merely to acquire money but as an escape. They need stimulus and nothing spurs them on more than an opportunity of getting something for nothing.

Modern society, with its streamlined life and mechanization, has created boredom in unprecedented measure. Gambling relieved people's tensions, trying to give some taste to a dull existence of everyday routine. Gambling is the artificial adventure for those unable to find the real adventure of life.

Dice-throwing is one of the most ancient of games. It was even enjoyed in primitive times. And yet, apart from a few refinements, it has changed little for more than 5,000 years. The earliest dice were in the simple form of knucklebones and pebbles.

The antiquity of the game is documented by countless finds all over the world, in graves, on inscriptions and in historic records. Cheating at dice is almost as old as the game itself. Ancient loaded dice have been found more than once.

The earliest dice were of two kinds and accordingly marked— those that promised good fortune and others that brought ill luck. Ancient Egyptians stamped their dice with small circles, each representing a unit. One of the most popular Greek games, especially among women, was played with five knucklebones. Simultaneously thrown into the air, the player tried to catch all of them on the back of one hand. If any of them dropped to the ground, an attempt had to be made to pick them up with the same hand, without dislodging those already caught.

Soon the four sides of the knucklebones were marked by four faces, so that there was no possibility of confusing them. The first face was convex, the second concave, the third almost flat, and the fourth a profile. Eventually, other materials replaced the rather macabre bone or primitive pebbles. Substitutes were of stone, wood, ivory, bronze, lead and sometimes amber.

Yet, in reality, originally the game of dice was not just a kind of amusement. It was believed that dice revealed the will of the gods! The way they fell showed their favor or disapproval, predicted success or failure, victory or defeat.

Playing Cards

The devil himself has been credited with the invention of playing cards. However, that assertion and all it implies is rather unap - preciative of the good cards have done, notwithstanding their obvious evil. They have provided people with relaxation and, as psychologists have pointed out, even more so, have helped them to direct their aggressive instincts into innocent channels.

One tradition claims that society owes playing cards to itiner- ant gypsies who had first devised them for their fortune-telling. The fact that a French craftsman was commissioned in 1392 to paint a set of cards for Charles the Mad led to a third suggestion— that cards originated as a kind of occupational therapy. They had been invented to soothe the king's nerves—whenever he had a bout of insanity.

Actually, playing cards stem from China, where they first appeared more than 1,000 years ago. A claim that they had been invented during the reign of twelfth-century Emperor Seun-Ho to keep his concubines amused is probably nothing but malicious gossip.

The Chinese used cards made from various kinds of wood or plant fiber. Simple in design, they were painted in rich colors. From the East, cards eventually reached Europe via Arabs.

Some of the oldest specimens of cards in existence came from Venice. They, too, were painted, but lacked numerals and special names. At first, the European cards pictured a whole galaxy of emblems and figures, which included the sun, the moon and a star; the emperor and empress; the wheel of fortune; Justice; "the lovers" and "the hanging man." They also showed the fool, the mountebank and the devil.

Only then did people start to number the cards and divide them into suits. These distinguished cups (representing faith), swords (justice), money (charity) and clubs (fortitude). The painting of cards became a special craft and their supply a monopoly and—for the state—a special source of revenue by taxation.

From Italy and Spain cardplaying spread to France, where it created an industry. Though there is no record of the date on which cards were introduced into Britain, they certainly were known there by 1480. A royal decree, issued fifteen years later, prohibited cardplaying by servants and apprentices, except during the Christmas holidays. Yet even the Puritans could not suppress the love of the game. King James I, who was an addict, had two courtiers in constant attendance, one to hold his cards and the other to suggest which one to play.

Cards were now elaborately decorated and illuminated with gold and silver. With the passing of time and the increased popularity of the game, the original simple collection of cards thus became numerous and complicated. Eventually, however, the pack was again reduced and limited to the present number of fifty-two, apart from the joker, with various countries adopting their own names and figures.

Spain and Portugal retained the original Italian cups, swords, money and batons. The Germans and other northern European nations preferred to have hearts, bells, leaves and acorns. From France, England chose hearts, diamonds, spades and clubs.

Practical considerations were responsible for a further development. Painted cards were rather expensive and not easy to shuffle, so people began to have them stencilled and, finally, printed. They were bought not in ready-made packs but in sheets, with several cards printed on each of them, to be cut out by the players.

In the excitement of the game, some players were at a disadvantage. As those sitting on the "opposite" side could not at once recognize a card's value when it was thrown onto the table, an ingenious Frenchman in the nineteenth century thought of a remedy. Instead of picturing a whole-length picture, he introduced the double-headed one, equally recognizable from either side of the table.

Though present-day playing cards evolved from the early fortune-telling pack, they differ in various aspects and reveal interesting changes and adaptations.

Originally, the king, queen and knave, because of the elaborate robes they wore, were known as "coat" cards. It was so easy to err in this case by their association with the royal court. Soon they were mispronounced and erroneously called "court" cards, which they have remained ever since.

The modern "trump" goes back much further. It is a telling monument of early triumph in warfare, recalling the triumphal processions by which Roman generals celebrated their victories. The pictures on the cards were never updated and thus continue to reflect the fashion, the way of life and symbolism of the time in which the cards came into existence.

To begin with, the four suits were meant to represent the four social classes which made up medieval society. The present-day "clubs," "hearts," "spades" and "diamonds" are a later evolution and partially a misunderstood interpretation of the early designs. To indicate the four strata of society for which they stood, these showed chalices for the clergy, swords for the nobility, coins for the merchants and staffs or wands for the peasantry.

In spite of their apparent appropriateness, the "spades" have nothing to do with the agricultural tools used to dig up the ground. From the Spanish *espada*, it referred to the "sword" and as such symbolized the warrior class. Oddly, the English retained the old Spanish word and possibly did so because the shape of this sword looked very much like a spade.

The early chalice or communion cup was not retained. It was replaced by the heart. It is not certain what actually caused this substitution. Some believe that it was to express the supreme position of ecclesiastical power. Were not the bishops and clergy the very "heart" of the community? Their station in life would bring home the message so much better than a communion cup. "Clubs" were not, as the word might suggest, wooden implements used as weapons. They were trefoil symbols, meant to remind the player of the three-leafed clover, and thus represented the peasant, significantly doing so in a luck-spelling way of the trinity. "Diamonds" seem so plainly to be associated with the moneymaking merchant class. But they, too, are not what they appear to be. They recall the checkred floor of diamond-shaped stones of the exchanges where the important business trans-actions took place.

Few players realize that in every pack one of the aces is specially ornamented. There was a valid and costly reason for this and, to players at the time the "decoration" was first introduced, not a welcome one.

Governments, always anxious to raise funds, do so primarily by raising taxes and never seem to be at a loss to find new avenues for their revenues. Eighteenth-century Britain put a levy on playing cards and, adding insult to injury, the duty stamp was incorporated artistically inside the ace of spades which thus metaphorically dug into players' pockets. That the tax has been paid for a pack of cards is nowadays indicated by a sticker on the wrapper outside. Nevertheless, the modern packs retain the original "tax receipt," and it continues to take part in every game and in cartomancy in general.

The earliest European cards preserved (of which there are alto-gether seventeen) stem from a pack painted in Paris in 1392 for therapeutic purposes. They had been made for King Charles the Mad of France in the first stages of his mental sickness. It was hoped that they would help to relax and distract his mind. Despite the unfortunate circumstances, the mere fact that cards played some part in the royal household gave them standing and led to their vast popularity.

Their association with both gambling and divination, however, caused their use to be prohibited by official edicts. The ban was welcomed by many. Aristocrats had lost huge sums of money gambling with them and were threatened with bankruptcy.

Unfaithful spouses and corrupt officials in high quarters, believing in the efficacy of the new art of cartomancy, feared that the "pack" might bring to light what they tried to keep dark: their adulteries and dishonesties. But the prohibitive measures were counterproductive.

The very desire and effort to suppress cards publicized them all the more and gave them a special attraction. Card reading and playing became the fashion, and people have never lost their fascination for them.

The Ace

The single "spot" on dice and cards is known as the ace. In spite of its apparent simplicity, its genealogy is quite considerable and its ancestry rather dubious.

An ancient tradition has it that the Celts invented the ace which they called "as," because in their tongue this word described the first of all things, the source of being, the origin. More plausible is the explanation that the ace came from the Romans. They referred to it in their Latin as the unit, the "one"—*unus*. Greeks corrupted this numeral into *onos* and Germans adapted it into *Ass*, which eventually deteriorated into ace.

Most likely is a third suggestion—that ace originated from the Roman coin called the *as*, which also served as a unit of weight.

A French writer, however, was convinced that the ace of cards and on dice was so called because it pointed directly to an ass—a fool.

Love in Tennis

Many people have been puzzled by the fact that "no score" in tennis is announced as love. This practice goes back at least to the year 1742. Seeking an explanation of the expression, some have thought that anyone failing to score must be playing the game for love.

However, it is much more likely that "love" in tennis may have had its roots in France, just as the game (and its name) originated in that country, the word tennis being derived from the French *tenez*, meaning "take it" or "play."

Nil, or nothing, is zero, the figure whose shape resembles an egg. The French, always subtle and quick on the uptake, adopted their word for egg, *l'oeuf*, to announce "no score." Crossing the Channel, the *l'oeuf* was adapted to British tongues by being rendered love.

The Crossword Puzzle

The crossword puzzle is of comparatively recent origin and to solve the mystery of its first appearance is therefore not so difficult. The credit belongs to America. The puzzle was invented by Arthur Winn and published for the first time in the *New York World* on December 21, 1913.

Actually, it was a development of the old word-square. This consisted of a set of words of an identical number of letters which had to be found and so arranged in a square that they read the same horizontally and vertically.

The new and ingenious kind of puzzle in the Supplement of the Sunday edition of the *New York World* was welcomed so enthusiastically that it was retained as a weekly feature. Eleven years later the first book of crossword puzzles appeared on the market. It proved an immediate success. More so, almost overnight a craze for the new brainteaser swept America and then spread throughout the world. Newspapers everywhere adopted the crossword puzzle as a standard feature.

Britain succumbed to it in 1925 and soon developed her own style, pattern and definitions. Crosswords now exist in almost every language except those, like Chinese, which do not lend themselves to this kind of up and down manipulation of words.

It was only in 1930 that "crossword" was included in dictionaries as a legitimate word. It was a deserved recognition of what had become an institution. After all, it was those very puzzles that had boosted the sale of dictionaries in unprecedented measure.

The Quiz

Quiz is a modern word. It has the distinction of being the only one added to dictionaries as the direct result of a bet. More surprising is the fact that when the word was first coined, it was intended to mean exactly—nothing. Quiz, as a word, was born in Ireland about 1780. Its parents were a Mr. Daly, the manager of a Dublin theater, and some of his friends.

When one night they discussed the gullibility of people, Daly asserted that "the mob" could be made to believe and accept well-nigh anything.

His friends maintained that people were not as stupid as all that. But Daly was adamant and said he was prepared to prove his point. He claimed he would make the masses adopt a new word—a meaningless chain of letters—just overnight. He was ready to take a bet on this. His friends felt quite safe in agreeing to the wager.

All night they rushed through the streets of Dublin with pails of paint and brushes. Next morning, Dubliners found wherever they went—on houses, pavements and fences—four mysterious letters: Q U I Z.

Everyone asked what they meant. Later, the quiz spread from Dublin all over the world. Introduced to prove people's foolishness, it is now used to demonstrate the extent of their knowledge, which is yet another paradox of life. Some people, on the other hand, have seen in the quiz an abbreviation of the word inquisition, and therefore denoted "questioning."

Blue for First Prize

The Blue Ribbon is an ancient distinguishing mark of merit. As the sky, which was the highest people could see, was blue, its color was chosen as a symbol of distinction.

Ribbons are the traditional badge of an Order of Knighthood. That is why those honored by the Order of the Garter, the most noble and famous decoration awarded by the British Crown, established by King Edward III in 1348, wear a broad dark blue ribbon.

Eventually, the "blue ribbon" came to be used to highlight outstanding achievements in many other spheres of life as well.

Benjamin Disraeli is said to have coined the expression the "blue ribbon of the turf" as a description of the Derby, the famous English horse-race.

It was on the occasion when Lord George Bentinck, one of his friends, was complaining to him that a horse he had sold had subsequently won the Derby. As Disraeli seemed unsympathetic, Bentinck accused him of not even knowing what the Derby was, which made the Prime Minister promptly reply, "Indeed I do. It is 'the blue ribbon of the turf.'"

The same tradition is responsible for the awarding of a "blue ribbon" to the liner fastest in crossing the Atlantic Ocean and of the first prize in shows.

The Clue

The clue that helps to unravel a problem, solve a puzzle or a crime, goes back to an early mythological guide-line! The original "clue" (spelled clew) was an enchanted "ball" of yarn that helped Theseus, the Greek hero, to find his way in and out of the labyrinth on the island of Crete.

The ball of thread was given to him by Ariadne, the Cretan king's daughter who had fallen in love with him and was determined to save him from being devoured by the Minotaur. He fastened one end of the yarn to the door's lintel. Another version, more romantically, claims that, in fact, Ariadne herself held it in her hand, anxiously waiting for her hero's return after having slain the dreaded monster, instead of being devoured by it.

Unwinding the ball, Theseus was magically led through the twists and turns of the maze to reach its very center, to confront there and kill the Minotaur. To find his way out again, all he had to do was to rewind the clue.

Clues continue to show the way, though in less lethal circumstances they do so in a variety of puzzling and perplexing situations. Literally, one "threads" one's way through difficulties.

The Jigsaw Puzzle

The modern jigsaw puzzle was invented not as a game but as a teaching aid! It was first devised to help in the teaching of geography.

A map, mounted on wood, was cut into irregular pieces by means of a jigsaw, the tool best suited for the task. By fitting the various parts together, pupils playfully learned their geography lesson.

To begin with, these cut-up pieces were marketed as "Dissected Maps." Later on, however, they were described by the instrument used to shape them—the jigsaw.

The name stuck to the map, even when the tool was no longer used. Geography tuition through jigsaw maps, too, was abandoned, but the joy of the pursuit was not lost. Enterprising manufacturers applied the principle to make pictorial "jigsaws" with no one realizing their ancestry or the reason for their name.

The earliest specimen of the original jigsaw (map) dates back to the late 1760s. It is a hand-colored engraved map of "England and Wales Divided into their Counties" and was published by its inventor, John Spilsbury of Russell Court, Drury Lane, London, who described his firm as "Engravers and Map Dissectors in Wood."

Backgammon

One of the significant and frustrating features of backgammon has been responsible for the present name of this dice game, one of the oldest of its kind. Because in certain circumstances a player must return a piece to its starting place to be moved forward all over again, the pastime (originally and until the seventeenth century known in England as "Tables") came to be called the "back-game," backgammon, with Gamen the Old English for "game."

Smoking Cigarettes

The name of the cigarette is derived from the Spanish *cigarro* which, in turn, is believed to have its root in the Mayan *sicar* for "to smoke." However, it has also been suggested that it was called after the cicada, either because its shape resembled that of the insect or puffing it made a sound reminiscent of the cicada's chirp.

The Holy Land, it is claimed, was not only the source of the three world religions of monotheist faith, but the place where man enjoyed his first "modern" cigarette. This occurred in Acre in 1832 and in a strange combination of circumstances.

During the Turko-Egyptian war and the siege of Acre, Egyptian forces occupied the city. It had been invested by the British, who were aiding the Turks. During the bombardment of the fortress a cannon ball made a direct hit on a store of hookahs and totally destroyed it. Known in their more primitive form as hubble-bubbles, hookahs are the Oriental kind of pipe, in which the smoke is drawn through water by means of a flexible tube.

The loss was soon felt by the Egyptian soldiers. One of them, longing to have a smoke, improvised a new way of enjoying tobacco. Picking up discarded containers of gunpowder (known as "Dutch tubes"), he used them as wrappers around tobacco and smoked this new device—the first cigarette. The experiment succeeded. Once again, necessity had been the mother of invention.

Some twenty years later, British soldiers serving in the Crimea smoked the "little cigars" and took the vogue to England. Inventions, however, have a peculiar way of their own and "famous firsts" are often proved to be not so original after all. This certainly applies to the Oriental claim of the first cigarette.

It is known that thousands of years earlier natives in the West Indies and Mexico smoked what could be regarded as the authentic forerunner of the cigarette. They used thin palm bark or maize husks as the wrapper. It was part of the old Mayan culture to blow tobacco smoke towards the sun and the four points of the compass. The Aztecs used reeds filled with tobacco for this purpose.

Sixteenth-century Spanish explorers first discovered this ancient habit in the New World. They adopted it and through them it spread over all the Mediterranean countries, as far as Asia Minor—the future Turkey. At that early stage, Spaniards started experimenting with all types of wrappers, including paper, which became popular in the seventeenth century.

Perhaps—giving the Egyptians the benefit of the doubt—the habit of smoking cigarettes was lost to be rediscovered that fateful morning in the fortress city of Acre.

CHAPTER 20

On the Stage

A critic once wrote of a poor play that "It opened at 8:40 sharp and closed at 10:40 dull." The theater can truly excite and bore, exalt and debase. Tragedies have agitated the soul, and comedies, at their best, have provoked "thoughtful laughter." The theater is as old as humans themselves. Play-acting has been an instinct from earliest days. In the beginning, however, the theater was not meant to entertain. It was a matter of life and death. Among primitive tribes and in early civilization, the theater was not a pastime but part of life and religion.

The word theater comes from the Greek and means "a place for looking." Originally, plays were performed not to be heard but to be seen. A drama, therefore, is literally something "acted" in the way of a mime.

Drama's 3,000 years of history tell about humans themselves, their tears and laughter, their fears and loves, the strange quirks life can play and its many paradoxes.

The Theater

Long before the actual birth of the theater, people play-acted. They did so, however, not to amuse themselves or others, but to survive.

The theater originated in one of the most primitive forms of religious worship—sympathetic magic. This believes that if one properly acts something, one can make it really happen. If one wants to ensnare a beast, or see one's fields and cattle prosper, or kill a man, one can achieve those aims by "remote control." One merely has to enact the scene and, by magic, fiction will be translated into fact.

Hunting tribes, for example, lacking meat, would enact a hunting scene, with some men representing the game and others the successful party of huntsmen. Fertility rites were the earliest "theater." Dances then performed were thought to promote magically the falling of rain and, consequently, the growth of vegetation and the increase of cattle. Primitive people were convinced that on such play-acting depended their prosperity or adversity.

A theater resembled a sacred shrine, and the actors were the priests whose dramatic performances magically directed nature and the gods to do their bidding. Thus early "productions" were not restricted to a limited circle of art lovers, but concerned all the people. They were a communal event, second to none in importance.

The noise the "actors" made while moving rhythmically (with their feet and swaying body) in their mimic dances eventually led to tribal chants, the chorus, and ultimately to poetry. It is, therefore, not an accident that the measure of a verse is the "foot" and that there is a close affinity between the ballet and the ballad. Dramatic performances gave not just aesthetic pleasure but, much more so, roused religious passion and sensuous excitement.

The Tragedy

The theater, as it is now known, grew out of a popular celebration held in Athens more than 2,500 years ago. It took place once a year in honor of Dionysus, the god of nature and wine. This, in turn, was an adaptation of an even more ancient Egyptian festival whose theme was the death and rebirth of nature.

Thousands of people from all over Greece flocked to Athens to participate in this event. It was meant to celebrate and propitiate procreative powers, with the singing of obscene songs and a greatly enlarged replica of the phallus being carried around in procession.

The educated class now rebelled against the low level of those celebrations and all they implied in orgies and licentious living in praise of god. They demanded restraint, decency and a ritual altogether more fitting for the occasion. As a result, lyric choruses were introduced. They were sung by a choir of fifty men and boys, and with it the stage was set for the future theater.

The tragedy, as the first dramatic form to come into existence, developed from that earliest choral lyric performance at the festival of Dionysus. *Tragedy* literally means a "goat-song." The origin of this peculiar term for a play of a serious nature with a disastrous or fatal ending is obscure and has given rise to many and varied interpretations.

It has been pointed out that the men and boys in the choir were disguised as Satyrs and dressed in goat-skins. Hence their song and performance were referred to as a "goat-song." There is also the opinion that the odd name derived from the fact that the original religious festival included as one of its main features the sacrifice of a goat to Dionysus and that the chorus was sung over the goat's body.

Finally, it has been suggested that the tragedy, as a goat-song, received its name because of the prize offered at the annual "art festival" of classical Greece. This trophy was not in the form of a shield, a cup or a wreath, but of a *tragos*—a goat! The winner had the privilege of offering it as a sacrifice to the god. Its slaying was the climax of the play. Therefore it is not so far-fetched that any theater performance that ends with the death of the hero is linked with that ancient goat sacrifice and still called a tragedy.

What a world of difference there is between this early goat-song of the tragedy and present-day "acting the goat."

The Pit and the Stalls

In the seventeenth century, the ground floor of the theater was known as "the pit." From it, and under the open sky, the audience watched the play standing up. Later, they were seated on wooden benches without backboards to lean against. There was still no roof to shelter the spectators from inclement weather. They must have been so absorbed in the play that they just did not care for or notice their own discomfort. This alone is evidence of the popularity of many of those early stage productions. The name pit has another significance. The first performances of dramatic art in England took place in arenas previously used for cockfights. Obviously, the pit is a survival of the cockpit, the place in which birds were *pitted* against each other. London's first theater, built in 1618, where Shakespeare's plays were performed, stood on the site of a famous cockpit in Drury Lane.

Centuries passed, architecture developed, and the theater changed into a refined center of culture. Auditoriums were no longer remembered as former arenas, and the audience demanded comfort.

Theater managers obliged. As the seats nearest the stage were favored most, they were also the dearest. Only well-to-do people could afford to reserve them. To cater for these patrons' tastes and at the same time give them value for money, front seats were most luxuriously equipped. Appropriately, the former pit was now called by the fashionable French word *fauteuils*, meaning "armchairs." Soon the French term was Anglicized and became "stalls."

Yet as if to remind the unsuspecting, comfortably placed spectator of what went before, the stall still recalls, at least etymologically, the former cockpit. The word stall is derived from an Old English term which meant "standing room." Thus, to speak of a stall seat is really a contradiction in terms. Literally it suggests sitting down on something that denotes "standing room" only! This is yet another symbol of the make-believe world that is the theater, so full of paradox, where "the play's the thing"!

CHAPTER 21

In the Way of Speaking

Sooner of later practically everyone uses two ways of speaking their mother tongue. One is more or less grammatically formal and the other is slang.

Colloquially speaking, people like to "call a spade a spade" and good slang "hits the nail on the head." It conveys one's meaning succinctly, vigorously and to the point. Certainly, slang words and phrases have to struggle for their existence but the apt ones survive. Eventually, they become accepted and a respectable part of the vocabulary. Popular expressions above all prove that a language lives. Nothing can take their place. Napoleon was astonished what power words have over people, and modern dictators, following him, have made use of that knowledge.

Words and phrases offer a mine of information. What is "fair dinkum" to the Australian might be "O.K." to Americans, though to find "the real McCoy" is at times very difficult.

The Real McCoy

It is very rare that the person responsible for a phrase himself explained its origin. But, according to one version, this is the case regarding the "real McCoy."

He was a famous boxer, Charles ("Kid") McCoy, a one-time world welterweight champion, who died in 1940. For many years he was unbeatable in his class and so his name became a legend. The real McCoy came to mean the real thing, the genuine article! It was the finest praise anyone or anything could receive. People came to speak of the real McCoy in every sphere of life, whenever they wished to describe the best of its kind or someone who excelled in their class, profession or sport.

Yet this did not assure happiness for the real McCoy, once so celebrated and adored by the American people. He accidentally killed his sweetheart and was sentenced to serve a prison term at San Quentin. While there, he rescued a pilot whose plane had crashed near a road gang of prisoners and as a reward, and recalling the ex-boxer's former happier days, the warden presented him with a pair of boxing gloves and a punching bag to use when not busy with prison duties.

While serving his sentence (he received his parole in 1932), he had many friendly talks with Warden Duffy. On one occasion McCoy gave his own version of how his name came to be perpetuated in American speech. Duffy relates the story in his book, *88 Men and Two Women*.

Duffy says McCoy told him that while having a drink with a lady friend in a saloon, a man accosted the woman. Trying to brush off the intruder without much fuss, McCoy asked him to go, adding as a warning which needed no further explanation, "I'm Kid McCoy!" But the man persisted in pestering the lady, not believing that McCoy was the American champion fighter. He remarked with scorn, "Yeah? Well, I'm George Washington!" McCoy said he struck the man once and quite lightly. The man collapsed and when, ten minutes later, he regained his senses, he rubbed his eyes and called out, "Jeez, it was the real McCoy!" And so, according to Kid, it was this incident that gave birth to the now commonly used phrase of approbation.

It is sad to know that the life of the real McCoy, whose name had come to stand for the finest and best, ended tragically. After his release from San Quentin, he worked for the Ford Motor Company in Detroit. In 1940, whilst looking forward to his tenth marriage, he died from an overdose of sleeping tablets.

Nevertheless, in spite of McCoy's own testimony, there are other intriguing claims and definitions of the phrase's origin.

The Irish were not slow to recognize in his name one of their own kind and took the phrase as a general tribute to Irishmen's honesty and excellence. Their people were famous as fighters. No one could match them. A ballad of the 1870s tells of an Irish woman who had beaten her husband mercilessly—just to prove that she was "a real McCoy."

There is also the claim that the phrase relates to the days of prohibition in the U.S.A., when bootleggers prospered. Some took advantage of the fact that, even should they defraud their thirsty customers, they could not claim any compensation or take their dishonest suppliers to a court of law. Therefore the greater proportion of illegal liquor sold as the real thing was heavily diluted with all kinds of substitutes.

One bootlegger named McCoy, however, refused to cheat his clients and supplied only the best quality, undiluted imported whisky. His name became a trademark and a recommendation and his product was referred to as "the real McCoy." The phrase soon caught on and survived prohibition and bootlegging days to become a general term of praise.

Fair Dinkum

"Fair dinkum," describing something as really genuine, is usually said to be an indigenously Australian saying. Yet research shows that it may well go back to English colloquial speech where, in provincial dialect, it meant "fair play."

Intriguing, though not so factual, is an alternative explanation that still links the origin of the term with Australia, its gold-digging days and associated with the early influx of foreigners.

Australians always liked to drink and to gamble, especially after a day's hard work in search of gold. On the goldfields around Ballarat they persuaded their newcomer friends from abroad to join them in their pastime. However, it did not take those "diggers" from overseas long to realize that a mind befuddled by liquor was no good for gambling and that to keep sober, at least until the game was over, meant also to keep one's money, or even add to it. So they refrained from drinking till afterward.

The locals, faced with heavy losses, were not slow in finding out what was happening. They demanded "fair play," which, to them, implied "fair drinking" as well. That is why eventually, to show their good intentions, the foreign diggers assured their Australian partners that there would be "fair drinking" all round: not only after, but before, the game.

Somehow (so the story goes) by their accent they made their promise sound like "fair dinkum." The "Aussies," highly amused at their mispronunciation, took a liking to it and adopted it themselves. So, fair dinkum, a foreign contribution to the Australian language, came to be known as a dinkum Australian word!

"O.K."

Winston Churchill was convinced that the short words are the best. "O.K." is now the universal slang to say that "it's all right." No one will mistake the meaning of these two capital letters. Yet views differ as to how they first came into existence as a vivid term of approval and approbation.

This shortest and internationally adopted expression supplies one of the longest lists of possible explanations. Illiteracy, political slander, a clever election campaign, bureaucratic efficiency, an American Indian chief and the French, they all, in turn, have been credited as the originator of the "O.K."

America's presidents are no mere figureheads. Frequently, they have been known as the policy makers of their country, directing the course of their nation's history. However, none of them has had the distinction of having been a word maker as well, except Andrew Jackson, the seventh president of the United States. He has been called the "father of the O.K."

This claim was not made by his admirers, but by those who sought to discredit him during the presidential campaign in 1838 as a completely illiterate man and not qualified to lead the nation.

His enemies spread the rumor that Jackson, then a general and one of the candidates, so lacked even the rudiments of ordinary education that he used the abbreviation of "O.K." for "All Correct," as he, being untutored and ignorant, thought that the words were spelled "Orl Kerrect"!

It is quite possible that Jackson was fond of calling things that were correct "O.K." But if he did so, it was not because of any lack of education or faulty spelling. It is said that he derived it from the Choctaw Indian word *okeh*, which they used to emphasize the validity of a statement or the hope that what they said would come true, in much the same way as Amen is used.

Other authorities claim that the creation of "O.K." was linked with a different American presidential election campaign, during which it was invented as a slogan, not to malign an opponent, but to boost a candidate. A catchy phrase, if cleverly chosen, is worth thousands of votes where mere policy speeches go unheeded. Disraeli rightly stated that "with words we govern men."

When in 1840 Martin van Buren was standing for a second

term as president, with his chances of success being doubtful, his followers tried every possible means to get him votes. What they needed most was a good slogan.

Van Buren was born in the township of Old Kinderhook in the state of New York. By combining the initials of its otherwise rather cumbersome name, supporters referred to him as "O.K." Soon those two letters became a rallying call. In New York his party even organized an "O.K. Club," further to popularize the cause and—quite unintentionally—the new "word."

As it happened, the "Old Fox of O.K.," as he was also known, was not re-elected, but the two letters survived van Buren's defeat to become a favorite colloquialism among all English-speaking people.

To further add to the confusion, another view stated that "O.K." stems from the American Indians, although it was not one of their actual words. It represented the initials of *Old Keokuk*, the name of one of their famous chiefs who, believing that time was money, saved it by signing treaties with his initials instead of his full name.

So "O.K." came to stand among the Indians as an affirmation of things said or done: the final approval. Unfortunately, none of the documents is preserved to verify or disprove the claim.

Other explanations of the "O.K." are interesting, yet most unlikely. One attributes the expression to an old French term. The other suggests that, in reality, the "O.K." is altogether an error. Originally, the letters were not "O.K." at all but "O.R.," which stood for "Order Recorded," a once customary endorsement of documents.

Certainly, there is ample choice of possible explanations for the "O.K.," but one is left to wonder which is truly O.K.

CHAPTER 22

The Beginnings of Writing

People have always wondered how writing first came into existence. From earliest times myth and legend have tried to give an answer.

Egyptians believed that only a god could have revealed the art of writing and they called their script hieroglyphics, meaning "sacred carvings." They worshipped Toth as the giver of script and, for this reason, always presented this bird-headed deity as holding a reed brush and ink palette in his hands.

The Chinese attributed the invention of the alphabet to the four-eyed dragon-faced god T'sang Chien and said he took the pattern of his symbols from nature—the footprints of birds, the marks on the back of a turtle, and so on.

According to Hindu myth, the god Brahma created the letters. He wished to write down his teachings on leaves of gold. But as there was no alphabet in existence, he had to invent it. He did so mostly by copying some of the peculiar tracings formed by the seams in the human skull.

The known facts about writing are, of course, less exciting, though still fascinating.

Clearly, a *manuscript* literally means "written by hand," though nowadays it is mostly typed. However, many other terms and implements of writing do not disclose their background and story so easily. To understand their past enlightens their present.

A *pen*, in any shape, recalls the original quill. The word is derived from a Latin root, meaning "feather." Any text is words "woven" together to display some pattern of thought.

The Alphabet

The alphabet, as many other benefits of Western civilization, came from the Orient. Just as the Ten Commandments were revealed on the Sinai Peninsula, so—as discoveries of inscriptions have suggested—one of the earliest alphabets. It was conceived in that very region as well. There is no doubt that the desert land between Egypt and Babylonia, between the home of hieroglyphics and cuneiform, is the cradle of its creation. The approximate date of its birth is the second half of the second millennium B.C.

The alphabet's very name reflects its Semitic parents. It is derived from the fusion of the first two letters of the Greek alphabet—the *alpha* and *beta*—which in turn were phonetic imitations of the first two letters of the Phoenician and Hebrew alphabets—the *aleph*—and *beth*. Phoenicians, those most outstanding seafarers of the ancient world, brought them to Greece. The Greeks in their adaptation then spread them throughout Europe.

All letters developed from pictures. The prototypes of present-day writing are drawings of some common object, such as a fence, a camel, a hand, a head, a fish or a spear. In Oriental languages the letters are still called by their names, whose initial sounds represent the letters of the alphabet in most tongues to this day.

The letter *a* originally depicted the head of an ox (*aleph* in Hebrew); *b* was the simplified drawing of a house (*beth* in Hebrew); *g* derived from a camel (*jama* in Hebrew); in the *m* we can still recognize water, shown by one of its waves (*ma'yim* in Hebrew); and in the *o* the shape of an eye. The *t*, most obviously, is a cross.

The number of the letters in the alphabet differs slightly from nation to nation. Whilst the English alphabet, for instance, counts twenty-six letters, that of the Russian has thirty-six, of the Spanish twenty-seven and of the Hebrew twenty-two.

The reason for this fluctuation is easy to discover. The general rule of the alphabet is "one sound—one letter." People vary not only in the language they speak but in the kind of sounds they are able to produce. Arabs are even more guttural than the Germans. The Greek tongue could not make any use of the English *c* and *v*, whilst the letter *j* was "unpalatable" to the Romans.

The sounds represented in the earliest alphabets completely lacked any vowels. Originally, they consisted of consonants only, which complicated interpretation. The most simple text would baffle the readers, who had to decide for themselves where a vowel was intended and which one was needed. Take, for example, one of the best-known nursery rhymes. Written in the ancient manner it would appear as—

MR HD LTTL LMB

Even if it were indicated what this line of consonants represented, it would still take some considerable time to read into it that—

MaRy HaD a LiTTLe LaMB

But this is exactly how, in earliest times and for almost 2,000 years, people wrote. A simple three-letter word, for instance, made up of the consonants BRD presented a choice of many meanings. It could be read as—

BeaRD, BiRD, BReaD, BaRD, BReeD, BRoaD or BrooD

—to mention the most obvious possibilities.

It is not surprising, therefore, that this lack of vowels became a frequent source of misunderstanding and error, as actually "reading" was merely "guessing." When, finally, vowel signs were introduced, they were simple in form—Morse-like dots and dashes.

Other obvious features of present-day script are equally the result of thousands of years of evolution. To begin with, only capital letters were known; small or lower case letters were not developed until the Middle Ages. At first, all writing moved from right to left, as Hebrew and Arabic still do to this day. To unravel the above nursery rhyme would thus be an even greater problem—

BML LTTL DH RM

Another later development was punctuation, which for centuries was nonexistent. A further difficulty of early writing was that all words were strung together without spaces, in order not to waste precious writing material like papyrus and parchment. Applying the original way of writing, from right to left and without vowels and spacing, the verse would have been this short line of consonants—

BMLLTTLDHRM

No wonder that the reading of documents was confined to a small circle of experts!

It was one of the great innovations in the history of civilization when, for the first time, an unknown genius comprised the idea "literally" to pause between words and to separate them not only on his tongue but on whatever then took the place of paper.

The alphabet is one of the most revolutionary inventions made by humans in the cultural development. It came into existence not suddenly but, as has been shown, as the result of continuous growth and many stages of trial and error.

"To Mind One's P's and Q's"

The curious phrase "to mind one's p's and q's"—meaning to be careful in one's words and behavior—evolved from the shape of the letters themselves.

However, the letters as capitals provide no clue to the original reason for the saying. But once *p* and *q* are written or printed as small letters their similar appearance must strike the eye. Without special care, children learning the alphabet or inexperienced typesetters might easily confuse these characters. Young pupils and printers' apprentices were thus specially reminded not to miss but "to mind their p's and q's."

The most obvious answer need not always be the right one, and particularly so in this case. After all, the same danger of confusing similar shapes of letters applied to other characters as well. Further investigation confirms this assumption and offers two totally different interpretations of the phrase. These have nothing to do with either the art of calligraphy or of typesetting but belong to the social side of life.

One explanation leads straight into ale-houses of former times. Innkeepers then used to keep a score of what customers drank by chalking up on a board (or the wall) a record in pints and quarts, which they indicated by *P*'s and *Q*'s.

A careful drinker, anxious not to be overcharged, would remind the publican to be exact when chalking up the score—in other words, to mind his *P*'s and *Q*'s.

On the other hand, and this is no less likely, it could have been the innkeepers who, concerned that people should not drink above their (monetary) capacity, warned them, especially when they were well advanced in their rounds, to mind (the number of) pints and quarts, lest, when the final account was rendered, they were unable to pay.

More far-fetched, but still possible, is another origin of the phrase, which links it with French court etiquette of the seventeenth century. During the reign of Louis XIV men used to wear large wigs. When greeting members of a higher class, especially royalty, they bowed low, an act of courtesy which needed much practice as, doing so, they might stumble over their feet, or worse still, in the course of the bow their wig might become disarranged or even fall off altogether.

Dancing masters cautioned their pupils always to "mind their feet and wigs," in French their *pieds* (feet) and *queues* (wigs). When the English adopted the fashion and caution, always being practical and perhaps not too sure of the correct accent, they shortened the French "feet" and "wigs" to their mere initials, resulting in people ever since speaking of minding one's p's and q's.

The Question Mark

The question mark has a fascinating past. In Latin a query was indicated by the word *questio*, meaning "question," which was placed at the end of a sentence. However, this took up valuable space on the page.

An unknown economist in the art of writing, who might also be considered an early pioneer in shorthand, had the idea to abbreviate QUESTIO to QO. But this was not satisfactory, since it could be mistaken for the ending of a word. Writers began to place the Q on top of the O. It did not take long for the Q to deteriorate into a squiggle and the O to contract into a dot. The present-day question mark was the result.

Paper

The origin of paper goes back thousands of years to two centers of ancient civilization, far removed from each other.

The word "paper" comes from Egypt's papyrus, that tall straight reed once covering acres of marsh to a height of 19 feet. In wild thickets and later in cultivated fields, Egyptian workers used to cut the papyrus stems individually for their "factories."

Papyrus was then the raw material for many things. Its base was eaten as a delicacy. Its rind made loin-cloths for the lower classes and its inner pith was used for sails, boats, baskets, ropes and sandals. Above all, however, it served as the source of writing material.

The choice of the old Egyptian word papyrus as the name of this plant had special significance. Meaning "the royal," it proclaimed the reed as royal property and the manufacture of "paper" as a strictly guarded state monopoly.

For centuries papyrus was the only substance in the world from which paper was made. The Egyptians wrote on it as long ago as 3000 B.C. Reaching the Greco-Roman world, it was used there for more than 1,000 years.

Yet it had disadvantages. One of them was that the supply of papyrus was limited to those regions where the plant could be grown or exported from in sufficient quantity. Furthermore, it yellowed with time and was brittle.

That is why it was replaced by parchment, made of animal skin and called after the city of Pergamon in Asia Minor, where parchment became a substitute for papyrus in the second century B.C., when King Ptolemy stopped its export from Egypt.

Parchment then surpassed the unobtainable paper in many ways. It was much tougher, lasted longer and could take twice the amount of writing, as both sides could be used. But it was still expensive and only the rich could afford it. Nevertheless, it conquered the world and, for the next 1,200 years, was most favored by Europe's scribes, monks and scholars.

During all that time, though unknown to the West, a much cheaper writing material was available in the Far East—real paper, invented in ancient China.

For once luck willed it that the name of the man who is said to have invented it is known, as well as his profession and the year in which he did so. T'sai Lun manufactured the world's first paper in A.D. 105 after many experiments with varieties of bark, fibre and waste. The astonishing fact is that T'sai Lun's own profession had nothing to do with learning. He belonged to the imperial palace and his appointment was that of Chief Eunuch to the Emperor Ho Ti.

For hundreds of years the use of paper was restricted to the Far East. In the eighth century Chinese prisoners revealed the art of paper-making to their Arab captors. These, in turn, introduced it into Europe where—in 1340—the first paper mill was established in the town of Fabriano in Italy.

The ancient "royal" name of the Egyptian papyrus was then welded to the "modern" Chinese material, and paper took over the name of its earliest predecessor. Thus the East and the West combined in bringing enlightenment to the entire world. Literary knowledge was no longer restricted to a small coterie of scholars but available to all the people. It was the new kind of paper that made possible the invention of printing in 1450.

Foolscap

An old watermark and a corrupted Italian term have both been cited as the origin of "foolscap" paper, which now measures 13 inches by 8 inches. The earliest known specimen dates from 1540. For many years, until the seventeenth century, the head of a jester with cap and bells was used in Britain as the watermark of paper of this special size, which most probably made people refer to the paper as that of a fool's cap.

Opinions differ as to how the watermark was introduced. Least probable is the suggestion that Herr Spielmann (later Sir John Spilman), a German resident in Britain, started it. Jeweler to Queen Elizabeth's court, he established a paper mill at Dartford in 1580, the second in England, and to mark his product, made use of his name. In German a Spielmann is a person who acts or plays. Why could it not be a man who played the fool, he reasoned. It must be remembered that, between the thirteenth and seventeenth centuries, jesters were a privileged class, employed by courtiers and the nobility. Their emblem was a cap and bells. All these circumstances made Herr Spielmann decide to choose this sign as a trademark for his paper.

Another unlikely explanation links the introduction of the fool's cap as a watermark with history. The story is told that when

King Charles I found his coffers empty, he explored every means of raising funds, one of them being the granting of privileges to people prepared to pay a high premium.

The monopoly of making paper was thus sold. At the time it bore the royal arms as its exclusive watermark. With the defeat of the Royalists, Oliver Cromwell and the Rump Parliament were determined to express their break with the past in every possible way. It included the order to remove the royal sign wherever it was found, even from notepaper, but especially from the large-sized pages of the Parliamentary Journal, where it was used as a watermark.

It is said that, to ridicule the former king and add further indignity to his memory, Cromwell substituted a fool's cap for the royal arms. However, with the prorogation of the Rump Parliament this mark of contempt was again removed. Yet, ever since, paper of the Journal's size has been referred to as foolscap.

Others believe that the description of paper as foolscap was based on a misunderstanding, a corruption of the Italian *foglia cape*, meaning a "first-sized sheet," a chief or large page. Like the English word foliage, the Italian *foglia* is derived from the leaf of a tree, when speaking of the leaves of a book.

Eventually, Britain replaced the watermark of the fool's cap with the figure of Britannia or that of a lion rampant, supporting the cap of liberty or a pole. But the original fool's cap survives, if not as a watermark, as a term for the paper it once distinguished.

Ink

An ancient Greek word for a branding iron is the basis of the modern word ink. Literally this means "burned in" and refers to the custom of sealing by heat both wounds—cauterizing them—and colors—fixing them more durably. The Greek *enkausston* and Latin *incaustum* became the names reserved for the (Tyrian) purple fluid with which Greek and Roman emperors signed official documents.

The earliest use of ink dates back to Egypt and the fourth millennium B.C., when it was not a liquid but a dry substance, made chiefly from soot scraped from cooking pots or, in the form of carbon, from charcoal. The ink was kept in small cakes and liquefied by mixing it with either water or gum.

Independently, the Chinese began to use carbon ink about 2000 B.C., traditionally invented by T'ien Chu. In both China and Japan pine soot and lampblack served as a base.

The use of ink is referred to only once in the Old Testament. It is in the passage in which Baruch, Jeremiah's secretary, relates how he recorded what the prophet dictated to him: "He pronounced all these words unto me with his mouth, and I wrote them with ink in the book."

Carbon ink of that early type could easily be washed off. Though additives of vinegar and wormwood were thought to make it more durable and to repel mice, drawbacks soon became apparent. Once mixed, the ink thickened in no time and clogged the pen. With the introduction of parchment as a writing material, the carbon-liquid proved even less satisfactory. Something more fluid and more permanent was needed.

Scribes realized that ink with a mineral mixture had the advantage of penetrating the material, although sometimes it also gradually destroyed it. To avoid this led to the introduction of an iron-gall liquid, known to the Hebrews as early as the sixth century B.C. and still retained in principle.

Colored inks were produced in most remote times as well, though, except for red, they were applied only to drawings. The Egyptians made their red ink from cinnabar and used it for several purposes. It indicated the final sum in their accounts, and marked the beginning of paragraphs in their writings. Not least, they wrote the names of evil creatures in red, for this was the color of hostile powers.

Blotting Paper

Blotting paper was discovered by accident. It was the result of a workman's forgetfulness. In charge of the mixing vats at a paper mill in Berkshire, England, one day he forgot to put in sizing, one of the essential ingredients in the making of paper.

The finished product, of which there was a large quantity, proved useless, but the factory proprietor, being a thrifty man, was reluctant to throw it away. If it was not saleable as paper, he thought, at least he would make use of it himself, for rough notes.

However, he found that this was not possible either, as the ink spread all over the sheets and was completely absorbed. This, in turn, gave him the idea that this peculiar fault might be the beginning of a novel line of business, offering a considerable market outlet.

For hundreds of years people had used sand to dry ink, a long and cumbersome process. Now the factory owner advertised the spoilt goods as "blotting paper." In no time he disposed of the complete stock and a thriving new industry had been born.

Originally, most blotting paper was produced in a pink or red color because of a wish to utilize matter which otherwise would have been of hardly any value. Red was a fast color and difficult to bleach. Though in paper-making red rags were not a paying proposition, for blotting paper any color would do, and red was as satisfactory as the purest white. Thus the law of economics determined the original color of blotting paper as well.

CHAPTER 23

Counting and Accounting

People have always felt the need to take the measure of things, and anything that could assist them to do so they gladly employed. That is why first of all they used parts of their body, such as the feet, for a measure, and the fingers for counting. The power of a horse and the weight of a stone were other aids. The sun, moon and stars helped them as ready reckoners of the passing of time.

Coins are unrivalled storytellers and an important source of historic data. Payment by money replaced the more primitive method of barter, a term that not accidentally also meant cheating.

The earliest currency did not consist of coins but of objects, such as knives, just as Roman soldiers were paid in salt, essential for life and still ingrained in the present-day "salary." The original type of money was not counted but weighed, which explains the English pound, at first describing a "load" of 7,680 well-dried grains of wheat.

It is often said that "money is the root of all evil." This is a misquotation from the New Testament, which says that it is the love of money that is the source of wickedness, and not money itself. Boldly Mark Twain amended this passage by stating that not love but lack of money was the root of all evil. Though it is good to remember that sometimes one can pay too much for money.

"Once in a Blue Moon"

When one speaks of "once in a blue moon" one means "very rarely indeed." Obviously, a blue moon is not an everyday occurrence.

The moon has been blamed—rightly or wrongly—for many things. She has given the vocabulary the lunatic and the tides. It is customary to speak of the moon as being yellow as cheese, though in reality the color is probably a dark brownish-black. The "blue moon" is an optical illusion.

All light of the moon is reflected sunshine, and the color in which it appears to the naked eye changes according to the atmosphere surrounding the earth through which the rays have to pass. That is why the moon may look bright yellow, whitish, orange or, very rarely, blue.

Any change in the atmosphere, which is caused by particles of dust or other matter being absorbed in it, immediately influences the color of the rays of light reflected by the moon from the sun.

That is why in 1883, for example, the world saw a blue moon. Nothing had happened to the moon, but on earth, the volcanic Indonesian island of Krakatoa had been blown almost into halves, and enormous clouds of dust and water vapor had been thrown into the atmosphere and were circling the earth for many weeks.

This changed the light rays reaching the earth from the moon, and made people believe that the moon was blue. Things are not always what they seem to be!

The Fortnight

If telegraphy had been invented at the time, one could have assumed that the word fortnight originated in the minds of thrifty people who, knowing that every word in a telegram was counted and charged for, were anxious to save money by making one word out of two.

Fortnight is the combination of two Old English words, fourteen nights. The fortnight's antiquity is indicated by the fact that its reference is to nights. That the calendar also originally took more note of lunar changes than of solar circumstances is apparent in several other terms in daily use. When speaking of a month—literally—it recalls the Old English monath for (the) moon, as in some cultures the beginning of a new month still coincides with the appearance of the new moon.

It is not surprising therefore that the starting of the celebration of Christmas on its eve relates to the early domination of night over day. This was first expressed and emphasized by the biblical story of Creation in which it is said, "there was evening and there was morning—one day." The day began at night!

A Baker's Dozen

Present-day business methods subject people to all kinds of temptations to buy certain goods. Most common is the promise of a free gift for the purchaser of an article thus advertised.

It might be assumed that it was also a wish to increase trade that made bakers give a customer buying twelve loaves of bread a thirteenth loaf free of charge. However, the baker's dozen is not the result of ancient trade-promotion. It is a survival of an early type of price-control.

Bread was the staple diet of the people who purchased it in the form of either cut pieces or whole loaves. Anticipating modern strict regulations, loaves were not only counted, but had to be of a certain weight. Heavy penalties threatened any baker selling short weight.

As bread, after it has become dry and shrunk, loses weight, the baker wisely started to add an extra loaf or piece of bread to every dozen sold. This was called the in-bread. What the baker thus lost on the swings, he got back on the roundabout. The gift of some extra dough in the proportion of one to twelve saved him from the loss of more precious "dough."

There is a suspicion that self-interest of another kind might have accounted for the baker's dozen. People were afraid of evil forces, ever ready to spoil their luck, unless they were given "protection money." To propitiate them, the baker, anxious to prosper in his trade, may have added the extra loaf. This gave rise to the saying "twelve for the baker and one for the devil."

"By Rule of Thumb"

When using the phrase "by rule of thumb," it is meant to say that a very rough-and-ready method is applied and certainly not an accurate and scientifically dependable procedure. There are several conjectures as to the origin of the expression.

In the early days, the thumb, like the foot, was an always-available instrument of measure. The last joint of the thumb was taken as approximately equal to one inch. It became a widely established custom, reminiscent of the baker's dozen, when measuring cloth to allow "a thumb" as an extra to one yard. And precisely because this was a very rough calculation, the rule of thumb came to signify that.

Another possible explanation leads back to Bordeaux in southern France and 1814. French contractors were then paid in Spanish dollars. To calculate their worth in francs, their own money, they often made notes on the thumb-nail, a method which highly amused the military. They were convinced that it was all pretense, and that it was impossible by such "rule of thumb" to accurately assess correct exchange of francs for dollars.

A third interpretation relates to the brewing of beer and has its birthplace in Yorkshire, England. To ascertain whether the infusion of malt had reached the right degree of fermentation, it was necessary to check the temperature of the mixture. As at the time no scientific instruments were available for the purpose, the thumb was dipped in the liquid. Thus, by "rule of the thumb," it was known more or less whether or not the brew was ready.

The Piggy Bank

A favorite medium for saving, both among children and adults, used to be the piggy bank for their coins. Made of pottery in the shape of a pig, it had a slot in its back. Why, people wanted to know, was the "coin holder," of all things, so called and shaped?

Pigs have been known for many things, but certainly never for being thrifty or concerned with the future, saving up for a rainy day.

Dogs bury bones. Camels are said (mistakenly) to store away water. But as for pigs, even the proverb says that one cannot make a silk purse out of a sow's ear, and the Bible admonishes people not to throw pearls to swine.

Indeed, there is no real link between a piggy bank and a pig that would justify the choice of name. Their association is due to a confusion of words.

During the Middle Ages metal was rarely used in the manufacture of common household utensils as it was too expensive. More economical and pliable was a type of clay then commonly known as *pygg*. This was so popular for dishes, pots and jars that eventually all earthenware was referred to as pygg.

Frugal housewives then, as now, put aside what they could save into one of these pots or jars. That is how, by a natural process of evolution, the container serving the purpose of the family "treasury" came to be known as the pyggy bank.

In time, however, the origin of the term was forgotten. In nineteenth-century England, potters, being excellent craftsmen but not good etymologists, did not realize the true meaning of pyggy— that ancient clay. Therefore, when customers ordered a pyggy bank, they erroneously produced a pig-shaped moneybox.

Mistakes always prosper. In no time the piggy bank caught people's imagination. Subconsciously they might have remembered the fertility of swine, hoping that their money would multiply likewise.

The Rim on Coins

Ever since the invention of money, there have been forgers. Modern counterfeiters have had their unworthy predecessors even at times when paper money was nonexistent and its precautionary watermarking could not be employed. Savage penalties like cutting off the hand of the offender, which was common for centuries after early Saxon times, did not deter them.

The earliest coins were handmade and, although of marked weights of gold, silver or bronze, could differ in shape. This allowed forgers to clip the rims of the coins and steal the metal thus gained. The practice had become so widespread and trouble-some during the reign of Henry V of England, that the monarch had it classified as treason and made punishable by death.

The rim around coins was introduced first not as an ornament. So to speak, it was a case of "milling vs clipping." Any coin lacking the grained rim was no longer acceptable as currency.

Obviously, some of the more persistent forgers must have tried—after clipping the coin—to provide the reduced disc with their own home-made edge.

Discovering this new ruse, Oliver Cromwell decreed that, instead of milling the edge, this should be inscribed with suitable mottoes. First these legends piously referred to God and faith. Eventually they became very explicit. In some cases they read: "THE PENALTY FOR CLIPPING THIS COIN IS DEATH." However, at the time of Charles II, the inscription became less threatening, saying briefly: "AN ORNAMENT AND A SAFE-GUARD."

Modern coinage is not valuable enough to tempt clipping, but the milled edge is kept as a tradition. Perhaps this might still serve as a safeguard, though of a different kind. It may help people to grasp the coin more firmly and thus enable them to hold it longer in their hands before, inevitably, it will roll away.

The Traveler's Check

When to carry large sums of cash had become a dangerous practice, "letters of credit" were introduced. They proved only partially successful. Few banks would cash them and they could easily be forged. To solve the problem a London banking company—in 1792—presented customers with what were called "circular notes," valued at £20 ($40) each. Arrangements were made with just under 100 institutions to honor them.

It was not an ideal solution. Though insured against loss or theft, the use of the notes was limited in the amount of money being carried.

An overseas trip in 1890 by James Fargo, the brother of famous William ("Wells") Fargo, and president of the American Express Company, was responsible for the invention of the modern traveler's check. Not burdening himself with lots of cash, he carried—as he thought—a sufficient number of letters of credit. To his dismay, he found that many European bankers refused to accept them and, consequently, Fargo was short of money.

On his return to New York, still irate by what had happened to him and thereby spoiling his trip, he lost no time in contacting Marcellus F. Barry, a member of the firm and renowned for his financial genius. He told him of his unhappy experience and asked him to work out a method which would avoid any recurrence of the problem. Barry—also nicknamed "the Edison of Finance"—set to work at once. Realizing how difficult it was to forge a signature, he presented Fargo with the idea of creating some document which was to carry its owner's signature and was to be valid only if, in the presence of responsible officials, he was able to countersign it. Any difference with the "original" signature would immediately be recognized.

Rather appropriately, the first such check (for the amount of $50) was cashed by Fargo's son William, which he did when visiting the German city of Leipzig.

The Pawnbroker's Three Brass Balls

As in all money matters an element of uncertainty is attached even to the pawnbrokers' sign of the three brass balls. It is generally acknowledged that their trademark originated as the emblem of Italian nobility, the Medici family, who came from Lombardy. They introduced moneylending into England, arriving there, it has been suggested, as financial agents of the early Popes, to collect their dues. They are known to have financed the kings of England to the time of Edward III.

To indicate their place of business, they displayed the three balls, their family crest, outside the house.

As moneylending on pledges proved a lucrative trade, it did not remain for long a monopoly of the Medicis. Soon other merchants entered the field, wisely copying the sign, which by then in people's minds had become identified with this type of financial transaction. Ever since, the three brass balls have served as a pawnbroker's trademark.

It is still a matter of doubt how in the first place the Medicis came to adopt their crest. One explanation is that the name Medici is derived from the art of medicine and that the early and prominent members of the family were physicians, for whom a pill was a trademark. In medieval times it was customary to gild pills to make them more acceptable to rich customers.

Even those who deny an early association of the Medicis with medicine maintain that the obvious pun, the mere similarity of sound, had led the family to adopt the three enlarged pills in their coat of arms.

Another theory relates the three balls not to the healing of the sick, but to the defeat of an enemy. Averardo de Medici, who served as a commander with Charlemagne, was famous for an encounter with Mugello, a giant, whom he slew in combat. After the battle he carried with him as a trophy the giant's club, weighted with three iron balls. To commemorate the victory Medici adopted the three balls as his coat of arms.

A further tradition is completely divorced from the Medicis and links the pawnbrokers' symbol with the emblem of St. Nicholas of Bari and three purses of gold he is said to have left three poor pious sisters, to help them find husbands.

To nickname a pawnbroker "uncle" is neither a family matter nor does it reflect any special familiarity. Actually, it introduces a note of corruption into this otherwise honest trade, though only in the way of speaking. This type of uncle is merely a mispronunciation. The word is derived from the Latin *uncus*, which described the "hook," once commonly used by pawnbrokers to store and remove the pledges.

Blackmail

Blackmail has a very sad history indeed. It has come down from most respectable circles, eventually to become mixed up with illegal extortion. It started in Scotland hundreds of years ago and involved hardworking but poverty-stricken farmers.

Most of the land there was then owned by the English, who charged high rents to the Scots cultivating the soil. This "tribute" paid to the absentee landlords was known as *mail*, at one time a Scottish term for rent and taxes.

A condition stipulated that the payment should be made in silver. This was referred to as *white* mail. Life was hard and many a time the farmers could not raise the money for the mail, in which case the English landlords agreed to take produce in lieu of silver. The goods became known as *black* mail. They were quite legal and no opprobrium was at first attached to the term.

However, dishonest creditors then began to take advantage of the farmers' distress, asking for goods far in excess in value of the money owed, backing their demands with threats. This resulted in the term blackmail deteriorating into meaning payment extorted by intimidation.

Another explanation equally associates the origin of the present-day use of the term with the Scots, but dates it back to the boundary warfare between England and Scotland. According to this interpretation, "blackmail" was the protection money paid, in the form of produce, by the border farmers to freebooters. These promised, in return, to guard them against plunder by rapacious chiefs on either side of the frontier.

CHAPTER 24

The Measurement of Time

Much of modern society is possessed by the notion that "time is money." Punctuality is praised as a virtue and split-second timing has become an essential in research, industry and almost every type of scientific and technological endeavor.

Life is ruled by the clock and regulated by schedules. Failure to be punctual may cost one's job, a courting male his date and a business executive their travel connections.

Primitive people certainly had no trains or planes to catch. They did not have to clock in at work or to attend a shareholders' meeting, scheduled to commence "on the dot." Nevertheless, they, too, had their own kind of appointments to keep, especially in the service of their tribe and their gods. How then did they know when to arrive and to worship their deity at just the right moment?

The calculation of dates of the calendar serves many aspects of endeavor. The calendar reflects various obligations of people, as well as their organizational talent. It fixes events and is a reminder that life does not stand still.

And yet the calendar, which seems so definite, fixed and of most ancient date, is full of errors, inexactitudes and incongruities. It is divided into two periods—the years preceding and those following the birth of Jesus. They are indicated accordingly by the common abbreviations of B.C. (Before Christ) and A.D. (*Anno Domini*, meaning "in the year of the Lord"). But somehow the year 0 got lost: the year A.D. 1 immediately follows the year 1 B.C., whilst the actual year of Christ's birth is missing. Above all, it is now generally assumed that Christ was born four years "Before Christ"!

That January 1 is the beginning of each year is taken for granted. Yet until 1752 not January 1 but March 25 was New Year's Day!

Originally, a month was a moonth—the time it took the moon to revolve around the earth, approximately twenty-nine days. Thousands of years ago, a method of measuring time by the sun was adopted. The term month, however, was retained, although a misnomer.

This is a Christian country and of an enlightened mind. But the naming of the months and days still reflect beliefs in astrology and pagan gods. It has been said that a calendar is always up to date. However, turning the pages backward, the exact opposite can be found.

Life would be dull if one day were like another. Then truly the calendar, with its changing dates, would merely impress the passing of time and make one melancholy.

That is why it is essential that one not only adds years to one's life but life to one's years. As if aware of this need, the calendar has provided annually recurring Red-letter Days. They interrupt the monotonous flow of time and give people a chance to let themselves go.

Each of these special dates has its own story. Their origin goes back into the distant past and is the result of people's battle with nature and their own complexes, fears and desires.

Some of the days and months of the year have become linked with certain mysterious notions and telling phrases. Not only are they part of the chronology, they are full of romance, the fanciful beginnings of which it is good to know.

The Calendar

Originally there were no lists of dates and, to start with, the term calendar did not relate to anything written down but to a herald's announcement! It explains why the calendar's name is derived from the Latin for "to call out." The beginning of each month was proclaimed by the lead-priest or another appointed official.

No one knew beforehand when exactly the new month would start. It had to coincide with the appearance of the new moon. Only when this had been observed could the official declaration be made. That is how initially the *calends* merely referred to the first day of each month.

The development of commerce and financial transactions led to the writing down of these significant dates which by then, through the ever-growing knowledge of the movements of the sun, the moon and the stars, could be determined far in advance.

Merchants and money-lenders thus began to keep their own calendars—tables listing the initial dates of each month which enabled them to know when accounts had to be settled and interest became due. Out of these early account-books of the Romans grew the now indispensable tabulation of the passing of time, whether fixed on the wall, put on the desk or, in the form of a diary, carried in one's pockets.

The Numbering of Years

Even the most primitive races needed some sort of calendar. To them it was almost a matter of life and death. It was essential for them to know the proper time for sowing and reaping; when to seek shelter from the heat or the cold, from wet seasons and dry and from the inundations of rivers. Hunters and fishermen depended on the annual migration of animals and fish. Not least, conscious of their total dependence on the will of the gods, they had to serve them at the right moment and therefore the timely celebration of feasts was a vital part of their religion.

Observation taught them that the seasons coincided with certain positions of heavenly bodies and other celestial phenomena, the very reason astronomy assumed such an important place in human life and became the fountainhead of all calendars. Indeed, the daily and annual movements of the sun, the moon and the stars served from the very start as a basis for the division of time and one can only wonder at the remarkable accuracy of early astronomical perception.

The rotation of the earth on its axis resulted in the divisions of day and night. The period of the revolution of the moon around the earth suggested the month. The time it took for the earth to rotate around the sun created the year.

To start with, years were not counted continuously, but related to some outstanding event, such as a flood, an earthquake or a conquest. Not least, people noted how many years had passed since those occurred. The calendar also used the date of the accession of rulers as its reference point. Thus early records (particularly in the Bible) tell that an event took place "in the year X of the reign of King Y."

With the further progress of civilization, continuous numbering of the years was introduced, with its starting point differing from nation to nation and largely dependent on the people's general outlook on life.

Ordinary Time

The Hebrews dated their calendar back to the creation of the world which they calculated had taken place 3760 years and three months B.C. To this day Jews follow this early (fictitious) scheme.

The sports-minded Greeks reckoned their time from the first Olympic Games in 776 B.C. The Romans initially chose the foundation of Rome in 753 B.C. as the beginning of their chronology. Julius Caesar then revised it in 46 B.C., bringing it "up to date." As this "Julian calendar" was in use when Christianity arose, the Church adopted it and for the ensuing five centuries, with the calendar of the modern Christian era counting the years from the date of the Incarnation of Christ, replacing it only in A.D. 530. Its introduction was due to Dionysius Exiguus, a learned monk in Rome, who based the starting point of the new epoch on the tradition that Jesus was born "in the twenty-eighth year of the reign of Augustus."

With the new style of numbering the years taking hold very slowly, in England the Christian era was inaugurated more than 100 years later, at the Synod of Whitby in A.D. 664.

The Months

The choice of the moon for the division of time was not accidental. This principal luminary of the night was worshipped by almost all primitive races. They considered it was a mysterious being which, unceasingly and regularly, had to pass through the stages of birth, full maturity, decay and death. The moon's revolutions around the earth were used as a measure of time for thousands of years. The day of the new moon, always anxiously looked out for, was celebrated as a holy day, the start of a new month.

The names of the months are derived from the Latin, each one of them due to the ancient Romans. They started the year, not as is done now—at the height of summer or the depth of winter, but in (their) spring. It was a natural choice, as the time of sowing. But being a bellicose people, they also used this month to prepare for their military campaigns.

Not surprisingly therefore, they named this month in honor of the god Mars. Originally, he had been linked with the fertility of the soil but later had become the god of war and death as well. Thus it was just the right time to protect their fields and homes from all foes—both physical and spiritual. That is why the year began with the worship of *Mars*, who is still honored in MARCH.

APRIL carries on the cycle of nature. From the Latin word meaning "to open," it marked the season when the Roman countryside began to blossom and the buds *opened* up.

In MAY, the following month, all plants were growing and, therefore, the choice of its name fell on *Maia*, the goddess of increase, to whom sacrifices were offered on its first day. Another interpretation claims that the month received its name in honor of the *Majores*, the Senate in the original constitution of Rome.

JUNE honors *Juno*, the queen of heaven and personification of womanhood, who was considered the guardian of marriage. According to another school of thought, June was named after the *Juniores*, the lesser branch of the Roman legislature. Yet a third theory claims that the name derives from *Junius* Brutus, one of Julius Caesar's murderers.

The following two months no longer commemorate gods or seasons, but honor famous historic figures. JULY is the birthmonth of *Julius* Caesar, in whose honor Mark Antony is said to have named it in the year of his assassination.

As *Augustus*, Caesar's nephew, followed him on the throne, so he does in the sequence of months. He himself gave AUGUST his name, as he had then celebrated some of his greatest triumphs and put an end to civil war.

Somehow the Romans must have lost interest in their gods and emperors after the sixth month of the year, as following it they just numbered them prosaically: SEPTEMBER (the *seventh*), OCTOBER (the *eighth*), NOVEMBER (the *ninth*) and DECEMBER (the *tenth*).

The original Roman calendar consisted of ten months only—from March to December. There was an uncounted gap in the winter between the years. Tradition relates that it was Numa Pompilius, the second king of Rome, who—in 713 B.C.—added the missing two months.

JANUARY was so called in honor of *Janus*, the Roman god of the beginning of things and the patron of birth. Logically, the beginning of the year was moved to this month. But, negligently, it was omitted to adjust the names of the numbered months, which no longer fitted. That is why the 9th month is still called "the seventh" (September), the 10th "the eighth" (October), the 11th "the ninth" (November) and the 12th "the tenth" (December). No one has had the courage or wisdom to put things right. Janus also was the deity of doors and gates. His two-faced head looked both forward and backward and, so fittingly at the start of a new year, could be said to simultaneously gaze at the past and to look into the future.

A Roman festival of atonement, held with special rites of purification on FEBRUARY 15, gave this month its name. It is derived from the Latin word meaning "to cleanse"—*februare*. Women who had proved barren were then beaten with thongs cut from the hides of two goats, sacrificed on the occasion. It was thought that this drastic treatment would purify the women and make them fertile.

The Days of the Week

While the years and months are the result of the observation of natural phenomena, the week owes its origin to early astrological and superstitious beliefs. There was nothing in the order of nature that suggested it, but merely people's vivid imagination, their limited knowledge and their assumption that their fate depended on the stars.

The figure 7 has always been considered holy and magical. Standing for completeness, it was thought to bring luck. The seven-day week, undoubtedly, goes back to ancient Babylonian astrology which linked each of the days with one of the seven known planets.

This scheme of dividing time into units of seven days was then adopted by the Hebrews. They did so probably during their Babylonian exile in the sixth century B.C., purifying it—temporarily —from its astrological associations.

Introducing it to Egypt, it is claimed, the country's priests were the first actually to name the seven days after the planets. They assumed that the heavenly body which was in charge of the first hour of a particular day controlled the day entirely, thereby obtaining a complete list of "regents" and days of the week, consisting of Saturn, Sun, Moon, Mars, Mercury, Jupiter and Venus.

From Egypt the week found its way to the Romans, to whom it had been unknown in pre-Christian days. From them it spread all over the continent of Europe, then to reach England.

In a strange kind of selection "up North" only some of the Roman names were retained, whilst others were replaced by their Nordic equivalent. Thus throughout every week, in a peculiar mixture pagan deities both of Roman and Teutonic lineage are recalled.

SATURDAY was *Saturn*'s day. The planet associated with the Roman deity of that name had taken the place of the Greek god of Time. Said to have devoured all his children except three, it was imagined for a long time that people born under his star were unlucky, as they had entered the world under an evil omen. It is perhaps more than a strange coincidence that many prohibitions appertaining to the Sabbath are paralleled by regulations concerning the Roman festival of Saturn, during which the law courts had to be closed, no public business could be transacted, schools went on holiday, no war could be started and even criminals could not be punished.

Obviously, SUNDAY is the day of the sun, which controls all its events. It was only in the fourth century that the Church declared it a holy day, doing so in commemoration of the Resurrection of Christ and replacing the observation of the Jewish Sabbath.

The moon's day became MONDAY.

For no known reason the English then changed their system and, for the remaining four days of the week, made use not of Roman but Norse mythology.

TUESDAY was so called by them in honor of Tiw, the Scandinavian god of war, formerly a daring Norse hero who had lost his hand in a fight.

WEDNESDAY paid tribute to the god Woden, the Anglo-Saxon rendering for the better-known Odin. The god of storms, he welcomed brave warriors to Valhalla, treating them there to the delights they had most desired on earth. His dominion extended to the realms of wisdom, poetry and agriculture. The latter accounts for the widespread and long-held belief that Wednesday was especially favorable for the sowing of crops.

THURSDAY was dedicated to Thor, Woden's son, the god of thunder. Strong, brutal and greedy, these very qualities endeared him to the people. He was famous for three possessions: his hammer, used to produce lightning and thunder; his belt of strength; and his iron glove which helped him in throwing the hammer.

FRIDAY was *Frigga*'s day. Woden's wife, she was the chief goddess and patroness of love, marriage and fertility. Originally a moon goddess, she travelled in a chariot drawn by two cats. Every week thus continues to honor the planet Saturn, to worship the sun and the moon, and to pay homage to wars, storms, brute force and love.

Red-letter Days

Red-letter Days are spoken of when wanting to stress or recollect some special joyous occasion. This colorful description of a momentous day always seems to be associated with some completely worldly matter. Yet the origin of the red-letter day is just the opposite.

It belonged to the Church and its most sacred and solemn occasions. It goes back to the time when the calendar conspicuously listed saints' days and holy days in red print. This distinguished them from all other days and, at the same time, indicated that special services for them were contained in the *Book of Common Prayer*. The rest of the year was shown on the calendar in ordinary, plain black type. The color was not chosen just because it caught the eye, but for its sacred association, especially in the minds of the pious. They were reminded by it of the blood shed by the martyrs.

April Fools' Day

Everyone loves a laugh. To do so at other people's expense is rightly considered uncivil and wrong. The calendar, however, has made provision to suspend this generally accepted rule once every year. On April 1, until noon, people are permitted to make fools of others. April Fools' Day is a unique institution—a holiday for laughter, with a great variety of explanations of its origin and real purpose.

Some people date the day back to Noah and think it was all his fault. They reason that, having spent much time in the Ark, he was anxiously waiting for the Flood to subside. When, mistakenly, he thought that at long last this had happened, he opened a window and sent out a dove. But it was on a fool's errand. Unable to find any land, the bird returned to the boat. It had been a futile mission.

This took place on a Hebrew date which is said to correspond to April 1. Ever since, this day has been appointed as All Fools' Day, the "all" being a corruption of the ancient *auld*, meaning "old." It is a reminder of the unfortunate circumstances of old Noah's time and perpetuates the memory of humanity's deliverance from the Flood.

Those who forgot the event and all it implies are punished by sending them on an ineffectual errand, just as Noah had done with the dove. This is intended to jerk their memory and teach them a lesson, so that never again will they ignore "April 1" and its message of the second chance given to people and their duty not to forfeit it.

One of the most significant occasions in ancient times was the celebration of the vernal equinox. Then, with laughter and joy, people welcomed the coming of spring. Happy that the winter was gone and exuberant at the rebirth of nature, they indulged in all kinds of frivolity and fun-making.

This festival fell on or about April 1 and people concluded that All Fools' Day owed its existence to those early pagan celebrations. Indians, too, at the coming of spring held their feast of Holi, during which they took great pleasure in sending people on fools' errands.

Others have claimed that the day is closely linked with the Roman Saturnalia, when the population in like manner loved fooling about and making fun of each other.

There has been a suggestion that April Fools' Day has nothing to do with the rejoicing at the arrival of spring, but commemorates special incidents in the passion of Christ, which also took place about that time. Christ's foes, determined to torment and mock him, enjoyed sending him backward and forward. Medieval mystery plays dramatized those tragic events. They showed how Jesus was asked to go from one person to another, from Annas to Caiaphas, from Caiaphas to Pilate, from Pilate to Herod, and then again back, from Herod to Pilate.

Some authorities believe it was through these religious, medieval productions that the custom arose of ridiculing people by sending them, without rhyme or reason, from place to place— just as had happened to Christ. Thus All Fools' Day was not intended to be a source of merriment. On the contrary, it was meant as a solemn reminder of the ridicule heaped on Christ at that season.

The Scots call April fools a cuckoo. In France they are known as an April fish—*un poisson d'Avril*. At that time of the year, it is felt, they act like young fish when they appear in French rivers. Lacking experience, they are easily caught. In colloquial English they would be referred to as suckers.

Yet another theory is that April Fools' Day originated from the practice of letting insane people be at large on April 1. The vulgar did this to amuse the crowds, asking the unfortunates to perform acts which obviously they could not accomplish.

All these interpretations are colorful, but perhaps unconvincing. Most probably, All Fools' Day goes back not to Noah's Ark or Christ's passion, but to sixteenth-century France, and was the result of a peculiar combination of circumstances. These included people's ancient delight in celebrating the New Year and the change of calendar then introduced. Other factors were playing on some people's forgetfulness and on others' rather perverted sense of humor.

The old Romans took pleasure on New Year's Day in visiting friends and taking them gifts. Throughout the Middle Ages, New Year fell on March 25. The fact that this date frequently coincided with Passion Week, or even Good Friday, caused the actual merriment to be postponed to April 1.

In 1564 the French adopted the reformed Gregorian Calendar

and, consequently, moved New Year's Day back to January 1. Many people at first could not get used to the change and forgot all about the new New Year. Taking advantage of their confusion, jokers paid them mock visits on April 1. The pranksters, being seriously received and welcomed, did not fail to make fools of the host.

Eventually, even the dullest persons realized that times had changed and April 1 was "out." Yet the custom of making fools of people on that day persisted. It was kept on even after its origin was no longer remembered. After all, it appealed to people's sense of fun.

The conservative English adopted the new calendar and, with it, All Fools' Day only in the eighteenth century.

No matter by whom and when April Fools' Day was first introduced, it has a strong social and psychological significance. In societies which are still at a comparatively low level, there is often an obsession to force all its members into one single mould. Still today, as a relic from times when the herd instinct ruled supreme, people sheepishly love uniformity and try to accuse anyone who differs or excels.

It is humiliating to be laughed at. Whoever makes a fool of a person, unconsciously wants them to keep in the background and hide in the anonymity of the crowd.

In his study "Laughter," Henri Bergson claimed as laughter's main function an attempt to intimidate individuals and thereby make them conform. Next to society's love of conformity, there is the individual's wish for superiority. By making other people ridiculous, one experiences the feeling of power. Practical jokers thus enjoy their egoism and, sending friends on a fool's errand, look upon them as puppets whose strings they pull.

All Fools' Day, most of all perhaps, serves as a wonderful means of relieving tension and for one day at least every year gives people a chance to forget their worries.

May Day

May Day—the first day of May—is principally celebrated nowadays as Labor Day, a holiday for the workers. Originally, however, it was a spring festival. It was observed to promote the fertility of all growing things on which human life depended.

Its ritual included magic and even the offering of human sacrifices. Bonfires, still lit in many places throughout Britain and Europe on May Day, are actually the remnants of "bone fires"— part of those ancient murderous practices.

The floral decorations and dances that characterize May Day are also relics that were performed in order to force the pace of nature. The ancient Celts used to dance around a living tree in an attempt to arouse its spirit. Moreover, the maypole recalls the primitive worship of the phallus as the source of reproduction.

Labor Day was proclaimed as late as 1889 at the International Workers' Congress, organized by French socialists in Paris. It stipulated that the day should be set aside as a workers' festival in all countries.

It became a worldwide tradition, marked by public meetings, parades and political speeches, and fostered primarily by trade unions and other representatives of working people. The immediate ancestor of May Day, however, is the Ancient Romans' Festival of Flowers—the Floralia.

Boxing Day

The day after Christmas is St. Stephen's Day, named in honor of Christianity's first martyr. In Britain and Commonwealth countries, however, it is known as Boxing Day.

The name has nothing to do with pugilists or prize-fighting. It relates to the ancient custom on that day of presenting a box containing a gift to anyone whom one owed a debt of gratitude.

Although the box has long been discarded, it is still customary to give a "Christmas box"—a well-deserved and expected gift. Its origin dates back to the Romans and their feast of Saturn, during which they gave each other presents as an expression of the merry spirit of the celebration of the winter solstice.

The association of the practice with paganism led the Church to denounce it and call on the faithful to discard it. Their appeal fell on deaf ears. Unable to destroy the heathen ways of giving, the religious authorities reinterpreted them. Their initial link with pagan revelry was suppressed (and then forgotten), to be replaced by a new and sacred tradition.

People should still give to others of what they had, not for sensuous enjoyment but for the sake of the soul. The Church provided special boxes to receive gifts, for masses to be said for the donors which by then were celebrated for almost every contingency of life. When, for instance, a ship was about to leave, priests placed on her a box which they dedicated to a saint under whose protection she would sail. Everyone on her was expected to make some contribution. The box was not opened until the ship's return, its contents then to be given to a priest to say mass for the men, so that their misdeeds during the voyage might be forgiven.

It was the earliest kind of *Christ's* Mass, with the receptacle containing voluntary offerings in payment of its celebration becoming known as Christ's Mass Box.

There were further developments of the now Christianized pagan custom. The box became the symbol of church charity. It was in every house of worship and was opened on Christmas Day after the morning service. Money in it was called "the dole of the Christmas box" or "box money." This was distributed by the parish priest next day, which appropriately assumed the name of Boxing Day.

The wheel then turned full circle and the religious custom to aid the poor and destitute again became secularized. At Christmas, apprentices now called on their masters' customers, carrying a box into which they expected them to place a small gratuity. Boxes have become redundant, nor is it only apprentices who expect this recognition of services rendered.

A far-fetched and totally different interpretation of the Christmas box sees in it a survival—etymologically as much as practically—of the Oriental *baksheesh*. During the Crusades, this theory alleges, knights returning from the East brought back from there both the word and the tipping practice.

The Clock

The alternation of day and night offered the earliest means of keeping time. But just to say, "We'll meet when it's dark" (or "light") was insufficient. In search of something to assist people in being more specific, looking up into the sky they duly noted the movement of the sun, perceiving that it travelled westward as the day advanced.

The first clock thus was God-made—the sun. The day was divided according to its position—whether it was high or low in the sky, in the east or the west, rising or setting. That is how people began to speak of dawn, morning, noon and evening. Actually, *Orient* still means (the) "rising" (sun), and in many languages the word for evening is derived from a term denoting the *West*.

People soon felt the need to become more exact and to divide the time of day into much smaller and more definite units. From the sky, they turned their eyes to the ground and discovered the shadow. They watched it with fear and trembling, seeing in it some kind of mysterious being which followed on their heels as long as the sun shone.

They also observed that the shadow's length and direction changed continuously throughout the day. When the sun was high, the shadow was short; when the sun was low, the shadow was long. During the first half of the day, when the sun was in the east, the shadow pointed to the west, and vice versa.

Most likely, it was the Babylonians who first took note of these significant facts and began to use the moving shadow in telling the time much more accurately than had ever been done before by merely watching the sun.

It led to their invention—in the second millennium B.C.—of the first man-made clock, the sundial. It was one of the simplest instruments ever devised, consisting of a stick stuck vertically in the ground. As the sun advanced, the stake's shadow told the time. The term *dial* comes from the Latin word for "day" and explains why the shadow-clock, as an instrument telling the time of day by means of the sun, came to be called a *sundial*.

The movement of the stake's shadow described a curve. It did not take long for people to realize that, for practical purposes, this curve could be divided into various parts. The obvious way to identify these was to allot them numbers. Each section was called an *hour*, a Greek word meaning "the time of day."

Another important question still to be settled was the number of segments most suitable for the division of time. For both religious and practical reasons the figure "12" had immediately suggested itself to the Babylonians. To them, it was a mystical number. They also found it most convenient to use, as it could be divided evenly by 2, 3, 4 or 6. That is how the twelve-hour day started!

Sundials were very useful. Yet they had obvious disadvantages. They worked only when the sun was shining but in the dark or on a cloudy day the hours vanished. Furthermore, the speed of the travelling shadow was most irregular and hence the length of the hours varied. Some hours were short and others long, according to the season of the year and the sundial's geographical location. What was needed was a timepiece which was independent of the sun and assured the division of time into regular hours.

The Egyptians led the way in achieving that aim by inventing the water clock. In its simplest form, it consisted of a pot with a hole in the bottom. As it always took the same time to empty the vessel, people could easily tell the hour of day and night by merely noting the water's level in the bowl.

From Egypt, the new clock spread all over the Mediterranean world. In the course of time people learned to improve its design. A floater was put on the water, now gathered in a vessel beneath, and linked to a gear which moved a pointer that turned in a circle. Placed behind this "hand" was a dial, marked off all around and at regular intervals with the old sundial's figures from 1 to 12.

The face of the modern clock had made its appearance! Yet water clocks, just like their predecessor, the sundial, still suffered from a disadvantage: they depended on the elements of nature. In a cold climate they were apt to freeze in winter and, with it, once again as it were, time stood still.

About the year 250 B.C. further progress in the search for a more reliable time-recorder was made by the invention of the hourglass. This replaced water by pure, dry sand. The quantity passing through a narrow neck between two globes indicated the time.

Opinions differ as to where, and for what purpose, the sand-clock was first devised. Some say that it originated on sailing ships. Others assert that the Roman army introduced it to measure "watches" in the night. A monk at Chartres, skilled in glassblowing, is credited with having created its final shape in the eighth century A.D.

The sand-clock was retained for thousands of years and served in diverse ways. It timed tournaments in the Middle Ages, helped housewives in boiling their eggs, and congregations in restricting the time of their parson's sermon by conspicuously placing an hourglass on the pulpit.

Even sand had its drawbacks. Its enemy was damp weather, in which it either got stuck or flowed so slowly that time began to drag. Where water and sand failed, the burning of a light (or, as among the Chinese, of incense) succeeded. Thus, a burning candle was used as yet another way of measuring time. The candle became shorter at a steady rate. All that was necessary was to mark the taper, before it was lit, according to the passing of hours. It was a simple and effective (yet more expensive) way of telling the time.

Early on therefore, the sundial, water-clock, hourglass and burning candle either displaced or supplemented each other. All of them, however, were crude devices of poor accuracy which gave only a very rough estimate of the passage of time.

There was still much room for improvement. Yet it was not until the Middle Ages that further advancement was made and the first mechanical clock designed. This applied the principle of the water-clock, but instead of using water to move the hand, it employed weights. The invention of the pendulum, the escapement and the spring completed the development of the clock which had extended over almost 5,000 years.

The Naming of the Clock

The clock owes its name to religious practice. Experience has shown that the progress of mechanization alienates people ever more from God. But not so in the case of the clock. It is now believed that the earliest mechanized timekeepers were invented specifically to help people in saying their prayers.

Prayers used to belong to everyday life and were a regular habit. It was not left to the individual to worship whenever the spirit moved them, which, after all, might never be. A ritual had to take place at the appropriate hour and a service had to be held at the right moment. That applied especially to those who had dedicated their lives to God—monks and nuns.

How could they know that the hour had come for devotion, particularly after nightfall? A clock that struck the hour was the answer. Thus the chiming of bells became part of the first mechanical clocks. The discipline of monastic orders and not necessities of civil life brought the modern striking-clock into being. Actually, the earliest models indicated the time not visually, but audibly, by means of bells.

The French word for bell is *cloche*. That is how, from the regulated and properly chimed hours of worship, and through the French tongue, the clock received its name.

The Watch

The first watch small enough to fit into one's pocket was invented in 1588. The choice of its name refers to its earliest purpose and the very reason for its existence.

To prevent crime and catch criminals, guards were appointed whose duty it was to patrol the streets and keep watch. These early policemen followed their "beat" rather haphazardly, both as to where they went and the time they took. After all, they could not know the exact hour of the day or night.

The birth of the drive-spring then revolutionized not only the working but the size of the clock. No longer weighted, it could now be carried. Its new small dimensions had changed it into a portable timepiece. The first, still rather clumsy, iron-cased pocket clocks began to appear everywhere. They were just what the guards needed to keep a definite schedule in their watching. Soon they prided themselves on owning the new device.

People naturally took due notice and it did not take them long to associate, in every sense of the *word*, their watchmen with the portable clocks they carried. Eventually, the small pocket clocks became completely identified with the men of the watch!

CHAPTER 25

Religion and its Symbols

Many religious customs have become part of everyday life and are followed automatically, not stopping to inquire about their purpose and meaning.

Mothers may have taught their children to join hands at prayer. People kneel in worship. The sound of church bells has long been synonymous with the call to Christian service. The halo seems to belong from the beginning to Christian saints and only to them.

But why, how and where did these and other religious traditions start? Opinions differ and have caused much dissension.

As if to echo the great controversies aroused in the name of religion, even the very word has been subject to arguments and disagreements. Its linguistic root, of course, is Latin. *Relegere* meant "to treat with care" and represented the opposite of neglect. In that sense, religion would suggest awe and fear, respect for the sacred and the punctilious performance of rites.

Others felt that the verb *lego* was responsible for the word. This signified "to pick" or "gather together," and as *relego,* "to read again." So explained, religion would refer to the close observation of omens and portents which, by being put together and read again, assisted people in their search for the right interpretation.

A further suggestion saw in the word a combination of *re* ("back") and *ligere* (to "bind") and consequently found in religion something that bound humans up with their gods, the forging of a link between the terrestrial and the celestial.

An inquiry into the beginning of religious customs reveals yet another bond. It shows how almost all of them, in some way or other, are shared among most varied faiths and are tied up with ancient, and sometimes primitive, beliefs.

The "Dog Collar"

The clergyman's badge of office—his collar worn back to front—is of comparatively recent origin and far from being ecclesiastical. To wear it is really contrary to the early wishes of Church authorities, who were strongly opposed to a priest putting on any distinctive kind of dress. Indeed, Pope Celestinus, in A.D. 428, reprimanded those bishops who dared to wear a costume that distinguished them from other people, which was considered a denial of the original democratic and nonprofessional character of Christianity.

Despite these views and directions, priests eventually appeared dressed differently from the laity, their clothes were not a new ecclesiastical type of uniform. On the contrary, they were a continuation of a pagan mode of attire! It did not originate in biblical teachings or traditions, but in old Roman custom.

When, in the sixth century, fashions changed and people abandoned the traditional Roman kind of apparel, the clergy, conservative in all things, did not follow suit. They refused to adopt the "modern" garment and continued to use the now outmoded dress.

Whilst laymen got used to putting on the new short tunics, trousers and cloaks, priests persisted in wearing the Roman toga and long type of tunic, still surviving today in the surplice, cassock and frock. Indeed, Pope Gregory the Great, determined to obstruct any change, decried the new fashion as barbaric and decreed retention of the Roman garb by his priests.

It was only in the ninth century that Christian authorities tried to add to this Roman way of secular dress some likeness to the ancient priestly vestments, worn by the Aaronites in King Solomon's Temple.

The clerical collar itself is a development or, more accurately, a relic, of that part of medieval "priestly" garb which was known as the amice, a square of white linen worn in the eleventh century by priests celebrating mass. Tied both at back and front with a series of strings, it formed a triangular type of scarf. Modified in Tudor times, it became a white neck cloth with long tag ends which, eventually, were dropped.

The original purpose of this "dog collar" had no religious association, but was most utilitarian. It was a sort of scarf (worn already by Roman public orators) to protect the throat and neck of speakers against cold and a very practical way of preventing the rest of the garment from being stained by perspiration.

The cloth is attached to a white collar, which was merely the old white neckband worn by everybody from the sixteenth century onward until the introduction of the modern collar in the late nineteenth century.

Joining Hands in Prayer

From earliest times, people have accompanied their spoken prayer with gestures and postures. Most common, and first in Hebrew and Christian worship, was the spreading of arms and hands towards heaven. Later on, this custom was reduced to the hands being folded or crossed on the breast, one wrist resting on the other.

The joining of hands, as it is done now, was then unknown. It is not mentioned anywhere in the Bible and did not appear in the Christian Church before the ninth century. Its origin is divorced from religion and far from peaceful. It leads back to people's eagerness to subjugate each other and developed out of the shackling of hands of prisoners!

Though the handcuffs eventually disappeared, the joining of hands remained as a symbol of servitude and submission and people's inability (or even lack of inclination) to grasp a weapon.

Many examples show how the custom—long before being accepted in Christian circles—had become a standard gesture. Indeed, it was used as the real or imaginary shackling among pagans. Tacitus relates, for instance, how a German tribe, the Semnones, venerated a sacred wood "into which none penetrated without being bound as a sign of dependence and as a public homage to the power of the gods." Greeks and Romans adopted the identical gesture as a magic means to bind the devil and other occult powers and thereby to compel their obedience. Feudal lords finally adopted the joining of hands for their vassals, who thus had to swear and indicate their loyalty.

It was from those various sources that Christianity adopted the gesture representing shackled hands as a sign of one's total obedience to divine power. It has also been suggested that there was

Indian influence at work, as Hindus for many centuries prior used to join hands at prayer. All other explanations are of a later date.

Prayer to be perfect demands complete relaxation, one's being at ease and at rest. To attain this mood, the body has to be comfortable and motionless. To keep thus the hands together avoided any fidgeting and assured a natural position of repose. People with their hands joined sloughed off the turmoil of daily life and were able to look inward with all the force of their spirit.

It is a well-known fact that their instincts, without people even realizing it, help them to reach certain goals. The pressing together of hands or the clenching of their fingers into a fist somehow generates in the body additional electric potentials and impulses. It may be that by joining hands forcefully or clasping the fingers people add considerably to the store of spiritual power as well and make prayers all the more potent and effective.

The study of comparative religion suggests yet another possible origin of the gesture. Idol-worshippers were accustomed to stretch out their arms and point with their fingers to the objects whose help they wished to invoke—towards the sea, the sun or a statue of one of their gods. Sometimes they even went so far as to touch and stroke the idol. It is possible that as a reaction and protest against these pagan habits, Christians made sure of avoiding any pointing by joining their hands in the shape of what has later been interpreted as that of a church steeple.

A final psychological observation may be added. The mere fact that the early Christian custom of spreading the arms far and wide has been replaced by the humble and inconspicuous gesture of joining the hands is indicative of the secularization of life. Once religion was a powerful force, proudly displayed with the passion of people who wished that their faith should embrace the world. Now it has become much less demonstrative, meek and mild, as it were, and its retiring posture seems almost apologetic.

Kneeling

Kneeling is a most ancient custom and well attested in Holy Scripture. King Solomon knelt when dedicating the Temple and Daniel went down on his knees in worship three times every day to give thanks to God. Jesus knelt in prayer on the Mount of Olives at the fateful hour preceding his arrest. To St. Paul kneeling and prayer were synonymous. In Hebrew the term for praise is rooted in the word "knee."

Kneeling is even more characteristic in Islam worship, which is accompanied by much genuflecting, a fact responsible for the very name of the Muslim sanctuary: *mosque*, meaning a place of "kneeling."

The custom itself stems from the Orient and Greeks decried it as such. It expressed a person's total submission to a higher power. In essence, kneeling itself is a survival and a small part of the complete prostration of one's body on the ground, of a vanquished foe before his conqueror, a vassal in front of his lord, and a subject before his king.

Originally this was not merely a symbolic gesture, but a humbling position in which a person was helpless and could not commit any aggression.

That religion adopted this posture was due to several reasons. God was the King of Kings, who demanded complete submission. In homage to him and in self-abasement, humans bent their knee and threw themselves down. Like an offering, they presented themselves to God. That is why St. Paul in his Letter to the Romans could say, "I beseech you that you present your bodies a living sacrifice, holy, acceptable unto God. . . ."

But religions also realized the close relationship between outward attitude and inward feeling. Kneeling thus not only symbolized but fostered a mood of humility, so essential for prayer. It was further felt that one's whole being had to participate in it: not only the mind but the body as well.

The Rosary

According to traditional belief it was twelfth-century St. Dominic who instituted the devotion of the rosary. He was "admonished by the Blessed Virgin" to preach it "as a special remedy against heresy and sin." In fact, however, rosaries were in existence—in Christianity—long before then. St. Dominic merely extended and popularized the custom which in reality originated in Asia and is very ancient. Hindus and Buddhists made use of it centuries before Catholicism. The oldest reference to a rosary has been traced to India, where it was used by Hindu monks. When Marco Polo visited the king of Malabar, he was surprised to watch the monarch worshipping with a rosary of more than 100 stones.

Some authorities claim that the Crusaders brought the custom to Europe, having adopted it in the East from the Muslims. Nevertheless, examples of rosaries of one kind or another were known in western Europe before then. Thus it is said that Lady Godiva of Coventry, who died before 1070, bequeathed to the monastery she established "a circlet of gems which she had threaded on a string in order that by fingering them one by one, as she successively recited her prayers, she might not fall short of the exact number."

The rosary was a simple device to keep count of prayers—an aid to memory. Appropriately, it was referred to in Sanskrit as "the muttering chaplet" or "the remembrancer" and, early in Europe, as "calculi" and "numeralia."

Devotion commands complete concentration. For the mind to wander, even for a moment, thinking of other things, would interrupt communion with God. According to ancient tradition, frequent repetition of prayers and their multiplication added to their efficacy. In the early days of the Church it was a well-known practice to recite privately all of the 150 Psalms and to repeat the Lord's Prayer fifty times. Centuries later, Knights Templar who could not attend choir had to say the Lord's Prayer fifty-seven times and, on the death of any of their brethren, were required to recite it a hundred times daily for a week.

The absence of prayer books made it most difficult to keep count of the many and varied petitions and Psalms the devout had to or wished to recite. To count and pray at the same time, even by using the fingers, was practically impossible. Mechanical help was needed. At first, most simple means were employed, such as discs of bone, fruit stones, berries, pebbles and knots in a cord. When, for instance, in the fourth century, Paul the Hermit imposed on himself the task of repeating daily 300 prayers, he collected an equal number of pebbles and threw them away, singly, at the end of each prayer. Monks of the Greek Church used cords with 100 knots to count their numerous genuflections and signs of the cross.

Bead simply means prayer. The word is derived from the Anglo-Saxon *bede*, also retained in the German *Gebet*. Hence people "said their beads." Lest they omit any, they tied knots in a string—one knot for each prayer. Eventually, they began to call each knot a prayer; that is, a bead. But to identify part of a string with a petition to God seemed unworthy. The crude knots were therefore discarded and replaced with precious stones and sometimes with little balls of gold. As these remained the symbol of prayer, they continued to be known as beads. The modern woman does not realize that her necklace of beads goes back to the worship of the desert fathers and recalls not precious ornamentation but fervent prayer, even in its literal sense.

There was another, psychological function of the rosary which is not always realized. People found it helpful to let their hands play with an object while their mind concentrated on an image or an idea. Somehow the activity, carried on almost unawares, intensified the thought process. Letting smooth round objects slide through their fingers released tension and soothed the mind. It increased their spiritual power and added to their creative spirit, in which the soul laid itself open to the divine.

The word rosary means "a garland" or "a wreath of roses." The term probably did not appear till the fifteenth century. Its origin has been explained by simple facts, symbolism and a legend.

Early on, so it is said, the beads were carved out of rosewood, and it was the choice of this material that was responsible for the name. Others have suggested *rosaire*, French for "bead," as the linguistic root. As there were so many beads strung together, people began to call the mechanical aid to prayer simply "the beads," using the Latinized form of the French word.

The rose was a symbol of beauty and perfection. Early and medieval Christians chose it as the emblem of the Virgin Mary— the rose of womanhood. Since, according to tradition, she herself handed the first chain of beads to St. Dominic, this has been called ever since by one of her titles, the *rosa mystica*.

At times, its individual beads were marked with her emblem, the rose, and that is how, it is further claimed, the rosary really received its name.

The "complete rosary" of Catholicism, consisting of 150 beads, goes back to the ancient desert fathers and their recital of the 150 Psalms of the Hebrew Bible.

During the Middle Ages praying-strings were frequently used

for the repeated recital of The Lord's Prayer and thus came to also be known as Paternosters, the prayer's first two words in Latin, "Our Father."

Manufacturers of the prayer-strings were called Paternosterers. They comprised a recognized craft-guild of considerable importance and their concentration in one London street is said to have given it its name—Paternoster Row. It is still in existence.

Fish on Friday

Paganism considered Friday the luckiest day of the week. It was ruled by the planet Venus, whose influence was thought to be most fortunate. Named in honor of Freya, the goddess of love, it was a day most propitious for marriage.

In Christian lands Friday has always had a gloomy association, brought about by traditions of both the Hebrew Bible and the New Testament. It was on a Friday that Adam and Eve were said to have eaten of the forbidden fruit, thus bringing sin into the world. And on a Friday they died. Jesus suffered and was crucified on a Friday. Hence, every Friday became a memorial of Good Friday, as every Sunday was a little Easter.

That is why it was thought to be unprofitable, even inviting disaster, to start a new task or journey on a Friday. For centuries sailors refused to leave port on that ominous day and at the beginning of the twentieth century statistics showed that in France bus takings were lowest and train travelers fewest on Fridays.

The story is told that when the reluctance of seamen to sail on a Friday had reached such proportions that it interfered with naval operations, the British Admiralty decided to prove once and for all the fallacy of the belief. The keel of a new vessel was laid on a Friday, she was launched on a Friday, and she was named HMS *Friday*. On her first voyage, beginning on a Friday, she was commanded by Captain James Friday. Everything had gone according to plan—up to that moment. The ship duly sailed. . . . Nothing, however, has been heard of her or her crew ever since.

In memory of the crucifixion, Catholicism made Friday a fast day and a day of abstinence. Anyone having reached the age of seven had to fast (that is, to limit the intake of food) and abstain from meat. Only in recent times was the decree modified and it was left to the individual to choose which form the penance would take. Actually, there is no passage in the New Testament that commands a fast. In fact, St. Paul (I Timothy 4:3) alludes to the abstention from meat as a mark of apostasy and a sign of weak faith in that it attaches importance to such comparatively trifling matters. The kingdom of God, he said, was not meat and drink, but righteousness, peace and joy in the Holy Spirit.

The idea of what constituted a fast has been understood differently by various faiths. Jews fast for twenty-four hours on their Day of Atonement, the only fast day expressly ordained in the Old Testament. During that period they do not eat, drink, smoke or have sexual relations.

Muslims keep a whole month—Ramadan—as a fast. They are not even allowed to swallow their own spittle or enjoy the fragrance of perfume. However, they observe the fast only during daylight, to partake of food during the night.

There are various reasons why Catholics consider a meatless day as a fast. Some of them are completely divorced from religious considerations.

It was a Jewish tradition to abstain from meat on days of sorrow and as a sign of penitence. Thus Daniel (10:2–3) refrained from all pleasant food for three weeks: "I ate no . . . bread neither came flesh . . . in my mouth." Ever since the destruction of the second Temple in A.D. 70, pious people refused to eat meat at any time because they felt that, as there was no longer an altar on which animals could be offered to God, no one should enjoy their flesh. Abstention from meat was to them a symbol of grief and a constant reminder of the tragedy that had befallen their people.

It was not difficult for Christianity to adopt this tradition, reserving it for one day a week only and linking it with the tragic death of Christ, instead of with the burning of the Temple.

There is a possibility that the (now discarded) custom of eating fish on a Friday (and during Lent) entered the Christian faith not from Jewish sources alone, but from the pagan world as well, and that it was entirely independent of ascetic motivation or ideas. Greek philosophers believed that a vegetarian diet was helpful to their faculties and contributed to clarity of thought.

It might well be that eating fish on Friday also continued an old pagan practice. Fish was said to be sacred to Aphrodite, the foam-born goddess of beauty and fertility, who was also worshipped as the goddess of the sea. The Romans identified her with Venus, to whom they dedicated Friday. It was in her honor that fish was then eaten, most probably in the belief that it promoted fruitfulness.

To refrain from eating meat expressed grief and reverence to Christ. His passion and death were thus remembered one day every week, not merely in one's thoughts, but in one's very way of life.

In ancient days it was believed that the eating of meat stimulated man's passions. Hence, a meatless diet made chastity easier. To conquer their fleshly lusts and enable them to concentrate on spiritual exercises, abstention from meat appeared as a most helpful means.

In much later years, political and economic reasons reinforced the peculiar kind of fast on Friday. These were purely mundane— to restrict the eating of meat and foster consumption of fish. This achieved several aims. A fish diet once a week was cheap and aided the poor without making them feel inferior. It helped to protect a valuable breed of cattle and controlled the meat price, keeping it at a moderate level.

On the other hand, it ensured an increase in the sale of fish, thus boosting the fishing trade, the building of boats and the number of men going to sea. Above all, it furthered the strength of the British navy, as men, whilst on fishing expeditions, caught the love of the sea, and when the Admiralty called for volunteers, they were only too happy to offer their services.

It was with those thoughts in mind, and "not to put holiness in one kind of meat and drink more than another," that in 1548, the second year of the reign of King Edward VI, an Act of Parliament ordered abstention from meat on the fast day and that, similarly, during the Elizabethan era, a proclamation commanded the keeping of "fish days."

The Communion Service

The Holy Communion service, with its bread and wine, began within the Synagogue. It is derived from the ancient Hebrew custom of offering special thanks to God at the beginning of every Sabbath and festival, which was always on their eve.

The head of the family praised God at the festival table, before the actual meal. He did so over wine and bread, which symbolized the bounty of the vineyard and the field. All present partook of the bread he broke and the cup of wine he blessed.

According to the Synoptic Gospels, Jesus's "Last Supper," his final meal on the night before the Crucifixion, took place on the eve of the Jewish Passover and was, therefore, the traditional Passover celebration.

This was held in every home all over Jerusalem and the Holy Land. Its ritual included the blessing of wine and bread. But instead of ordinary loaves, unleavened bread, known as *Matzah*, was broken, in memory of the Israelites' affliction and their exodus from Egypt.

As a Jew, Jesus followed meticulously the ancient practice of breaking the bread and blessing the wine and then sharing both with his twelve disciples. While doing so, the Gospel account relates, he referred mysteriously to the bread as his body and the wine as his blood.

The words and their interpretation caused much conflict and controversy. Their very brevity and obscurity laid them open to various explanations. Critical scholars were reminded of pagan sacramental rites in which, by means of a joint participation of sacred food, the eaters were knitted to their god and to one another.

Did Jesus intend, it was asked, to introduce similarly a mystical and sacramental idea into the Jewish practice, linking it with his forthcoming sacrificial death? Or, conscious of the forgetfulness of humans, was he concerned about giving his disciples and those who followed them some way of remembering him and of holding them together when he had gone?

An association of thought could serve as the best reminder. The substance of bread would suggest to them his body and the red color of the wine would bring to mind his blood.

No matter what Jesus really meant, the fact is that the Eucharist, which became a central act of Christian worship, is the perpetuation of his last Passover supper and of the Jewish practice of thanking God by breaking bread and blessing wine, still carried on in every Jewish home.

Indeed, its Jewish tradition survives in the very name of Holy

Communion, the Eucharist, meaning "to give thanks." The term itself is not found in the New Testament and stems from the Greek. That the thin wafer, used as the Host, must be unleavened, equally recalls its Hebrew origin: the unleavened bread of the Jewish Passover feast.

Covering the Head in a Synagogue

For a man to cover his head in a synagogue and generally at prayer is now accepted as a Jewish religious custom. Anyone entering a synagogue, Jew or Gentile alike, is expected to keep his hat on, or, if without one, to use a skull cap.

The fact that Christian Church dignitaries, including the Pope, wear the same type of skull cap, and that Muslim worshippers also cover their heads, shows not only the ubiquity of the custom but how it has spread from Judaism to its daughter religions.

In its origin, the covering of the head had no religious implication. The earliest Hebrews did not know the practice, and it is not mentioned anywhere in the Old Testament. The custom entered Judaism at a later date from the outside world, and possibly, first of all, for health reasons.

People in the East suffered from the frequent and considerable changes of temperature and felt the need to protect the head. Long before the establishment of the first synagogues, the Hebrews prayed in the open. In the Temple of old, the altar on which the sacrifices were offered stood in the open, and those participating in the ceremonial were exposed to the burning sun of the Orient. To cover the head and avoid sunstroke became a wise precaution.

The original, practical purpose was soon forgotten. The custom became a gesture of humility and submission, whilst bareheadedness, on the other hand, was considered a demonstration of defiance. Eventually, anyone standing before God began to cover his head.

At first only the priestly class were appointed to serve God. They did this on behalf of the people and mainly to offer sacrifices. They were distinguished by their headdress, the High Priest wearing a miter, a cloth of fine linen, coiled around his head like a turban. But after the Romans had destroyed the Temple in A.D. 70, with the altar gone, the offering of sacrifices became impossible.

Consequently, the chief office of priesthood lost its justification and ceased to exist.

Prayers came to take the place of animal sacrifice, and the whole of the Jewish people took over the task of the ancient priesthood. To indicate their assumption of priestly duties, they adopted the custom of covering the head.

While Western man raises his hat out of courtesy, Eastern tradition demands the opposite. When entering a home, one has to remove one's shoes, but keep one's head covered. A host, similarly, did not dare appear before his guests bareheaded, as that would be considered a breach of good manners. Eventually, the hat, or whatever took its place, acquired an almost sacred significance.

Whilst Western man swears by the Bible, the Arab does so by his head cover. By a natural process of assimilation, the Jews of the Orient adopted the custom of their environment, probably first in Babylonia, and covered their heads as a general symbol of deference and an act of civility. If one covered one's head to pay respect to humans, was it not more essential to do so when standing before one's God? That is how the custom became part of synagogue worship.

When the Jews migrated to Western lands, they continued to cover their heads, carrying with them the Eastern style though, in their new homes with their different code of etiquette, its original purpose had lost its meaning. They were no longer aware of its roots and it was given new interpretations and considered as a hallowed tradition. It had become one of the most noticeable, yet least significant, features of Jewish worship.

Church Bells

Church bells were unknown to Christians for at least the first five centuries—and for obvious reasons. Christianity at first was declared illegal by pagan authorities and its worship was punished. The devout had to gather clandestinely, doing so in the catacombs and at night.

Even when Christianity became a recognized faith, it was a blast of trumpets and not a peal of bells that summoned the faithful to worship. Bells came into general use in the church only after the eighteenth century.

Bells developed out of small pieces of concave metal which explains why their very name is derived from the Latin term for a foot-pan or basin. The original purpose of all bells was to make a loud, but not necessarily musical sound—to drive off evil spirits. It was for this reason that they were first introduced in places as varied as Hindu temples and Christian churches. As late as A.D. 1280 a theological work dealing with the Christian ritual recorded that "bells are rung in processions that demons may fear and flee. For when they hear the trumpets of the church militant, that is the bells, they are afraid."

And this first and most important function of bells survived for centuries in many customs. The "passing bell," tolled at funerals, for instance, is known today as the herald of death and draws attention to the fact that a soul is "passing" from this world to the next and asks for our prayers on its behalf. Originally, however, its sound was meant to drive away evil spirits hovering around the dying person, ready to pounce on their soul.

Bells, likewise, were struck at times of sickness and natural disaster. Both were ascribed to the presence of fiends which only loud noise could scare away. Accordingly, a blessing of church bells, suggested by Egbert, the eighth-century Archbishop of York and included in his Pontifical, read, "Wherever this bell sounds, let the power of enemies retreat, so also the shadow of phantoms, the assault of whirlwinds, the stroke of lightning, the harm of thunders . . . and every spirit of the storm winds." In modern times, French church authorities have had the bells rung to ward off the effect of lightning and, in 1852, the Bishop of Malta ordered the tolling of bells to "lay a gale of wind."

Roger Bacon, often quoted as the inventor of gunpowder, also recorded the prevalent belief of the demon-chasing quality of the sound of bells. "The great ringing of bells in popular cities," he stated, "charmed away thunder and also dissipated pestilential air." Being of a scientific bend of mind, however, he tried to rationalize the ancient superstition. It was not really the sound of the bells, he claimed, but the concussion of air caused by their tolling, which purified the atmosphere, driving away pestilence and turbulence.

It was firmly believed that the bigger the bell and the louder its sound, the further the spirits were compelled to flee. Thus ever-larger church bells were used to guard God's sanctuaries and to keep them unsullied and at peace.

The tolling of bells as a call to prayer is a comparatively late development. Many other functions of bells were added down the centuries. They make up a colorful list and have been subject to fascinating and, sometimes, even amusing interpretations.

In pre-Reformation days "churchgoing bells" were rung, not to make people leave their homes right away, but as an invitation to a preparatory prayer there to put them in the right frame of mind for divine service. Later on, bells were sounded not so much as a call for spiritual preparation but as a reminder that people should get ready and dress for service, due to commence only an hour later.

On the other hand, at one time it was also a custom to ring bells at the conclusion of the sermon or the end of the service. This has been variously explained. It was introduced, some said, to announce to those who had stayed away from worship that another sermon was to be preached or service held that same night, giving them a chance to make up for their lost opportunity. But then it was also interpreted as of special and nonspiritual benefit to the clergy, who were said to like a hot Sunday dinner. It was to let their cooks know that the priest was about to leave church and that they had to make sure the meal was ready. Appropriately, this particular tolling came to be known as "the pudding bell."

In Westmoreland bells were chimed during the service, immediately after the recitation of the Creed. It was to inform dissenters that, without any qualms of conscience, they could now join the congregation in worship. At St. Michael's in York bells were rung every morning at 6 o'clock. The practice went back to an early incident when people, wandering in the nearby forest, got lost. After spending a terrifying night in the woods, they discovered their whereabouts only next morning, when they heard the pealing of the bells of St. Michael's. Out of gratitude and to help any future lost travelers, they endowed a fund which provided for the tolling of bells as a "homing beacon" at the same hour each day.

The Halo

The halo is pagan, practical, and completely un-Christian in origin. Centuries before Christ, natives used to ornament their heads with a circle of feathers. They did so to symbolize their relationship with the sun-god, their own "halo" of feathers representing the circle of light that distinguished the shining divinity in the sky. Indeed, people came to believe that by adopting such a "nimbus" humans turned into a kind of sun themselves and into a divine being.

The circle of light eventually lost its obvious link with the sun and became symbolic of any god and not only of that identified with the solar body. Soon it expressed the essence of divine power generally.

That is how, in painting and sculpture, Greek and Roman deities were represented with a halo and in Indian art Buddha, too, was shown with a celestial aura of light surrounding his head.

The development did not end there. When Roman emperors began to imagine themselves as divine beings, they often appeared in public with a crown, which was meant to imitate the orb of light of the sun. It was a foregone conclusion that artists, when creating the emperor's image, likewise would surmount his head with the celestial ornamentation.

The practice of placing a shield behind the head of a victorious emperor on his triumphal procession was a further contributory cause in the creation of the halo. In the minds of the people it became a distinguishing mark of power and glory.

And yet, perhaps more than anything else, utilitarian considerations were responsible for the general introduction of that peculiar kind of disc. Statues were kept not in museums but in the open. Therefore they were subject to deterioration through various causes. To protect them from the droppings of birds, the rain and the snow, a circular plate—either of wood or brass—was fixed upon their heads!

Thus pagan worship of the sun and artistic concern for the preservation of objects of art combined in the creation of the halo. It is a fact that the early Christian Church, well aware of the original pagan association, at first carefully avoided the use of the halo altogether. When, finally—and only in the sixth century—ecclesiastic authorities adopted it, they did so, to begin with, for its usefulness as a kind of umbrella.

In the Middle Ages the round halo was used only for angels and saints. When attached to Christ, it had to bear in addition a cross or the monogram of Alpha and Omega. Modern Catholic regulation permits a halo only for persons who have been canonized or beatified, or whose worship has otherwise been authorized by the Church.

Just as the halo's significance is of a late date, so even its very name, now descriptive of celestial glory, once was most earthbound. Literally the halo was born on the threshing floor of the old Greeks!

Many centuries before Christ, they used very primitive methods, as was only to be expected, in threshing their grain. They heaped the sheaves of corn they had gathered on hard but level ground, over which they drove round and round a team of oxen. Their numerous circuits eventually created a round track, and it was this which the Greeks called a "halo"! In the sixteenth century astronomers resurrected the word, applying it to the luminous orb around celestial bodies. Hence, it was quite appropriate that theologians adopted it for the crowning of the heads of their saints!

Such is the most unexpected and fantastic story of the halo. In its simple shape it combines traditions of Greek farming, the Roman deification of megalomaniac rulers, medieval astronomy and an early protective measure against dirt and inclement weather.

The Cross

There is a language of symbols. More eloquent than words, they can rouse the human spirit and revolutionize life and society. That is why modern political movements have used such symbols as the clenched first, crooked cross and bundle of rods.

Thousands of years earlier, each of the three world religions, Judaism, Christianity and Islam, knew of the symbol's dynamic power. They realized that a picture could talk louder than words and its impact outlast them. Therefore they chose the Star, the Cross and the Crescent to represent their beliefs, spread their faith and conquer the hearts and minds of men and women, wherever they might be and no matter what their station.

The cross was a common pagan emblem, and it has been found as such, carved in stone in remote ages. The reason for its choice was that it was one of the simplest figures to draw, and expressive in its message. Its arms pointed upward, downward, and sideways. Therefore the cross became a sign of all-embracing space. The east was represented by its top, the north by its right limb, the south by its left branch and the west by its lower portion.

The arms of the cross came to depict the rays of the sun as well. The ancient Assyrians used it as a symbol of the sky and its god Anu, and from earliest times it symbolized solar power. Consequently, it became the sign of fire and of the suffering of existence, with eventually everything being burned up. Indeed, it is quite likely that the arms of the cross developed out of the two kindling sticks with which primitive people produced fire.

The cross, too, stood for the world axis—the bridge that linked heaven and earth; the ladder with which humans could reach out towards God. It became the symbol of the joining of opposites, the linking of the left and the right.

Also showing the division of the world into four quarters, whence rain came and the wind blew, it indicated the four cardinal points from which droughts and floods could bestow blessings or curses on nature and human life. The similarity of the cross to a simple sword associated it as well with a weapon wielded to kill all that was evil.

By pointing to the sources of warmth, storm and rain, the cross became a visible symbol of fertility. It assumed this role even more so as a wooden cross. Easily constructed from two simple branches, it was seen as the emblem of all that grew and prospered. It was the tree of life. Stuck into the earth in fertile soil, an apparently dead and withered twig would start sprouting, as is still experienced today in the case of the "living fences" on the islands of the South Pacific. No wonder, therefore, that such miraculous change from a dead branch into a living tree seemed to represent the power of life over death. The cross, first of all, became a symbol of resurrection.

The Fish

The sign of the fish was the original Christian symbol. It preceded that of the cross by many years. The first Christians, ostracized and persecuted by the Romans, needed a badge for recognizing each other and proclaiming their faith in Christ. Their creed was then still banned and to spread its message was considered high treason. Where there was no time for words, a simple sign, quickly drawn and easily identified, spoke for itself.

The choice of the fish was therefore, first of all, the result of political circumstances. It could be drawn in no time, it immediately caught the eye, and its message could be understood at once.

From the earliest days of Christianity there was a close association, literally and figuratively, between the new faith and the denizens of the sea.

Christ's first disciples were fishermen and it was natural that they should be described as fishers of men, spreading their nets to gather in followers from the surging ocean of a pagan world.

The story of the miracle of the fish—how a few nourished thousands of hungry people—was well known. This made the fish expressive of a faith that worked wonders.

Finally, the fish was not only a picture but a word with a mystical meaning. In its Greek form, the language in which the New Testament originally was written, it contained a summary of Christian faith in the form of an acrostic. The Greek word for fish, *ichthus*, spelt out the initial letters of the revolutionary new creed, speaking (in its English rendition) of *Jesus Christ, the Son of God, the Savior of man.*

Thus the fish, both in its image and name, became the perfect symbol of a new religion that challenged the world.

The Crescent Moon

Islam's symbol is the crescent moon. It represents the moon in a state of increase and, therefore points to the faith's growth from small beginnings until one day, so Muslims believe, it will fill the world "all round." This sign of the youngest of world religions is not indigenously Mohammedan. Like the cross and the star, it goes back to most ancient and pagan days.

People have always been puzzled and awed by what they saw in the sky. The waxing and waning of the moon indicated to them the presence of miraculous power that dwelled in the crescent—a germ of fertility. Like the moon's sickle, its replica, whether drawn on cloth or shaped in metal, was thought to ensure an increase of all that humans sought after most: first of their own fertility and that of their fields and cattle, and then of their wealth and power.

The figure of the crescent thus became not only a symbol of growth and prosperity, but also a magical means of attaining it. That is why ancient Egyptians and early Greeks decorated their gods with the emblem and Athenians of illustrious birth wore a crescent of ivory and silver. It was for the same reason that Romans chose it as their empire's symbol, hoping that, magically, it would foster her might.

It is said that an event in 339 B.C. gave the crescent moon an additional significance in Asia Minor and hence in the Middle East. Philip, father of Alexander the Great, experienced great difficulty in his attempt to conquer Byzantium, the future Constantinople.

Besieging the city, his forces were unable to scale its walls and he decided to enter the fortress through tunnels. At first all went well. But then, a crescent moon suddenly appeared and revealed to the Byzantian defenders men building tunnels. Byzantium was saved! In gratitude for their deliverance, thanks to the new moon, the citizens adopted the crescent as their badge.

Another story links the choice of the symbol with Othman, the Sultan. He is said to have seen in a vision a crescent moon whose horns grew ever wider until they extended from east to the far west. He chose the crescent for his standard, believing that under its sign his rule, likewise, would spread to the ends of the earth.

When the Turks came to rule the Byzantians, they took over the emblem of the figure of the waxing moon. And because the Turks adopted Islam, people soon forgot the original national meaning of the crescent moon and mistook it as the religious symbol of the faith of Islam.

The Christmas Tree

Few people realize that many Christian customs have their root not in Christianity but in paganism. The fact that Christmas is observed on December 25 (though generally so only since the fourth century) is revealing. Probably this is not the birthday of Jesus at all which, according to some early Christians, fell on May 20. December was chosen by the Church to counteract the

Saturnalia, the pagan festival celebrated with revelry at this season of the winter solstice in honor of Saturn, god of vegetation and husbandry.

Each of the beautiful customs of Christmas has its own background. It is interesting to learn their story and to see how the genius of the human mind has been able, through the centuries, to give them a different and sacred meaning.

The Christmas tree is German and its adoption in English lands was due merely to the fact that Queen Victoria married a German prince. In Germany the tree cannot be traced beyond the seventeenth century. Its origin, however, goes back into the far-distant past—long before the birth of Jesus.

It is a fact that the Christmas tree stems from primitive pagan customs. Its main features, green foliage and candles, were associated with the winter solstice when nature seemed dead, and green branches and trees were used in a magic rite to ensure the return of vegetation and the victory of light over darkness.

Later, the tree was seen as the direct descendant of the world tree of Norse mythology whose branches and roots joined together heaven, earth and hell. The tree became the symbol of enduring and renewed life and the green of its leaves the emblem of immortality.

Egyptians used palm branches with twelve shoots as sacred expressions of the completion of the year and of the triumph of life over death.

At the time of their Saturnalia the Romans decorated homes and temples with foliage on which they hung images of their gods! It was a season of goodwill towards all. Schools were closed. No battles could be fought. Punishment could not be inflicted on any criminal and distinctions of rank and class were put aside. It was the carnival of antiquity when all joined in a mad pursuit of pleasure.

The Jews celebrated, at this very season, the Feast of Lights and for eight consecutive days kindled flames on an eight-branched candlestick in their homes.

Christianity knew of all these traditions. The fathers of the Church realized the impossibility of abolishing them root and branch. Thus they wisely retained the ancient institution of the green tree and the burning lights but gave them a completely new interpretation. In justification, they quoted the prophet Isaiah who had spoken of the "righteous branch" and foreseen the day when "the glory of Lebanon shall come unto you: the fir tree, the pine tree, and the box tree, to beautify the place of My Sanctuary."

How the first modern Christmas tree came into being is related in numerous legends.

A Scandinavian story tells of the violent deaths of two lovers and a consequent occult occurrence. At the spot where the murders took place, a beautiful "tree" grew out of the blood-soaked soil. On it, flaming lights miraculously appeared annually. These could be seen from far away and nothing could put them out.

Germans explain the introduction of the Christmas tree by an incident said to have happened when Christianity was first brought to their country. When St. Boniface arrived from England in A.D. 718 to convert the pagans, he was determined to root out all that was heathen and, to this end, he cut down a sacred oak in the city of Geismar. To pacify the angry worshippers he planted a fir tree in its stead and declared this to be the symbol of their new faith. It so happened that this event took place on Christmas Eve.

Martin Luther, the father of the German Reformation, has also been credited with the introduction of the modern Christmas tree. Returning home on a snowy Christmas Eve in 1517, he was deeply moved by the beauty of the glittering stars overhead. Wishing to describe this inspiring spectacle to his wife and children, he dug up a small fir tree and put it into the nursery. He then lit up its branches with candles, just as the starlit trees outside had appeared to him on that cold winter night.

Thus at Christmas time the tree's lights came to illuminate every German home, and the evergreen of its branches symbolized the deathlessness of the spirit. At the depth of the European winter, with its shortening days and their darkness and cold, Christmas told of the rebirth of warmth and light, of the re-creation of nature and the eternal spring of hope. The gifts hanging from the branches of the Christmas tree provided a personal joy to young and old.

From Germany the custom spread to other parts of the world. It found its way to the United States either by immigrants who made their new home there, or sailors and merchants. The first

Christmas tree recorded in the U.S.A. was put up by Hessian soldiers in 1776. They were mercenaries hired from Prussia (now Germany) by King George III of England to fight in the Revolutionary War. The tree took root in Britain very slowly. Its earliest mention there among the British people was amid royalty. The first English Christmas tree appeared at a children's party held at Queen Caroline's court in 1821.

However, the British hesitated to adopt what Charles Dickens described as "the new German toy" until the year 1841. Then, the Prince Consort, to surprise the young Prince of Wales and in nostalgic remembrance of his German home, had a Christmas tree erected in Windsor Castle. This royal example was soon copied by the general public, and the custom then spread throughout the world.

Tinsel

The symbolism of light accounts for the custom of decorating the Christmas tree with glittering tinsel. Light in all forms—fire, candles, even a flashing jewel—was thought to magically ensure that the forces of darkness were powerless.

Christianity added its own message, weaving a beautiful legend around the origins of tinsel. It tells of a poor widow who was determined to give her large family a memorable Christmas. However, all she possessed was a tree. She spent many hours decorating it and finally, exhausted, fell asleep. Late that night, spiders wove webs all over the tree's branches. Then, to reward the widow's unselfishness, the Christ-child changed the spider webs into shining silver threads.

Legend also has it that, as a child, Jesus once decorated a tree. He was assisted in this task by angels whose hair, when they departed, was caught on the branches and turned into tinsel.

Holly

An evergreen, holly is meant to speak of the renewal of life. More so, each of its features was explained to recall some sacred memory. The red berries were like the drops of blood Jesus shed, and their color symbolized the burning love for God in the hearts of the faithful. Its prickly leaves were reminders of the crown of thorns mockingly placed on his head by the Roman soldiers—as "the king of the Jews."

Christmas Pudding

Lighting up the Christmas pudding with brandy-fed flames gives extra zest to both the eating of the pudding and the celebration. This fire is also pre-Christian in origin, recalling the fervent prayers and magic rituals aimed at helping the "dying" sun in its fight for survival during the dark northern winter.

The Mince Pie

Intriguing is both the name and symbolism of the traditional mince pie, a relished treat of the Christmas fare. The pie recalled Jesus's cradle.

Originally of oblong shape, it had a crusty cover which was indented at the center with a small pastry doll—the figure of the Christ-child—put into the hollow. It was so called because it was a meat pie, filled with minced lamb's tongue and mutton.

When on their return from the East, the Crusaders brought with them highly prized spices, these soon came to replace the meat in the pie. No longer oblong, it became round. With the symbolism lost and the justification for its name gone, the mince pie—a misnomer now—nevertheless, because of its long association with the festival, remained a favorite part of Christmas, so puzzling to those not knowing its origin and place in the Christmas story.

The X in Xmas

The X in Xmas is a relic from the ancient Greeks whose letter *chi* looked like an X, the initial of *Xristos* (Christos), the Greek word for Christ. And Christmas, of course, is a contraction of Christ's Mass.

Early scribes were busy people. Theirs was an arduous task and parchment was costly. For practical considerations therefore, they introduced their own shorthand, abbreviations for words and concepts that recurred frequently. This saved them effort, time and money. That is how they came to use not the entire name of Christos, but merely its initial—Greek—letter. Possibly, the peculiar way of spelling the festival's name was retained by the misconception that the X represented St. Andrew's cross.

The Christmas Card

The Christmas card was invented by Sir Henry Cole in 1843. A well-known London figure, he was responsible for many innovations in British life. These ranged from the inception of a postal system to the construction of the Albert Hall, from the arrangement of the Great Exhibition in 1851 to the inauguration of the Victoria and Albert Museum.

Most of all, Cole wanted to improve public taste. In this pursuit he opened an art shop in Old Bond Street, where he sold all kinds of objects meant to beautify life. Cole tried to give aesthetic treatment to almost everything. Nothing was too small or too trifling not to deserve his attention.

He believed that, apart from being useful, everyday things should also be tasteful and artistic. That is how his fertile mind conceived the idea of the first Christmas card which he felt would add further lustre to this sacred day. Three independent factors may have prompted Cole in this endeavor.

There was the example of the Valentine card, in existence for almost half a century. Next came the the simple method of conveying his Christmas wishes by verses printed on cards, started by an eighteenth-century Frenchman. Third, Cole must also have been aware of a custom that had been introduced in English schools. Near the end of the winter term—around Christmastime—the boys were asked to produce "Christmas Pieces." These had a twofold purpose: whilst sending seasonal greetings to their parents, simultaneously they indicated to the teachers their pupils' progress in the art of writing. Large sheets on which the pupils wrote their (copperplate) Christmas wishes, the "pieces" were decorated with colored borders and headings.

Cole's conception of the first Christmas card was a drawing which would lend color to greetings and wishes which at the time had become too stereotyped. He commissioned a well-known artist, J. C. Horsley, RA, to design the picture for the card, specimens of which are still preserved.

Adopting the common medieval artistic form of a triptych, this actually consisted of a set of three illustrations. The central piece depicted a jolly party of adults and children with plenty of food and drink—a fact that aroused severe criticism from the Temperance Movement in Cole's own time. Underneath the picture was expressed the seasonal greeting, wishing "a merry Christmas and a happy New Year to you." Each of the two side panels was a representation of good works—the clothing of the naked and the feeding of the hungry.

Cole, as well versed in the art of publicity as in that of beauty, did his utmost to popularize the new card, not for personal gain but for the improvement of public taste and the embellishment of the Christmas celebrations. However, his idea did not catch on until twenty years later when, in the 1860s, big business adopted the card with stationery firms producing thousands of Christmas cards. Cole's initial failure changed into a tremendous success. In three decades British printers supplied 163,000 varieties of Christmas cards. Now collected in 700 volumes, they weigh almost seven tonnes.

In acknowledgment of his many services to the nation Cole was knighted and as "Sir Henry," dying only in 1882, he must have still enjoyed the eventual phenomenal success of his idea.

The Christmas Stocking

A coincidence of date, a legend and a poem jointly are responsible for the Christmas stocking, which at first had no real connection with the actual holy day.

The legend concerns St. Nicholas, or Santa Claus. He was renowned for doing good, especially in secret. One day, according to this story, he heard of three lovely sisters who lived in a small house on the outskirts of a city. They were desperately poor and it was rumored that their poverty might tempt them to sell their bodies.

St. Nicholas was deeply concerned. One night he went to the girls' home and, unnoticed, dropped three pieces of gold through the smoke hole (chimneys did not exist at that time). The coins did not fall onto the hearth, as St. Nicholas had intended, but fell into the sisters' stockings which they had hung up near the fire to dry. The girls were overjoyed when they found the gold next morning.

Once the tale became widely known, other people, hopeful of similar pleasant surprises, began to hang up stockings.

The fact that December 25 was dedicated to the memory of St. Nicholas linked his life, his charity and the stocking with the celebration of the birth of Christ. The beauty of this legendary explanation is not destroyed if it is remembered that for many centuries it was customary to put one's savings into a stocking. Actually, before this, shoes had served the purpose. However, they were replaced by stockings, the elasticity of which made them more suitable.

The famous poem by Clement C. Moore, "A Visit from St. Nicholas," did most, perhaps, to popularize the custom of the Christmas stocking.

Good Friday

The anniversary of Christ's crucifixion, Good Friday, used to be kept as a day of fast, abstinence and penance. Its liturgical color was black, no bells were rung and the church organ was kept silent.

Numerous customs developed to express the tragic circumstances of the day. In Durham, England, for instance, blacksmiths would refuse to shoe a horse on Good Friday, as the hammer and nails were associated with the crucifixion. In Yorkshire, people walked barefoot to church lest the nails in their shoes left their mark in the ground. In the Scottish Highlands peasants would not plough their fields and, generally throughout the country, no graves were dug. Burials had to wait until Easter Saturday.

All these practices are easily understood because nails had been used to fix Christ onto the cross. But people have often asked why such a tragic festival should be known as Good Friday. Several reasons may account for this apparent misnomer.

It is possible that the appellative was chosen simply to distinguish the day from all the other Fridays throughout the year. Another explanation is based on the Christian dogma that Jesus's crucifixion became the direct cause of human salvation. It was his sacrificial death on the cross that atoned for the original sin. To stress the great good that thus has come out of evil may well be why that day of gloom became known as Good Friday. On the other hand, the term may merely be a corruption of *God's* Friday. Anglo-Saxons used to call it Long Friday, an allusion to the length of the church services, and in the Greek Church it is known as the Holy or Great Friday. The Germans refer to it as *Karfreitag*, stressing its sorrowful connotation.

Hot Cross Buns

The hot cross bun, eaten at Easter, is a pagan survival of bread once offered to idols! At the annual festival of spring, the ancient Saxons ate such buns in honor of Eostre, the Anglo-Saxon goddess of Spring. Long before that, Egyptians, Chinese and Greeks baked and ate the same sort of cake in honor of their gods.

The word "bun" is derived from the archaic description of a sacred ox (*boun*). This used to be sacrificed at the time of the spring equinox, and a symbol of its horns was stamped upon the celebratory cakes. Eventually, this mark became a cross and the early religious symbol took on a practical purpose as well. It made it easy to divide the cake into four equal parts, to be shared by the worshippers. Such cross-marked cakes antedate Christianity by many centuries. Some of them were found in the excavations at Herculaneum.

Ancient worship of the moon also contributed to the peculiar kind of indentations. The bun itself represented the full moon and the cross symbolized its four quarters. The fathers of the early Christian Church realized that it was almost impossible to wipe out ingrained pagan customs. Instead, they adopted and absorbed them. The oxhorn marks were reinterpreted as the sign of the cross.

New developments and explanations were added. The buns were kneaded from the very dough used for the baking of the consecrated host and therefore, it was said, to indicate the sacred association, they were marked with a cross. Priests distributed them to the communicants attending early mass. This enabled the worshippers to break their fast even before getting home, an anticipation of the breakfast.

New superstitions began to replace the old. The buns were credited with being charms against evil and, as such, people kept and displayed at least one or two of them in their homes after Good Friday. During the festive season and long afterwards, as a protection against shipwreck, fishermen used to carry an Easter bun in their boats.

The Easter Egg

The Easter egg now caters for the tastes of the young and the not-so-young. Who would think of it as a sacred symbol with a message of deep spirituality and creativity? For that is its real and only purpose and meaning.

The Easter egg is the emblem of renewed life after death and of resurrection. To all appearances an egg is lifeless matter. And yet, out of it can come a new creature. Just as a chicken is entombed, as it were, in the egg and brought to life in due course, so out of the grave will rise the dead to a new existence. That is why, from earliest times and in many cultures, the egg assumed cosmic significance and became a symbol of fertility and immortality.

The Greeks and Romans buried eggs, real or their replicas, in their tombs. Scenes on Athenian vases show how baskets of eggs were left on graves. Maoris used to put an egg in the hand of a dead person before burial. Still today, Jews present mourners on their return from the funeral of a relative with a dish of eggs as their first meal.

In the northern hemisphere Easter coincided with spring, the season of the renewal of nature. Out of the dead earth, so it seemed, sprang new life. It was the moment of creation and re-creation. Even as early as pagan times the egg symbolized the rebirth of nature at the time of the solar new year. The shape of the egg was emblematic of the shape of the earth.

Christianity took this ancient sign of rejoicing at rebirth and applied it to the resurrection of Jesus. The ritual of Pope Paul V included a prayer, in which the faithful acknowledged this very purpose of the Easter egg: "Eating it in thankfulness to Thee, on account of the resurrection of our Lord." Also, the fact that all through the fast of Lent eggs were forbidden made them all the more welcome on Easter Day.

The tradition of painting Easter eggs in bright colors may have its origin in a legend that tells that Simon of Cyrene, who carried Christ's cross, was an egg merchant. When he returned from Calvary to his basket of produce, which he had left by the roadside, he found all the eggs miraculously colored and adorned. A Polish legend traces the practice of dying the eggs for Easter to Jesus's early childhood. To give her son some extra joy, Mary had painted hard-boiled eggs in a variety of colors—yellow, green and red. Other mothers soon followed her example. Only when the egg became the symbol of resurrection was the custom restricted to the season of Easter.

The Easter Bunny

Bunnies jumping about are a vivid illustration of the joys of spring. Yet, originally, the Easter bunny was no bunny at all, but a hare. It was the animal sacred to the goddess Eostre. Born with its round eyes open, the animal was chosen as representing the full moon, which was so closely linked with this goddess's feast. As both rabbits and hares are prolific breeders, they symbolized fertility and abundance of life. No wonder, therefore, that both became associated with the festival that celebrated spring and the resurrection of Christ. The popularity of rabbits with children also helped to spread the tradition of the lucky Easter bunny. How the bunny got its name is a "tale of a tail." "Bun," originally, was another word for a tail, and "bunny" is its diminutive. A rabbit was so called because of its "little tail."

In the Lap of the Gods

People who feel that they have done everything within their power to obtain a certain objective and that therefore the final result is beyond their control, might say that the ultimate outcome now "lies in the lap of the gods."

The mere fact that the phrase speaks of gods, and hence reflects polytheism, shows its antiquity. No wonder that it occurs as early as in Homer's *Iliad* and *Odyssey*. According to ancient Greek custom, those anxious to see a wish fulfilled inscribed it on a wax tablet which they then deposited on the lap or the knees of the statue of a god, convinced that thus they would draw his attention to their need. The practice survives in the modern saying.

"Amen"

Amen is the most widely known and frequently used of all religious words. Jews, Christians and Muslims have made it a significant part of their worship. It concludes hymns, prayers, creeds and the recital of the first Sura of the Koran, the Muslims' Bible. Marking their ends, it is like a seal, affirming what has been said or sung before, promised or threatened.

The word Amen is found thirteen times in the Hebrew Bible and, strangely, occurs there first in the case of a jealous husband, suspecting his wife of adultery. An ancient ritual test demanded of her to drink "bitter waters." While she was doing so, a priest pronounced a curse to the effect that, should she be guilty, her belly would swell and her thigh sag. The woman, still protesting her innocence, then had to affirm the curse by twice uttering Amen.

In the New Testament Amen is mentioned 119 times. Whenever Jesus wished to emphasize the significance and solemnity of what he said, he prefaced his words with it.

Amen is a Hebrew word. Though commonly explained to mean "so be it," expressing simultaneously assent, agreement and a supplication, it is derived from a root that signifies "truth." Hence anyone saying Amen confirms all that has gone before in speech or song as being true, trustworthy and reliable.

Some, however, believe that even the Hebrew Bible is not the original source of this affirmation and that the Amen actually goes back to Amun, the name of an Egyptian deity of highest rank who, indeed, as "king of gods," at one time was worshipped all through the Middle East with his name meaning "the hidden one."

Amen might also have originated in polytheistic faith, when Egyptian pagan believers—just as Greeks and Romans did later on, still recalled in "By Jove"—invoked their god in the form of an oath, saying, "By Amun." Perhaps it was from those early Egyptian sources that the Hebrews adopted the Amen. Wisely, however, they gave it a new interpretation by linking it with all that was "true" and "established." Naturally, both the Church and the Mosque, as children of Judaism, continued the use of the

Amen which nevertheless carries concealed within itself the ancient Egyptian god.

Such a simple and common word as the Amen "affirms" the mystery and paradox that make up life, when modern believers in a spiritual divinity endorse their prayers by the very word that once described a pagan deity!

INDEX

Accident, invention of wine 93; of champagne 94; of blotting paper 259
Acre, first cigarette 240
A.D. 269
Adam, his rib 28
Adam and Eve, four-leafed clover 7; marriage 28; dress 98; forbidden fruit on Friday 293
Adam's apple 82
Adams, John, and American flag 191
Aesculapius 158; Caesarean 158
Albatross 214
Alcohol, in Bible 85
Alexander the Great, beards 129
Alphabet 251
Amen 316
America, United States of, cocktails 88; painting of nails 125; flag of 191; Anthem 198
American flag 192; O.K. 249
Amun (Amon), Egyptian deity 316
Andrew, St, sign of kiss 31
Anecdotes, on etiquette 73; on Welsh rabbit 79; on toast 87; on first cocktail 88; on champagne 94; on invention of glass 97; on Frank Lloyd Wright 143; on witch's broom 155; on "God save the King" 196; on "Tell it to the Marines" 215; on Khaki 219; on "the blue ribbon of the turf" 239; on ill luck on Friday 293; on emblem of crescent 305
Anglo-Indians, grass widow 66
Anglo-Saxons, red hair 19; bride's veil 37; wedding cake 45; divorce 50; meals 74; handkerchief 107; the flea 134; ordeal 163
Animal, horse 7; cat 14, 136, 137, 139, 140; rabbit 15, 315; dog 18, 132, 137; crocodile 65; pig 83; and cocktail 88; elephant, white 132, as ornament 153; flea 134; owl 132; bull 133; hog 135; hare 135; kittens 137; goat, as sacrifice on Jewish Day of Atonement 172; Greek tragedy 244; albatross 214; Easter bunny 315
Anointment, of kings 181
Anthem, national 194–5; of Britain 195;

of United States of America 198, 200; of Israel 200
Antigonus, stumbling 13
Anti-transporatation League, of Australia, and Australian flag 189
ANZAC 225
Anzac Day 226
Aphrodite, and fish 294
Apollo, and Caesarean 158
Applause, in theater 179; in Parliament 179
April 273
April Fools' Day 277
Apron, as first dress 98
Arabs, color blue 25; belching 68; checkmate 231; head cover 298
Architecture 143
Army, buttons on sleeve 104; gauntlet 116; beards 129; the soldier 218; the private 218; the tank 218; martial 219; the baton 220; the drum-major's staff 220; the busby 221; its Australian emblem 223; the digger 224; the slouch hat 224; volleys over grave 228
Artemis, and candles 26
Asia, Central, and trousers 99
Astrology, and weekdays 274
Athens, and attic 145
Attic 145
Augustus, Emperor, passport 202; August 273
Australia, Aborigines' diet 83; her name 190; her flag 189; Waltzing Matilda 197; her army badge 223; the digger 224; the slouch hat 224; fair dinkum 248
Aztecs, the cocktail 88; cigarette 241

Babies, stork 24
Babylonia, beer 92; glass 97; painting of lips 122; weekdays 274
Bacchus, and Caesarean 158
Bacon, Roger, on bells 299
Bag, let the cat out of 136
Baker's dozen 263
Baldur, and figure "13" 4

318

Ballarat, Australian flag 190
Band, for mourning 57; around hat 114
Bands, military 220
Baptism, salt 1; crossing the line 212
Barbarian 185
Barber's pole 126
Bast, and cat 14
Bath, and the toast 86
Baton 220
B.C. 269
Beanes, William, the American Anthem 199
Beard 127
Becket, Thomas, forks 75
Bed, on the wrong side of 10
Bee, busy 131
Beer 91; brewing and rule of thumb, 263
Beethoven, L. von, waistcoat 102; on British Anthem 196
Bell, and, ship 210
Bells, horse 210; high priest 211, 227; at funeral 228; church 298
Bentinck, Lord George, the Derby, 239
Bergson, Henri, on laughter 279
Best man 36
Bethel, coronation stone 181
Bib, sailor's 207
Bible, red hair 19; kissing 29; veil 37; ring 40; on shoe 43; the helpmate 48; divorce 50; sneezing 71; the apple in 82; alcohol 85, 93; drunkenness 96; first dress 98; perfume 119; soap 125; hair 128;
on excretion 147; the scapegoat 172; shedding of blood 177; the flag 185; "God save the King" 195; Israeli Anthem 200; passport 201; tattooing 207; dice 231; ink 259; numbering of years 272; Friday 293; swearing by the 297; Amen 316
Bifocals 117
Birdwood, General, ANZAC 225; first Anzac Day 226
Birth, its customs 24–27
Birthday, celebration of 24; cake 26; candles 26; Queen's 27
Black, cat 14; mourning 56
Blackmail 268
Blood, barber's pole 126; mace 177; Communion service 182; Christening of ships 205; red-letter days 276
Bloomer, Amelia 167; bloomers 167
Blossoms, orange 38
Blotting paper 259
Blue, for boys 25; heaven 193; Peter 209;

for first prize 238; once in a blue moon 261
Boleyn, Anne 58
Bonfire 186
Boniface, St, Christmas tree 307
Boxing, and our language 227
Boxing Day 280
Boycott, Captain Charles C. 170
Brahms J., and British Anthem 196
Brandon, John, buttons on sleeve 103
Brass balls, three 267
Breakfast 74
Breaking of mirror 8
Brewers, and salt 2
Bridal 92
Bride, on left side of groom 37; her veil 37; capturing of 44; carrying over threshold 46; purchase of 49
Bridget, St, and leap year proposal 35
Britain, kicking of bucket 52; colored trousers 100; her Anthem 195
Broomstick, witch's 154
Bucket, to kick the 52
Bull, red rag to 133
Bull, Dr. John, British Anthem 196
Bun 313
Buren, Martin van, O.K. 249
Burgundy 144
Burial 58
Burma, slouch hat 225
Burton, Charles, and pram 26
Busby 221
Busby, Dr. Richard 221
Buttons, on waistcoast 101; on sleeve 103; on uniform 104; difference of buttoning 105
Byzantium, the crescent 305

Caesar, Julius, on trousers in Britain 100; the Lombards 146; Caesarean 158; Tsar 167; Kaiser 180; calendar 269; July 273
Caesarean 158
Cain, mark of 56
Cake, birthday 26; wedding 45
Calendar, the fortnight 262; the month 273; its inaccuracies 269
California, grass widows 66
Candles, birthday 26; death 58
Cannibalism 82
Canute, King, passport 202
Card, Valentine 52, 310; Christmas 310
Carey, Henry, British Anthem 196
Carpet, magic 154

Carrol, Lewis, on curtsy 70
Carrying bride over threshold 46
Cat, black 14, 131; o'nine tails 131; out of bag 136; raining cats and dogs 137; nine lives of 139; no room to swing a 140
Caterling, and Cheshire cat 152
Catgut 141
Catholics, candles 58; rosary 290; fast 293
Caucasus, and wine 93
Celestinus, Pope, clerical collar 287
Certificate, marriage 49; divorce 50; when crossing line 212
Chamberlain, Neville, and Umbrella at Munich 113
Champagne 94; and Christening of ships 205
Charles I, King, monopoly of paper 258
Charles II, King, Royal Marines 216; inscription on rim of coins 265
Charles the Mad, and cards 232, 235
Charm, of spittle 20
Checkmate 231
Cheshire cat 152
Chess 229
Chinese, mirror 9; their mourning color 56; chopsticks 76; their tea pots 77; fan 111; painting of nails 124; white elephant 133; the three wise monkeys 156; doctors 157; the flag 186; gunpowder 218; chess 231; playing cards 233; writing 251; paper 256
Chopsticks 76
Christ, *see* Jesus
Christening of ships 204
Christianity, ladder 10; marriage cerificate 50; number nine 139; counting of years 269, 270; All Fool's Day 278; prayer 288; symbol of fish 303; Christmas tree 305; Good Friday 312; Easter 313
Christmas, begins on eve 262; tree 305; card 310; stocking 311
Chrysostomos, on cosmetics 118
Church, salt 1; lighting three cigarettes with one match 12; Valentine card 32; wedding ring 40, 41, 42; beer 92; clerical collar 115, 287; wigs 116; bells 298; red-letter days 276
Churchill, Sir Winston, on building homes 143; describing lie in Parliament 174; on Israeli flag 193; on war and peace 218; on benefit of short words 249
Cicero, and stumbling 13

Cigarettes, lighting three with one match 12
Civilization 229
Clement of Alexandria, on cosmetics 118
Clergy, trousers 100; mace 177; "dog collar" 287
Clinking of glasses 87
Clock, stopping at death 54
Clover, four-leafed 6
Club, origin of mace 177; in cards 234-35
Cock-fighting, white feather 222
Cockpit 229; theater 244
Cocktail 88, 89
Coctel, and cocktail 91
Coffee pots and tea pots 77
Coffin 59
Coins, milling of 265
Cole, Sir Henry, Christmas card 310
Coleridge, Samuel, albatross 215
Collar, sailor's 208; clerical 115, 287
Colors, *black,* cat 14; for mourning 56; *red* hair 19; to the bull 135; paper 259; letter days 276; *blue* for boys 25; for heaven 193; Peter 209; for first prize 238; *pink,* for girls 25; *white,* for purity 193; for mourning 56; for cowardice 222; to sail under false 204; of sailor's uniform 207; of Easter eggs 314
Communion service 295
Communion, red flag 194
Confetti 42
Confucius, and his divorce 76
Contact lenses 117
Cook, Captain James, flag in Australia 190; tattoo 206
Coronation Stone 180
Corpse, its washing 58
Cortège 64
Coryate, Thomas 75
Cosmetics, *see* Beauty culture
Courtesies 68
Courting and marriage 28
Cresecent moon 304
Cretans, and W.C. 147
Crimean war, one match for three cigarettes 11
Crocodile tears 65
Cromwell, Oliver, foolscap 258; milling of coins 265
Cross, touching wood 6; of St. Andrew, and kiss 31; of St. George 187; Australian flag and Southern 190; symbol of 302; hot buns 313
Crossing of knife and fork 75

Crossword puzzle 237
Crown 183
Crucifixion, salt 2; unlucky "13" 3;
    touching wood 6; ladder 10; on Friday
    293; the cross 302
Crusaders, flag 186; medals 222
Cubit 210
Cumming, Alexander 148
Curtsy 70

Danes, red hair 19
Daniel, meatless diet 294
Dates, Queen's Birthday 27;
    St. Valentine's Day 32; February 29th,
    32; Anzac Day 226; New Year 274; All
    Fool's Day 277; May Day 279; Boxing
    Day 280
Days of the week 274
Death, pointing 21; mourning 52;
    stopping clocks 54; candles 58
December 273
De la Mare, Sir Peter 177
Derrick 167
Destiny, Stone of 181
Diamond, on cards 235
Dice 231
Dickens, Charles, on Christmas tree 308
Digger 224
Dillion, J., and Boycott 171
Dinner 74
Dionysius Exiguus, calendar 272
Dionysius, tragedy 244
Disraeli, Benjamin, the Derby 239
Divorce 50
Doctor, 157; staff and serpent 157;
    surgeon 158
Dog, howling 18; hearing 132
Dogwatch 211
Dominic, St, rosary 290
Doorstep, bride 46
Dozen, baker's 263
Drama 242
Drawing room 145
Dress, history of 98
Drinking customs 85
Drum-major's staff 220
Dryden, helpmate 48
Dunstan, St, horseshoe 7
Dwelling, story of 142

Ear, flea in one's 134
East India Company, the "senior service"
    217
Easter 312; egg 314; bunny 315
Eating habits 73

Edward I, King, Coronation Chair 181
Edward III, King, St. George 187, 188;
    the blue ribbon 238
Egbert, Archbishop of York, church bells
    299
Egg, tennis 237; symbolism 314
Egypt, cat 14, 137; the bucket 52; the
    West 53; wreaths 62; pigs 84; beer 91;
    wine 93; wigs 109; the fan 110;
    perfume 120; painted nails 124; soap
    125; the pyramid 143; darkness of her
    law courts 163; the flag 185; passport
    202; chess 231; hieroglyphic 251;
    paper 256; ink 258; water-clock 283;
    Christmas tree 306; the Amen 316
Elephant, memory, 131; white 132
Elephantine, Egypt, and marriage
    certificate 49
Elijah, fasting 40 days 161
Elizabeth II, Queen, birthday 27
Erne, Lord, and Boycott 170
Escoffier, G. A., peach Melba 80
Eskimos, kissing 30; shoes 43
Essex, Earl of, and Derrick 167
Etiquette 68
Eumaeus, and his dogs 19
Eureka Stockade, Australian flag 190
Evans, Sir Arthur, evacavation at Knossos
    148
Evanston, U.S.A., and Sundae 78
Evening 282
Everitt, Charles, "digger" 224
Execution, by derrick 167; by lynching
    168; by guillotine 171
Eye-paint 122
Eyebrows, shaving of 122

Fair dinkum 248
Fallacy, spilling of salt 2; red hair 19; ring
    finger 41; help-mate 48; watches and
    electricity 54; crocodile tears 65; apple
    as forbidden fruit 82; breeches worn
    by Adam and Eve 98; elephant's
    memory 131; busy bee 131; white
    elephant 132; bull's dislike of red 133;
    judge's black cap 162; stripes on
    sailor's collar 208; piggy bank 264
Fan 110
Fasting 293, 294
Fathom 210
Feather, white 222
February 274
Fertility, shoe 43; confetti 43
Fig leaves 98
Figureheads, of ships 204

Fish, and All Fools' Day 278; on Friday
    293; as a symbol 303
Fishing trade, meatless days 295
Flag, at half mast 57; its story as national
    symbol 185; the Union Jack 187;
    Australian 189; the Stars and Stripes
    191; Israel's 193; red 194; Blue Peter
    209
Flanagan, Betsy, cocktail 89
Flea, in one's ear 134
Flemings, gauntlet 116
Floralia, Roman, and May Day 280
Fools' Day, April 277
Foolscap 257
Foot, rabbit 115; measure 210
Footman 11
Fork 75
Fortnight 262
Forty, quarantine 160
Four-leafed clover 6
Fox-hunting, Parliament 178
Fox, Samuel 113
Franklin, Benjamin, spectacles 117
French, wedding cake 45; horse meat 83;
    trousers 100; handkerchief 107;
    gauntlet 116; jerry-built 151; red flag
    194; crossing the line 214; nitro-
    glycerine 218; minding P's and Q's
    255; rule of thumb 264;
    All Fools' Day 278; naming of
    clock 285
Freud, S., and "3" 8
Friday 276; fish on 293
Frigga, goddess of love 276
Funeral 58; procession 64; volleys at 228

Gaelic, and whisky 85
Gallipolli 225, 226
Games 229; chess 229; dice 231;
    knucklebones 232; playing cards 232
Gatty, F. A., and khaki 219
Gauntlet, to run the 116
George V, King, and tattooing 207
George, St. 187
Germans, the stork 24; birthday candles
    26; forks 74; joined hands 288;
    Christmas tree 306
Ghent, and gauntlet 116
Girls, pink for 26
Gladstone, W. E., tax on soap 126
Glass 97; host pouring wine 86; clinking
    of 87
Goat, as sacrifice 173; and tragedy 244
"God bless you" 71
"God save the King" 195

Godiva, Lady, rosary 291
Goethe, J. W. von, eyebrows 123
Good Friday 312
Gospels, on Judas 2; spitting 21; the
    figure "9" 139; on money 261; on
    fasting 293;
    Amen 316
Gothic 149
Gracchus, Tiberius, stumbling 13
Grass widow 66
Grave, volley over 228
Greek, stork 24; coffin 59; theater 242;
    ink 258; hour 282; halo 301; fish 304
Greeks, birthday candles 26; ring 40;
    laurels 62; wigs 109; "raining cats and
    dogs" 138; the jury 165; the flag 185;
    dice 232; tragedy 243; numbering of
    years 272
Gregory the Great, Pope, sneezing 71;
    priestly garb 287
Guillotin, Dr. Joseph I. 171
Guillotine 171
Gunpowder 195; plot and British Anthem
    195

Hair, locket of 16; red 19; attraction of
    109, 127; parting of 129; raising;
    "standing on end" 130
Half-mast 57
Halo 300
Hand, to cover mouth 72
Handkerchief 107
Hands, shaking of 69; joined at prayer
    288
Hanway, Jonas 112
Hare, mad March 135
Harington, Sir John, the W.C. 148
Hat, raising of 70; to eat one's 82; band
    114; slouch 224
Hatter, mad 115
Hawke, Sir Edward, blue Peter 209
Haydn, F. J., and British Anthem 196
Head, taboo 10; covering of in synagogue
    297
"Hear! Hear!" 179
Hearse 62
Hearts, on cards 234
Hebrew, stork 24; helpmate 48; Messiah
    181; origin of the alphabet 252; Amen
    316
Hecate, and dogs 19
Heine, H., on building of cathedrals 143
Helpmate 48
Henry II, King, and jury 166
Henry VIII, King, white for mourning 56;

waistcoat 102
Herodotus, on pigs in Egypt 84
Herzl, Theodor, Israeli flag 193
Hieroglyphics, circle 40; bucket 53
Hindus, tattooing 207; letters 251; rosary 291
Hitler, Adolf, umbrella 114
Hittites, soap 125
Hog, to go the whole 135
Honey, as aphrodisiac 47
Honeymoon 46
Honors list, Queen's birthday 27
Hood, Thomas, on honeymoon 47
Hopkinson, Francis, and the American flag 191
Horse, shoe, lucky 7; meat 83; bells 210
Horus, wine 93
Host, pouring wine 86
Hot cross buns 313
Hour 282
Howling, of dogs 18
Hugo, Victor, on death 52
Hungerford, Sir Thomas, Speaker 177
Hunting, terms in our language 229
Hutton, General Sir Edward, and Australian army badge 223

Idiot 185
Ill luck, figure "13" 3; getting out of bed 10; open umbrella 12; stumbling 13; black cat 14; howling of dogs 18; tattooing 205; albatross 214; Friday 293
Imber, N. H., Israeli Anthem 200
Incense 120, 121
India, grass widow 66; mutiny and khaki 219; chess 230
Indians, red, and scalping 130
Ink 258
Innocent III, Pope, and ordeal 165
Ireland, Coronation Stone 181; St. Patrick 188
Isabella, Queen of Spain, pram 26
Isis, cat 14; brewing 92
Islam, magic carpet 154; kneeling 290; mosque 290; rosary 291; its fast 294; the crescent 304; Amen 316
Israel, flag 193; Anthem 200
Israelites, and banners 285
Italian, confetti 42; keeping wine 86

Jack, as name of flag 189
Jackson, Andrew, and O.K. 249
Jacob, his courting 28; his stone 180
Jam-Sheed, and wine 93

James I, King, flag 188, 189; playing cards 233
January 269, 274
Janus, Roman god 274
Jeremiah, Prophet, soap 125; jerry-built 151
Jericho 151
Jerry-built 150
Jesus, figure "13" 5; touching wood 6; walking under ladder 10; spittle 21; candles in tomb 58; figure "40" 161; as Christ 181; as King of the Jews 181; date of birth 269; Incarnation and calendar 272; passion and Fools' Day 278; kneeling 289; Friday 293
Jews, wedding ring 41; marriage certificate 49; divorce 51; sneezing 71; the pig 83; their toast 86; mourning 106; development of ink 259; counting of years 272; seven-day week 275; at prayer 288; *see* also Judaism
Jezebel, Queen, painting face 118
Johnson, Dr. S., grass widow 66; on lunch 74
Jonson, Ben, on shoe 43
Joseph, ring 41
Judaism, candles for the dead 58, 60; wigs for married women 110; scapegoat 173; praying shawl and flag 193; fasting 294; origin of Communion service 295; covering of head 297; symbol of egg 314; the Amen 316
Judas Iscariot, spilling of salt 2; red hair 20
July 273
June 273
Juno, marriage 32; June 273
Jury 165; its 12 men 166
Justice, sources of 162

Kaiser 180
Kephiyeh, and hatband 114
Key, Francis Scott, American Anthem 199
Khaki 219
King's birthday 27
Kipling, Rudyard, on scents 121
Kiss 29
Kittens, to have 137
Kneeling 289
Knife 74; crossing of knife and fork 75
Knights, hats 70; fleas 134, 135; the use of the cross and flag 187
Knocking on wood 6
Knucklebones, game of 231
Koran, magic carpet 154; Amen 316

Krakatoa, island of, blue moon 261
Kreuger, Ivar, and three cigarettes with
    one match 12

Ladder, walking under 10
Ladies, curtsy 70; walk "inside" 148
Lapel, slit in 106
Last Supper, spilling of salt 2; unlucky
    "13," 4, 5; Passover night 5
Lateran Council, on priest and ordeal 165
Latin, for left 11; pram 26; umbrella 111;
    source of perfume 121; Caesarean 159
Laugh up one's sleeve 104
Law 162
League of Nations, passport 203
Leap year proposals 34
Leeman, of Manchester, and khaki 219
Left, handedness 11; bride on, of groom
    37; medals on 222
Legends, four-leafed clover 6;
    St. Dunstan and the horseshoe 7;
    babies and stork 24; blue for boys and
    pink for girls 25; Adam and Eve 28;
    leap years proposals 34; orange
    blossoms 38; wedding cake 45;
    sneezing 71; the Adam's apple 82;
    drink 85; invention of wine 93; first
    fan 110; man and flea 132; white
    elephant 132; magic carpet 154;
    invention of the alphabet 251; rosary
    290; Christmas tree 305; Christmas
    stocking 311; colored Easter eggs 315
Leicester, Earl of, Parliament 174
Lenses, contact 117
Lent, figure "40" 161; fish 294
Leo X Pope, spectacles 117
Leonardo da Vinci, spilled salt 3
Lincoln, Bishop of, and King's anointment
    182
Line, crossing of 212
Lipstick 121
Little, Sergeant K. M., Anzac 226
Locket of hair 16
Lombards, lumber-room 146
Lombroso, Cesare 11
Lottery, on marriage 33
Louis XIII, King, wig 109
Love, in tennis 236
Loving cup, and toast 87
Luck, clover 6; horseshoe 7; third time 7;
    black cat 14; rabbit's foot 15; locket of
    hair 16; blue 25; shoe 43
Lumber-room 146
Lunch 74
Luther, Martin, Christmas tree 307

Lydda, St. George 187
Lynching 168

McCoy, the real 246
McCoy, Charles ("Kid") 246
Mace 177
Macpherson, C., Waltzing Matilda 197
Mad Hatter 115
Mad March hare 135
Magic, and mirror 9; getting out of bed
    10; whistling 17; pointing 22; candles
    26; ring 40; shoe 43; stopping of clock
    at death 54; birth 137, 152; carpet
    154; figure "40" 161; anointment 182;
    scepter 184; flag 186; tattoo mark 206;
    bells 211; figure "7" 274; crescent 305
Magna Carta, passport 202
Maia, goddess of increase 273
Maiden speech 174
Manuscript 251
Maoris, kissing 30; egg 314
March, hare 135; month of 273
Margaret, Queen, leap year 34
Marines, tell it to the 215
Mark, of Cain 56
Marriage, as wedlock 28; certificate 49;
    wig 110; infidelity 316
Mars, martial 219; March 273
Matsah, and Communion service 296
May 273
May Day, May pole 280
Meals, three daily 74
Measurements 210
Meat, abstention from 293
Medals, on left 222
Medici, pawnbroker's emblem 267
Medicine, perfume 119; soap 125; playing
    cards 232; pawnbroking 267; meatless
    diet 315
Melba, Dame Nellie, toast 81
Melba, peach 80
Mesopotamia, and wine 93
Messiah, and Christ 181; oil 182;
    expectation of, and Israeli flag 193
Mexico, cocktail 89; cigarettes 241
Milling of coins 266
Minos, King, the W.C. 148
Mirror, breaking of 8
"Mister," surgeons as 158
Mitre 297
Mohammed, and perfume 120
Mohammedanism, *see* Islam
Monash, General Sir John, and Anzac
    Day 227
Monday 275

Money, the piggy bank 264; traveler's checks 266, blackmail 268
Monkeys, three wise 156
Month 272, names of 273
Moon, month 46; once in a blue 261; Monday 275; crescent 304
Moore, Clement C., and Christmas stocking 312
Moses, the figure "40" 160; Five Books of, as "the Law" 162
Mosque 290
Mourning 52; tear in garment 106
Mouth, yawning 72; evil spirits 122
Music, army 220

Nails, painting of 224
Nandi, tribes, and brides 49
Napoleon, stumbling 13; doctors 157; drum-major 221; power of words 246
Navy, half-mast 57; jerry-built 150; the Jack 187, 189; customs 204; tattooing 205; sailor's uniform 207; ship's bell 210; as Senior Service 217
Nelson, Admiral Lord, and sailor's collar 208
Neptune, crossing the line 214
Nero, Emperor, the palace 144
New Testament, *see* Gospels
Newgate prison, going West 54
Nicholas, St. 311
Nine, lives of a cat 139; symbolism of figure 139
Nitro-glycerine 218
Noah, wine 93; April Fools' Day 277
Nomads, trousers 99
Norfolk, Va., U.S.A., and Sundae 78
Nose, rubbing of 29
November 273
Nufer, Jacob 159
Numa Pompilius, and Caesarean 159
Numbers, symbolism of "13" 3; baker's dozen 263; "3," third time lucky 7; cigarettes and one match 11; daily meals 74; volleys 288; "4," clover 6; "9" 139; "40" 160; "12" 166
Nurse 157

Octel, cocktail 89
October 273
Odin, dogs 138
Odyssey, howling dogs 19
Oil, anointment 182
O.K. 249
Old Bailey 163
Oliphant L., Israeli Anthem 200

Operation, first 157
Opposition, H.M.'s 175
Orange blossoms 38
Ordeal 163
Orient 282
Othman, Sultan, the crescent 305
Owl, its sight 132

P's and Q's, to mind one's 254
Paganism, pointing 22; Valentine card 32; horse 83; hair 129; ships 204; gestures at prayer 288; fish 293; Christmas 305; Easter 313
Palace 144
Palatine Hill 144
Paper and papyrus 256
Paradise, clover 7
Parchment 256
Park, Mungo, stumbling 13
Parker, Sir Peter, blue Peter 209
Parliament, British, wigs 109; Bill on cosmetics 118; applause in 179; Act on meatless days 295
Partridge, Eric, Cheshire cat 142
Pasht, *see* Bast
Passover, Communion service 296
Passport 201
Pastimes 229
Paternoster 293
Paterson, A. B. "Banjo" 197
Patrick, St, leap year 35; flag 188
Paul V, Pope, Easter egg 314
Paul, St., kneeling 290; fasting 294
Pawnbroking 267
Peach Melba 80
Pepys, beauty-patches 118; Royal Marines 216
Perfume 119
Pergamum, parchment 256
Perignon, Dom, champagne 94
Perrers, Dame Alice, the Speaker 176
Persepolis, wine 93
Persians, Caesarean 158
Peter, blue 209
Petrie, Sir Flinders, glass 97
Pharaohs, ring 41; passport 202
Philadephia, U.S.A., American flag 191
Philip of Macedonia, the crescent 305
Philochorus, birthday cake 26
Phoenicians, glass 97; soap 125
Pig 83
Piggy bank 264
Pilgrim Fathers, beer 93
Pilot 204
Pink, for girls 26

Pit, in theater 244
Playing cards 232
Pliny, the Elder, spitting 21; glass 97; soap 126; "raining cats and dogs" 138; Caesarean 158
Pointing 21
Polo, Marco, rosary 291
Polynesian, tattoo 206
Pompeii, soap factory 125
Pork 83
Poseidon, crossing the line 214
Potamon of Alexandra, passport 202
Pots, coffee and tea 77
Pram 26
Prayer, kneeling 289; joining hands 288; use of rosary 291
Priests, ordeal 165; clerical collar 287
Private, army 218
Proposals, leap year 34
Psychoanalysis, ring ceremony 41
Psychology, stumbling 13; carrying of bride across threshold 46; mourning 52; perfume 119; the invention of the guillotine 171; gestures of prayer 288; use of rosary 291
Pyramids 52, 143
Pythagoras, salt 2; figure "3" 8

Quarantine 160
Queen's birthday 27
Question mark 255
Quiros, Pedro F. de, Australia 190
Quisling 167
Quiz 218

Rabbit, foot 15; Welsh 79; Easter bunny 315
Rabies, howling dogs 19
Rachel, and Jacob's wooing 28
Raining, cats and dogs 137
Ramadan, month of 294
Rameses III, Pharaoh, beer 92
Rationalization, stopping clock 54; mourning color 56; clinking of glasses 87
Rebecca, bride's veil 38
Rechabites 96
Red, color of, hair 19; rag to bull 133; flag 194; wine for Christening ships 205; blotting paper 259; letter days 276
Regalia, Royal 174
Religion, perfume 121; beards 127; as guardian of the law 162; stones 180; ships 204; meaning of word 286

Resurrection, coffin 61; symbol of cross 303; egg 314
Revolution, French, trousers 100; red flag 194
Ribbon, blue 238
Ring, wedding 40; finger 41
Romans, nailing of evil 7; "sinister" left side 11; wedding cake 45; threshold 46; divorce 51; candles 58; laurels 62; sneezing 71; mind's power over body 157; Caesarean 158; scepter 184; flag 185; passport 202; the numbering of years 272; All Fools' Day 277; May Day 280; clerical collar 287; fish on Friday 295
Romulus 144
Ropes, to know the 204
Rosary 290
Ross, Betsy, U.S. flag 192
Royalty, the pram 26; bottom button of waistcoat 102; regalia 180; tattooing 207
Rule of thumb 263
Russell, Betrand, leisure time 229
Russia, red flag 194

Sacrifice, salt 1; incense 121; goat 244; human; and Christening of ships 205
Sade, count of 167
Sailors, "no room to swing a cat" 140; tattooing 205; bib 207; albatross 214
Salary 261
Salt, sacrifice 1; spilling 1
Samuel, anointing Saul 182
Sandwich, Earl of, 167
Sandwich Islands, spittle 20
Sanskrit, mace 178; rosary 291
Santa Claus, stocking 311
Saturday 275
Saturn 275
Saturnalia, Fools' Day 277; Christmas tree 305
Saul, King, his anointment 182
Savoy Hotel, London, peach Melba 80; Melba toast 81
Sax, Adolphe 167
Saxophone 167
Scalping 130
Scandinavians, best man 36; honeymoon 46; Christmas tree 305
Scapegoat 172
Scepter 184
Scipio Africanus, Caesarean 159
Scone, the stone of 181
Scots, salt in brewing 2; leap year 34;

gauntlet 116; Coronation stone 181; St. Andrew 187; blackmail 268; Fools' Day 278

Scott, Sir Walter, stumbling 13

Sea, whistling at 17; demons 211

Seneca, on curing disease 157

Senior Service 217

September 273

Serpent, symbol of 158

Serviette 77

Seven, symbolism of 274

Sex, ring ceremony 41; shoes 43; dress 98; perfume 119; cats ; witch's broomstick 154; tattooing 206; May pole 280; Easter bunny 315

Shakespeare, stumbling 13; evil 167; the pit 244

Shaking of hands 69

Shaving 128; crossing the line 212

Shaw, George Bernard, credulity 9

Shepheard's Hotel, Cairo, Anzac 225

Ships, as "she" 204; Christening of 204; figureheads 204

Shoe, throwing of 43

Sillery, Marquis of, champagne 95

Sleeve, buttons on 103; to laugh up one's 104; length of 104

Slit, in lapel 113

Slouch hat 224

Smetana B., Israeli Anthem 201

Sneezing 71

Soap 125

Soldier 218

Solomon, King, magic carpet 154; chess 229; kneeling 289

Soul, spittle 20; yawning 72

South African War, lighting of cigarettes 12; the digger 224

South Sea Islanders, forks 75; launching of ships 205

Spade, in cards 234

Spaniards, painting of nails 124

Speaker, in Parliament, his Chair 176

Spectacles 117

Spilling, salt 1

Spilman, Sir John, foolscap 257

Spitting 20

Spooning 31

St. Dunstan, horseshoe 7

Staff, serpent 157; drum-major's 220

Stalls, in theater 244

Star of David 193

Star-spangled banner 198

Stars and Stripes 191

Stocking, Christmas 311

Stones, role in religion 180

Stork, babies 24

Stumbling 13

Suicide, bucket 52

Suits, four of playing cards 234

Sumerians, soap 125; doctors 157

Sun emblem of rising 223; Sunday 275; dial 283

Sundae 78

Sunday 275

Superstitions 1; clocks at death 54; pregnant women 137; tattooing 205; albatross 214

Surgeons, as "Mister" 158

Sweden, best man 36; gauntlet 116

Symbolism, salt 2, 3; clover 6; horseshoe 7; color white 38, 56, 222; ring 40; shoe 43; staff and serpent 157; scepter 184; Southern Cross 190; "rising" sun 223; blue 193; clerical collar 287; hands at prayer 288; kneeling 289; covering head at worship 297; halo 300; cross 302; fish 303; star of David 193; crescent 304; egg 314

Table manners 73

Taboos, pork 83; bodily function 146

Tacitus, binding of hands 288

Tahitians, tattoo 206

Tank 218

Tattooing 205

Taxation, soap 126

Tea pots, coffee pots 77

Tears, crocodile 65

Teetotaller 96

Temple, destruction of 294

Tennis, love in 236

Teutons, jury 165; baton 220

Theater, applause 179; drama 242, tragedy 243; stalls and pit 244

Thirteen, unlucky 3

Thor, god of thunder 276

Three, the perfect 8; cigarettes and one match 12; volleys at funeral 228

Threshold, carrying bride across 46

Throwing of shoe 43

Thumb, by rule of 263

Thursday 276

Time, its measurement 269

Tiw, god 275

Toast 86

Tomb, of Christ and candles 58

Tombstone 64

Totemism, rabbit's foot 15; eating of pork 83; flag 185

Toth, giver of script 251
Tragedy 243
Trial by jury 165
Triangle 10
Trichinosis, pork 84
Trinity, ladder 10; three cigarettes 12; ring
   ceremony 42; volleys over grave 228
Trousers 99
T'sai Lun, paper 256
T'sang Chien, alphabet 251
Tsar 167, 180
Tuesday 275
Tullia, light 58
Turner, Richard, teetotalism 96
Turn-ups 100
Tutankhamen, tomb of and perfume 120
Twain, Mark, "waltzing" 197; money
   261
Twelve jurymen 165

Umbrella, opened indoors 12, 111
Union Jack, 187

Vadjra, deity 156
Valentine, St, marriage card 32
Veil, bride's 37
Venetians, quarantine 161
Venus, fish 295
Versailless, Palace of, etiquette 69
Vespasian, spittle 21
Vesta, threshold 46
Victoria, Queen, pram 26; painted nails
   124; sailor's bib 208; Christmas tree
   306
Vikings, flag 285; Christening of ships
   204
Vulgate, excretion 147

Wagstaff, Major, Anzac 226
Waistcoat 101; bottom button 102
Wales, spooning 31
Walking under ladder 10
Waltzing Matilda 197
War, *Crimean*, smoking 12; slouch hat
   224; digger 224; *World War I*, "on
   going West" 53; white feather 222;
   digger 224; Anzac 225; *American-
   Mexican*, cocktail 89; *Crusades*, flag
   187; medal 222; *of American
   Independence*, the Stars and Stripes
   191; *World War II*, Israeli flag 193;

American, the Star-spangled banner
   198; *Indian Mutiny*, khaki 219; *Turko-
   Egyptian*, first cigarette 241
Washington, George, American flag 191
Watch 285
W.C. 146
Wedding, best man 36; procession 37;
   orange blossoms 38; ring 40; confetti
   42; cake 45
Wedlock 28
Wednesday 276
Week, length 274; days 275
Wellington, Duke of, trousers 100
Welsh, rabbit 79
West, to go 53
West Indies, cigarettes 241
Whips 178
Whisky 85
Whistling, at sea 17; girl 18
Whitby, Synod of 272
White, Lt. A. T., Anzac 226
White, for mourning, 56; feather 222
Whitman, Walt, handkerchief 107
Wigs 109
William I, King, jury system 166
Window 149
Wine 93; at Last Supper 85; the pouring
   of 86; Christening of ship 205
Winn, Arthur, crossword 237
Winton, Qld., Waltzing Matilda 197
Witch's broom, 154
Witchcraft, spittle 20; perfume 120;
   kittens 137
Witchetty grubs, their taste 83
Woden, god 276
Wood, knocking on 6
Worship, joining of hands 288; kneeling
   289; rosary 290; Communion service
   295; covering of head 297
Wreath 61
Wright, Frank Lloyd 143
Writing, beginnings of 251
Wycliffe, the helpmate 48

X, for kiss 31; cross of St. Andrew 187
Yawning 72
Years, the numbering of 271

Zionist congress, Israeli flag 193; Israeli
   Anthem 201
Zochitl, cocktail 88